D1598691

Sociolinguistic Variation
in American Sign Language

THE SOCIOLINGUISTICS IN DEAF COMMUNITIES SERIES

Ceil Lucas, General Editor

Sociolinguistic Variation

in American

Sign Language

Ceil Lucas, Robert Bayley,
and Clayton Valli

In collaboration with Mary Rose,
Alyssa Wulf, Paul Dudis, Susan
Schatz, and Laura Sanheim

GALLAUDET UNIVERSITY PRESS

Washington, D.C.

Sociolinguistics in Deaf Communities

A Series Edited by Ceil Lucas

Gallaudet University Press
Washington, D.C. 20002

ISBN 1-56368-113-7
ISSN 1080-5494

♾ The paper used in this publication meets the minimum requirements of American National Standard for Information Sciences—Permanence of Paper for Printed Library Materials, ANSI Z39.48-1984.

This book is dedicated to the memory of William C. Stokoe and to Roger Shuy and William Labov.

Contents

CHAPTER NINE:

Sociolinguistic Variation in American Sign Language, 192

Foreword

Sociolinguistics emerged prominently in the 1960s, celebrating the heterogeneity of language based not only on linguistic constraints but also on variation occasioned by the race, ethnicity, age, gender, and social status of its speakers. Before that, the task of the linguist was a whole lot simpler. Most language teachers needed to pretend that there was such a thing as "a language" that was unified enough to be taught and learned despite the way speakers tended to wander off from the textbook norms.

Overlooking variation may make linguistics simpler, but sooner or later, somebody is going to notice that people don't use language the way the grammars prescribe it. My own first experience with this phenomenon, as a seventh-grade language arts teacher in 1957, is a case in point. My textbook insisted that "which" should be pronounced with "a puff of air preceding the w." I had never myself distinguished phonologically between the noun "witch" and a relative pronoun. Nor did anyone else in my part of the country, including our mayor and his entire city council. A quick look at the title page of the text showed me that the book was published in Boston, where "hw," the Northern variant, is considered the standard way to begin words like "which." My students and I shrugged our shoulders and went on pronouncing it the way standard English was pronounced in our own area. Acceptable variation always trumps stereotyped standards. Sociolinguistics was a new concept at that time, a few years earlier than the blossoming studies of social variation in the sixties.

Sociolinguistics has come a long way in the past forty years, beginning with phonological and morphological variation, then followed by analyses of syntactic variation and discourse interaction features. In the early years of sociolinguistics, primary attention was given to English variability, but this soon expanded to other languages and other parts of the world.

About the same time that sociolinguistics was emerging, a small cadre of linguists, led by William Stokoe, faced an infinitely larger task, that of proving to a skeptical world that American Sign Language (ASL) was indeed a full-fledged language. In retrospect, it appears that early accurate descriptions of variation in ASL actually worked against the primary goal of getting it accepted as a real language. Pretty much the same thing happened with the early descriptions of English vernaculars, which were often misunderstood to be proof of cognitive deficits of their speakers. But such is the folly of assuming that variation, even ASL variation, is not patterned and systematic. It seems that linguists perpetually need to remind (or inform) the general public that variation is not only healthy for keeping a language vital and changing, as the authors point out, but that it is also an important factor in our humanity, opening the door to the creativity that permits such things as poetry. Equally important is the message to linguistic laypersons that language variations are structured, systematic, and living proof that those who use one variety have just as much cognitive ability as those who use another one.

With the advent of an increasing number of sociolinguists who specialize in ASL, it is only natural that this now accepted real language would get the deserved attention that this book provides. Its uniqueness comes from the fact that a unified exposition of ASL sociolinguistics has hitherto not been put forth. It is natural for developing specializations to begin with scattered articles on parts of the issue. Later, with the maturation and a coming together of like-minded people, the pieces and parts are put together in this way.

The standard methodology of sociolinguistics is to gather as much data as possible and let the data drive the analysis. This contrasts with approaches used in some other fields, which often begin with a hypothesis and then find data to either prove or disprove it. There may always be questions about whether sociolinguistic samples are representative, adequate, or unusual in other ways. But, whatever qualms an experimental researcher might have had about this type of research, there can be no question but that we learn very important things in the process. This project is to be congratulated for videotaping representatives from different areas of the United States, different ethnicities, different ASL backgrounds, different ages, different socioeconomic statuses, and different genders. That data of such excellent quality were produced is a tribute to the sensitive and creative approach taken by the authors.

It should also be pointed out that the product of this research is not a dictionary or an encyclopedia of all types of extant ASL variation. To do so would be a lifetime work, similar to the *Dictionary of American Regional English* or the *Oxford English Dictionary*. Instead, the researchers focus on targets, in this case targets of phonological and morphosyntactic variables that have been studied earlier in smaller studies. These target variables are representative of other features in their categories, ones that future researchers might wish to study further. Proceeding in this way is reminiscent of the early work in Vernacular Black English by Labov (1966) and by Wolfram (1969), in which a small number of target features were studied in a large sample of speakers in New York and Detroit, respectively.

Language attitudes and policies are also an important aspect of sociolinguistic research. The authors of this study provide a brief and poignant description of the subjective reactions and policies of various schools for deaf people, information crucial to the actual production of ASL by the representatives of those schools. As the authors point out, policies are often a product of the influence of individuals. This too is not unusual. Perhaps it is not surprising that the first known policy for accepting ASL to meet a graduate school language requirement was created in the early 1970s at Georgetown University, a direct result of the persuasiveness of individuals on the sociolinguistic faculty at that university.

Some of the findings of this book are not surprising. For example, sociolinguists will not be shocked to learn that the variation found here is systematic and regular, just as we found it to be in Vernacular Black English in the 1960s. It is also not too surprising that internal linguistic constraints and external social constraints on variation, such as those found in spoken languages, are also present in a manually signed language. Those who knew all along that ASL was a real language are not at all shocked to learn that ASL behaves much like a spoken language, but it is very nice to have empirical proof of this. To be sure, there are important differences in the details of the variations and the social and interactive factors that cause them, one of the most interesting aspects of this book.

On the other hand, it is somewhat surprising that the distribution of such regularity does not always follow the predictable regional lines found in dialects of spoken American English. It is surprising that some phonological variables in Virginia and Washington are more like each other than they are to more neighboring signers. As usual, however, the authors explain the reason for this. And even the veteran sociolinguist might be surprised at the authors' discovery of the strong role of grammatical function in ASL phonological variation.

This book is a fitting tribute to the work of the late William Stokoe of Gallaudet University who, despite his brilliance and his clarity, had ideas that were apparently too revolutionary to be fully appreciated during his lifetime. He would be proud that the work evidenced by this volume is made available, for he is the one who paved the way and on whose shoulders we all try to stand. Although the last word on ASL sociolinguistics has not been said here, this book sends us on our way with a flourish.

Roger W. Shuy
Georgetown University

Introduction

This book is the seventh volume in the Sociolinguistics in Deaf Communities series. It represents the culmination of a seven-year project on sociolinguistic variation in American Sign Language (ASL) funded by the National Science Foundation (SBR # 9310116 and SBR # 9709522). The idea for the project grew directly out of my training and research experience in spoken language variation. The original idea was to provide a comprehensive description of the variables and constraints at work in sign language variation, with the four decades of research on spoken language variation as the foundation. This kind of research requires large amounts of videotaped data, so the project was therefore, by definition, a huge team effort. Its success was made possible by the willing participation and support of many individuals.

Data were collected in seven sites around the United States, and this data collection simply would not have been possible without the contact people in each area: in Virginia, Mike Marzolf, Frances Marzolf, and Charity Reedy; in Maryland, Anne Marie Baer, Paula Ammons-Woodall, Arlene Blumenthal Kelly, and Malcolm Peters; in Boston, Yvonne Dunkle, Nancy Becker, and Lynn Marshall of The Learning Center for Deaf Children in Framingham; in Olathe and Kansas City, Missouri, Nancy Eades, Arden McDowell, and Irvine Stewart; in Fremont and San Jose, California, Sue Saline and Anita VanderCourt; in Washington, Glen and Betty Bocock and Larry Petersen; and in New Orleans, Anthony Aramburo, Ester McAllister, and Liz Heurtin. These people recruited participants for the study and made all of the practical arrangements for data collection in each site. Also central to the data collection process was Ruth Reed, who conducted all of the interviews with the African American signers and has presented project findings many times at the annual meeting of National Black Deaf Advocates and other venues.

The project also benefited from valuable institutional support. At Gallaudet, this support was provided by a variety of individuals: Mike Karchmer and Tom Allen, deans of the Graduate School and Research during the period of the project; Bill Moses and Pat Cox, deans of the School of Communication also during the project; Stan Matelski, Judy Newhouser, and Christine Katsapis of the Office of Sponsored Programs; Mike Lockhart in Contracts and Purchasing; Michel Nau and Deborah

DaSilva in Accounting; and Ulf Hedberg, Mike Olson, and the staff of the Gallaudet University Archives, and Patrick Harris of Television and Media Production Services. Institutional support also came from James Tucker at the Maryland School for the Deaf, from Kim Brown and Kim Beardslee at Johnson County Community College in Overland Park, Kansas, and from the California School for the Deaf in Fremont. Many technical problems were handled by Eugene Lewis of the Technical Support Office at Gallaudet University, while Chip Reilly of the Gallaudet Research Institute provided the benefit of his experience during the crucial early equipment-purchasing stages of the project. Further institutional support came in the form of the Schaefer Fellowship given to me for the 1999–2000 academic year with the benefit of release time and the University of Texas-San Antonio faculty research grant given to Robert Bayley.

A number of graduate students in the linguistics program in the Department of ASL, Linguistics, and Interpretation at Gallaudet University did crucial work as data coders: Leslie Saline (who was also involved in data collection), Jim Van Manen, Noni Warner, Rob Hoopes, Alison Jacoby, Raychelle Harris, and Tashi Bradford. Keiji Goto and Myisha Blackman worked on digitizing the data. Ethylyn DeStefano, administrative secretary in the same department, cheerfully handled all of the paperwork involved in the purchase of equipment, travel for five researchers to seven sites and to conferences and workshops, and the payment of salaries and honoraria.

Colleagues who provided essential feedback on the work at various stages include Walt Wolfram, Greg Guy, Peter Patrick, Claire Ramsey, and Ben Bahan. Dennis Preston, Ron Butters, Alan Metcalf, and the American Dialect Society twice provided a forum for the presentation of the findings. At the National Science Foundation, Paul Chapin, Fernanda Ferreira, and Cathy Ball gave steadfast encouragement and support.

Tom Witte, our computer consultant, has earned special recognition. We met in December 1994 and began a year-long dialogue that resulted in the development of the database for the project, which involved getting the videoplayer and the computer to talk to each other, developing a database that could be learned and used efficiently by a number of people, and developing techniques for then extracting the data in a useable way. Tom spent countless hours developing and testing all aspects of the system central to the success of the project and pretty much maintained his sense of humor throughout.

The writing of the volume also represents a team effort. Clayton Valli and I served as principal investigators for the project, and Susan Schatz, Mary Rose, Alyssa Wulf, Paul Dudis, and Laura Sanheim worked as research assistants. Robert Bayley joined the project in January 1997 as a VARBRUL consultant and quickly became centrally involved in the analysis and writing. Chapters 1 and 2 are written by Robert Bayley, Clayton Valli, Susan Schatz, and myself. Laura Sanheim did the research for chapter 3 and was joined by Robert Bayley and myself in the writing. Mary Rose focused on the analysis of 1 handshape variation and wrote chapter 4 with Robert Bayley and myself, and the three of us also collaborated on the analysis of DEAF and location signs and the writing of chapters 5 and 6. Alyssa Wulf and Paul Dudis were responsible for the analysis in chapter 7 and co-wrote it with Robert Bayley and myself, while Susan Schatz and I collaborated on chapter 8. Finally, I wrote chapter 9.

We are deeply grateful to those individuals responsible for the production of this book: Jayne McKenzie, the secretary in the Department of ASL, Linguistics, and Interpretation, typed the entire manuscript of the volume; Robert Walker did the drawings of signs for which MJ Bienvenu served as a model; Ivey Wallace, Deirdre Mullervy, and Carol Hoke of Gallaudet University Press edited and produced the volume, and John Van Cleve and Dan Wallace, also of the Press, have shown consistent support for the series as a whole.

Finally, we acknowledge our significant others: wives, husbands, partners, and friends who followed our progress with interest and supported us all the way through.

Ceil Lucas

Chapter 1

Sociolinguistic Variation and

Sign Languages: A Framework for Research

The 1960s witnessed the development of two subfields in linguistics, the systematic study of language variation, pioneered by William Labov (1963, 1966), and the scientific study of sign languages, developed initially by William Stokoe (1960). The theoretical framework and rigorous methodology of Labov's early studies on Martha's Vineyard and in New York City were soon extended to numerous other sites around the world. Research in many communities has shown that all human languages are characterized by what Weinreich, Labov, and Herzog termed *orderly heterogeneity* (1968, 100). That is, although variation is characteristic of all languages, it is not random. Rather, language users' choices between variable linguistic forms are systematically constrained by multiple linguistic and social factors that reflect underlying grammatical systems. Moreover, speakers' and signers' choices between variable linguistic forms both reflect and partially constitute the social organization of the communities to which users of the language belong.

Like Labov's work on linguistic variation, Stokoe's initial work on the linguistic structure of sign languages was soon taken up by other researchers. His early monograph on sign language structure was followed by the *Dictionary of American Sign Language* (DASL) (Stokoe, Casterline, and Croneberg 1965). Other researchers examined the structure of American Sign Language (ASL) (e.g., Klima and Bellugi 1979; Liddell 1980), the acquisition of ASL by Deaf children (e.g., Meier and Newport 1985), as well as sociolinguistic aspects of ASL such as the differences between African American and Caucasian signing (Woodward 1976) and the effects of language contact on the production of Deaf signers (Lucas and Valli 1992). Taken together, these studies, as well as many others that we might name, established the status of ASL—and by extension other sign languages—as a fully developed language, equal to spoken languages in grammatical complexity and expressive power.

However, sign language researchers have not previously availed themselves of the insights to be gained by adapting the framework and methodology of quantitative sociolinguistics to the study of ASL or any other sign language.

This book describes a large project designed to examine whether variation in ASL is subject to the same types of constraints that operate in spoken languages. In this first chapter we describe the variationist framework within which the project was conducted. To establish that framework, we first discuss general concepts in the study of variation. We then explain the overall goals of the project and provide a review of studies of variation in ASL. Finally, we discuss what we expected to discover about sociolinguistic variation in ASL at the outset of the project, based on what we already knew about variation in both spoken and sign languages.

LINGUISTIC AND SOCIOLINGUISTIC VARIATION

Even casual observation reveals that language users sometimes have different ways of saying or signing the same thing. Variation may be realized at all different levels of a language. English, for example, contains numerous examples of variation in the lexicon. Some speakers use the word *couch*, whereas others say *sofa* or *davenport*. ASL also exhibits numerous examples of lexical variation. For example, a number of signs exist for the concepts BIRTHDAY, PICNIC, or HALLOWEEN.

At the phonological level, variation exists in the individual segments that make up words or signs or in parts of those segments. For example, speakers of a wide range of English dialects sometimes delete the final consonant of words that end in consonant clusters such as *test, round,* or *past,* the result being *tes', roun',* and *pas'* (Labov et al. 1968; Guy 1980). In ASL, phonological variation can be seen in signs such as BORED or DEAF, usually signed with a 1 handshape (index finger extended, all other fingers closed) but sometimes produced with both the index finger and the pinky finger extended (Hoopes 1998).

Variation may also occur in the morphological and syntactic components of language. For example, in African American Vernacular English (AAVE), the copula *be* is variably deleted, and the sentences *He is my brother* and *He Ø my brother* both occur. The example of consonant cluster reduction given earlier also concerns morphological variation because the final consonant deleted is often a past-tense morpheme (i.e., a meaningful unit). For example, the phonetic realization of the English word *passed* is [pæst], and the /t/ is the past-tense morpheme that may be variably deleted.

Morphological and syntactic variation in ASL has not yet been extensively explored. However, the variable realization of subject pronouns may serve as an illustration of this type of variation. The ASL verb THINK, for example, can be produced with an overt subject pronoun, as in the sentence PRO.1 THINK, 'I think.' ASL, however, is what is known as a *pro-drop language,* and verbs that can have overt subject pronouns are sometimes produced without them, so that the preceding sentence can be produced simply as THINK, '(I) THINK.' That is, the production of subject pronouns is variable and is likely to be a fruitful area for research, as it has been in languages such as Portuguese and Spanish (see e.g., Cameron 1996; Naro 1981).

Sociolinguistic variation takes into account the fact that the different linguistic variants may correlate with social factors including age, socioeconomic class, gender, ethnic background, region, and sexual orientation. For example, older people may use more of a given variant than younger people; women may use less of a given variant than men; a given variant may occur more in the language used by working-class people than in the language of middle-class users.

Several researchers have offered useful explanations of the concept of a *sociolinguistic variable.* Drawing upon the work of Labov (1966), Fasold characterized the sociolinguistic variable as "a set of alternative ways of saying the same thing, although the alternatives will have social significance" (1990, 223–24). Milroy referred to the "bits of language" that "are associated with sex, area and age subgroups in an extremely complicated way" (1987, 131), the "bits of language" being sociolinguistic variables. She defined a sociolinguistic variable as "a linguistic element (phonological usually, in practice), which covaries, not only with other linguistic elements, but also with a number of extra-linguistic independent social variables such as social class, age, sex, ethnic group or contextual style" (1987, 10). Wolfram defined a linguistic variable as a "convenient construct employed to unite a class of fluctuating variants within some specified language set" (1991, 23). He distinguished between a linguistic variable, which has to do with the linguistic constraints on variation, and a sociolinguistic variable, a construct that unifies the correlation of internal variables and external constraints. Internal constraints are features of a linguistic nature—a sound, a handshape, a syntactic structure—that favor or disfavor a speaker or signer's choice of a particular variant. External constraints are the factors of a social nature that may correlate with the behavior of the linguistic variables. For example, the variable (ING) (in the pronunciation of words such as *working* as *workin'*) has been studied in many dialects of English. Research has shown that (ING) is subject to both internal and external constraints. Thus, the alveolar nasal variant /n/ is associated with verbal categories, and the velar nasal variant /ŋ/ with nominal ones, an internal constraint (Houston 1991). The choice between /n/ and /ŋ/ is also subject to external constraints. Thus, women tend to use the /ŋ/ variant, the standard form, more frequently than men of the same social class (Trudgill 1974).

In spoken languages, other internal constraints on linguistic variation may include the preceding or following segment, the grammatical structure in which the variable item occurs, and syllable stress. In sign languages, internal constraints may include the handshape of the preceding or following sign, for example. We will return to the nature of internal and external constraints in more detail in a later section.

The interaction between linguistic forms and the immediate linguistic environment and between social factors and linguistic forms has been explored extensively in spoken languages for over 40 years, beginning with Fischer's (1958) study of (ING) in the speech of New England school children and further developed by Labov (1966, 1969) in New York City. Other representative studies include Shuy, Wolfram, and Riley's (1968) and Wolfram's (1969) work in Detroit, Sankoff and Cedergren's study of Montreal French (1972), Cedergren's (1973a) dissertation on Panamanian Spanish, and Trudgill's (1974) study of variation in the dialect of Norwich, England. Somewhat later, Rickford (1979, 1987) studied Guyanese Creole, Lesley Milroy (1980) reported on variation in the English of Belfast, Northern Ireland, and James Milroy (1992) proposed a model of language change.

Turning to sign languages, since William C. Stokoe's pioneering work in the 1960s, linguists have recognized that natural sign languages are autonomous linguistic systems, structurally independent of the spoken languages with which they may coexist in any given community. This recognition has brought about extensive research into different aspects of ASL structure and resulted in the recognition that, because natural sign languages are full-fledged autonomous linguistic systems shared by communities of users, the sociolinguistics of sign languages can be described in ways that parallel the description of spoken languages. It follows that sign languages must exhibit sociolinguistic variation similar to that seen in spoken languages.

Indeed, there have been some investigations of sociolinguistic variation in ASL, but these have generally focused on only small numbers of signers, have used a wide variety of methods to collect data, and have looked at a disparate collection of linguistic features. Patrick and Metzger (1996), for example, reviewed 50 sociolinguistic studies of sign languages conducted between 1971 and 1994. They found that more than half of the studies involved 10 or fewer signers and that one-third included only one or two signers. Only nine studies involved 50 or more signers, and a number of these drew on the same data set. Patrick and Metzger found that although the number of sociolinguistic studies increased during the period they surveyed, the proportion of quantitative studies declined from approximately half during the period from 1972 to 1982 to between one-third and one-quarter during the period from 1983 to 1993. The percentage of studies involving large samples (50+ signers) also declined from 33 percent during the first period to a mere 6 percent during the latter period. The result is that we do not yet have a complete picture of what kinds of units may be variable in ASL and of what kinds of internal and external constraints might be operating on these variable units. However, as Padden and Humphries (1988) observed, Deaf people in the United States are aware of variation in ASL even though no one has fully described it from a linguistic perspective.

Padden and Humphries describe "a particular group of deaf people who share a language—American Sign Language (ASL)—and a culture. The members of this group reside in the United States and Canada, have inherited their sign language, use it as a primary means of communication among themselves, and hold a set of beliefs about themselves and their connection to the larger society." They continue, "this . . . is not simply a camaraderie with others who have a similar physical condition, but is, like many other cultures in the traditional sense of the term, historically created and actively transmitted across generations" (1988, 2). Certainly, then, there is an ever-growing awareness among its users of the existence and use of a language that is independent and different from the majority language, English. ASL users are also aware of sociolinguistic variation in ASL. However, many aspects of that variation have yet to be explored. In terms of linguistic structure, most of the studies to date focus on lexical variation, with some studies of phonological variation, and very few of morphological or syntactic variation. In terms of social factors, the major focus has been on regional variation, with some attention paid to ethnicity, age, gender, and factors that may play a particular role in the deaf community, such as audiological status of parents, age at which ASL was acquired, and educational background (e.g., residential schooling as opposed to mainstreaming).

No one has yet examined the interaction of socioeconomic status and variation in a systematic way. So, for example, widespread perception exists among ASL users that there are "grassroots" Deaf people (Jacobs 1980) whose educational backgrounds, employment patterns, and life experiences differ from those of middle-class Deaf professionals and that both groups use ASL. Accompanying this perception is the belief that each group exhibits differences in their signing. However, the sociolinguistic reality of these perceptions has yet to be explored. In this regard Padden and Humphries state that "even within the population of Deaf people in Boston, Chicago, Los Angeles, and Edmonton, Alberta, [smaller groups] have their own distinct identities. Within these local communities, there are smaller groups organized by class, profession, ethnicity, or race, each of which has yet another set of distinct characteristics" (1988, 4).

SOCIOLINGUISTIC VARIATION IN ASL: PROJECT GOALS

The project this book describes aimed to provide a general overview of variation in ASL at the phonological, lexical, morphological, and syntactic levels and to understand which social groups were more likely to use particular variants and which groups were likely to use other variants. That is, we sought to provide for ASL the kind of overview of variation that exists for many spoken languages. Two basic theoretical questions guided our work:

1. Can internal constraints on variation such as those defined and described in spoken languages be identified and described for variation in ASL?
2. Can the external social constraints on variation such as those defined and described in spoken languages be identified and described in ASL?

The answers to these questions are important for two reasons. First, to understand ASL and other sign languages, we need to understand how variation functions in those languages at all linguistic levels. Second, a comparison of variation in ASL with variation in spoken languages has the potential to contribute to what is known about variation in human languages in general. We want to know whether a comparison of variation in sign languages and spoken languages will enable us to define overall characteristics of linguistic variation regardless of modality. We also want to know whether variation in sign languages is characterized by unique features not found in spoken language variation. These are the fundamental issues that underlie the work described in this book. In the remainder of this chapter, we review the work that has already been accomplished on variation in ASL and provide a basic framework within which to consider variation in sign languages. We then define what we expected to find in our data, based on what we already knew about variation in general and variation in sign languages in particular.

PREVIOUS RESEARCH ON VARIATION IN ASL

Users and observers of ASL have clearly been aware of the existence of variation in the language for a long time, and evidence of this awareness can be seen in writings about deaf people's language use. For example, in the proceedings of the fourth Convention of American Instructors of the Deaf held at the Staunton, Virginia, school in 1856, J. R. Keep describes how "teachers of the Deaf and Dumb" should acquire knowledge of signing:

> It is answered in this inquiry that there is *a language of signs; a language having its own peculiar laws, and, like other languages, natural and native to those who know no other.* . . . There may be different signs or motions for the same objects, yet all are intelligible and legitimate, provided they serve to recall those objects to the mind of the person with whom we are communicating. As a matter of fact, however, although the Deaf and Dumb, when they come to our public Institutions, use signs differing in many respects from those in use in the Institutions, yet they soon drop their peculiarities, and we have the spectacle of an entire community recalling objects by the same motions (emphasis added) (1857, 133)

In a response to Keep's remarks, Dunlap (in Keep) compares the signs used at the Indiana School for the Deaf with those used at the Ohio and

Virginia schools and states that there is a need for uniformity "not only in Institutions widely separated but among teachers in the same Institution" (1857, 138). In another response to Keep's remarks, Peet (in Keep) refers to Deaf signers as "those to whom the language is *vernacular*" (emphasis added) and in a discussion of a class of signs described in current theory as classifier predicates states "Here is room for difference of dialects. One Deaf Mute may fall upon one sign and another upon another sign, for the same object, both natural" (1857, 144–146).

In 1875 Warring Wilkinson, principal of the California School for the Deaf in Berkeley, wrote about how "the sign language" comes about:

> The deaf mute child has mental pictures. He wants to convey similar pictures to his friends. Has speech a genesis in any other fact or need? In the natural order of thought the concrete always precedes the abstract, the subject its attribute, the actor the act. So the deaf mute, like the primitive man, deals primarily with things. He points to an object, and seizing upon some characteristic or dominant feature makes a sign for it. When he has occasion to refer to that object in its absence, he will reproduce the gesture, which will be readily understood, because the symbol has been tacitly agreed upon. Another deaf mute, seeing the same thing, is struck by another peculiarity, and makes another and different sign. Thus half a dozen or more symbols may be devised to represent one and the same thing, and then the principle of the 'survival of the fittest' comes in, and the best sign becomes established in usage. (CSD 1875, 37)

These writings provide an indication of early awareness of sign structure and variation, although formal research on the topic did not begin until the 1960s.

Early Research on Variation in ASL

THE DICTIONARY OF AMERICAN SIGN LANGUAGE

Any review of systematic research in variation must take its departure from Carl Croneberg's two appendices to the 1965 *Dictionary of American Sign Language (DASL)* by William Stokoe, Dorothy Casterline, and Croneberg. "The Linguistic Community" (Appendix C) describes the cultural and social aspects of the Deaf community and discusses the issues of economic status, patterns of social contact, and the factors that contribute to group cohesion. These factors include the extensive networks of both a personal and organizational nature that ensure frequent contact even among people who live on opposite sides of the country. Croneberg noted that "there are close ties also between deaf individuals or groups of individuals as far apart as California and New York. Deaf people from New York on vacation in California stop and visit deaf friends there or at least make it a practice to visit the club for the deaf in San Francisco or Los Angeles. . . . The deaf as a group have social ties with each other that extend farther across the nation than similar ties of perhaps any other American minority group" (1965, 310). Croneberg pointed out that these personal ties are reinforced by membership in national organizations such as the National Association of the Deaf (NAD), the National Fraternal Society of the Deaf (NFSD), and the National Congress of Jewish Deaf (NCJD). These personal and organizational patterns of interaction, of course, are central to understanding patterns of language use and variation in ASL. Specifically, as we will discuss in more detail in chapter 3, while ASL is definitely variable at a number of different linguistic levels, there is at the same time the reality and the recognition of a cohesive community of ASL users that extends across the United States.

In "Sign Language Dialects" (Appendix D) Croneberg dealt with sociolinguistic variation, specifically as it pertains to the preparation of a dictionary. He observed, "One of the problems that early confronts the lexicographers of a language is dialect, and this problem is particularly acute when the language has never before been written. They must try to determine whether an item in the language is *standard*, that is, used by the majority of a given population, or *dialect*, that is, used by a particular section of the population" (1965, 313). He outlined the difference between what he termed *horizontal* variation (regional variation) and *vertical* variation (variation that occurs in the language of groups separated by social stratification) and stated that ASL exhibits both. He then described the results of a study of lexical variation undertaken in North Carolina, Virginia, Maine, New Hampshire, and Vermont using a 134-item sign vocabulary list. He found that for ASL, the state boundaries between North Carolina and Virginia also constituted dialect boundaries. North Carolina signs were not found in Virginia and vice versa. He found the three New England states to be less internally standardized (i.e., people within each of the three states exhibited a wide range of variants for each item) and the state boundaries in New England to be much less important, with considerable overlap in lexical choice observed among the three states. Pointing out the key role of the residential schools in the dissemination of dialects, he stated, "At such a school, the young deaf learn ASL in the particular variety characteristic of the local region. The school is also a source of local innovations, for each school generation comes up with some new signs or modifications of old ones" (1965, 314).

In his discussion of vertical variation, Croneberg mentioned the influence of age, ethnicity, gender, religion, and status. His definition of status encompassed economic level, occupation, relative leadership within the Deaf community, and educational background. He further noted that professionally employed individuals who were financially prosperous graduates of Gallaudet College "tend to seek each other out and form a group. Frequently they use certain signs that are considered superior to the signs used locally for the same thing. Examples of such signs are Gallaudet signs, transmitted by one or more graduates of Gallaudet who are now teaching at a school for the deaf, and who are members of the local elite. The sign may or may not later be incorporated in the sign language of the local or regional community" (1965, 318).

Finally, Croneberg commented on what a *standard* sign language might be and stated that "few have paid any attention to the term *standard* in the sense of 'statistically most frequent.' The tendency has been to divide sign language into good and bad" (1965, 318), with older signers and educators of the deaf maintaining the superiority of their respective signs for various reasons. He neatly captured the essence of the difference between prescriptive and descriptive perspectives on language when he wrote, "What signs the deaf population actually uses and what certain individuals consider good signs are thus very often two completely different things" (1965, 319).

LEXICAL VARIATION

The years following the publication of the *DASL* witnessed a number of studies of variation in ASL. At the lexical level, for example, Woodward (1976) examined differences between African American and Caucasian signing. His data, based on a small number of signers, included both direct elicitation and spontaneous language production. He suggested that African Americans tended to use the older forms of signs (i.e., the signs that do not show evidence of phonological processes such as assimilation).

In 1984 Shroyer and Shroyer published their influential work on lexical variation, which drew on signers across the United States. They collected data on 130 words (the criterion for inclusion of a word was the existence of three signs for the same word) from thirty-eight Caucasian signers in twenty-five states. Their findings also included instances of phonological variation, but they did not discuss them as such. They collected a total of 1,200 sign forms for the 130 words, which included nouns, verbs, and some adverbs. Because this study was the point of departure for one portion of our data collection, we will review it in more detail in the chapter on lexical variation.

Other early studies of variation focused on the phonological, morphological, and syntactic levels.

PHONOLOGICAL VARIATION

In the mid-1970s Battison, Markowicz, and Woodward (1975) examined variation in thumb extension in signs such as FUNNY, BLACK, BORING, and CUTE. All of these signs may be produced with the thumb either closed or extended to the side. Thirty-nine deaf signers participated in the study. The social factors determining participant selection were gender, parental audiological status, and the age at which the signer learned to sign (before or after age six). Signers provided intuitive responses about whether they would extend their thumb in certain signs. They were also asked to sign ten sentences under three conditions: as if to a deaf friend, as if to a hearing teacher, and as if in a practice situation. In the third condition, signers were asked to practice the sentences and were videotaped doing so without their knowledge. Six internal constraints on thumb extension were reported to distinguish the signs being investigated: (1) indexicality (i.e., is the sign produced contiguous to its referent, as in a pronoun or determiner?); (2) bending of fingers (i.e., do the other fingers involved in the sign bend, as in FUNNY?); (3) middle finger extension (i.e., is the middle finger extended as part of the sign?); (4) twisting movement (i.e., does the hand twist during the production of the sign, as in BORING?); (5) whether the sign is produced on the face, as in BLACK or FUNNY; and (6) whether the sign is made in the center of one of four major areas of the body.

All of these features are what Wolfram (personal communication, 1993) would call *compositional,* that is, features of the signs themselves that may be playing a role in the variation. The analysis found that signs that were indexic, such as the second-person pronoun PRO.2 ('you'), had the most thumb extension, followed by signs with bending, such as

FUNNY. Signs produced in the center of the signing space, such as PRO.1 ('I'), had less thumb extension. The analysis found no correlation between the linguistic variation and the social factors used to select participants.

Another study of phonological variation, conducted by Woodward, Erting, and Oliver (1976), focused on face-to-hand variation—that is, certain signs that are produced on the face in some regions are produced on the hands in other regions. Such signs include MOVIE, RABBIT, LEMON, COLOR, SILLY, PEACH, and PEANUT. Deaf signers from New Orleans were compared with signers from Atlanta, and data were collected by means of a questionnaire. Results from forty-five respondents suggested that New Orleans signers produced signs on the face that Atlanta signers produced on the hands.

Phonological variation is also evident in the one-handed and two-handed form of the same sign. Woodward and DeSantis (1977b), for example, examined a subset of such signs produced on the face, including CAT, CHINESE, COW, and FAMOUS. They proposed that the features conditioning the variation included outward movement of the sign, high facial location as opposed to low facial location, and complex movement—again all compositional features. On the basis of questionnaire data, they claimed that the signs that tended to become one-handed were those with no outward movement, made in a salient facial area, produced lower on the face, and characterized by complex movement. They also reported that Southerners used two-handed forms more than non-Southerners, that older signers used two-handed signs more than younger signers, and that African American signers tended to use the older two-handed signs more often than Caucasian signers of the same age.

Finally, DeSantis (1977) examined variation in signs that can be produced on the hands or at the elbow, such as HELP or PUNISH. The analysis was based on videotapes of free conversation and on responses to a questionnaire. Data for the study were collected in France in the summer of 1975 and in the United States in the spring of 1976. Ninety-nine deaf signers participated, including 60 from France and 39 from Atlanta. The results were similar for both French and American signers. Men used the hand versions of the signs; women used the elbow versions more frequently.

MORPHOLOGICAL AND SYNTACTIC
VARIATION

At the levels of syntax and morphology, Woodward (1973b, 1973c, 1974) and Woodward and DeSantis (1977a) explored the variable use of three morphosyntactic rules: negative incorporation, agent-beneficiary directionality, and verb reduplication. *Negative incorporation* is a rule in ASL whereby negation is indicated in a verb by outward movement, as in DON'T-KNOW, DON'T-WANT, and DON'T-LIKE, as opposed to KNOW, WANT, and LIKE. *Agent-beneficiary directionality* is the term Woodward and De-Santis used for verb agreement. For example, in the verb "1st-person-GIVE-to-2nd-person," the hand moves from the signer to a space in front of the signer; in "2nd-person-GIVE-to-1st-person," the hand moves from a space in front of the signer to the signer. What Woodward and DeSantis refer to as *verb reduplication* entails the repetition of the movement of the verb as a function of aspect, as in STUDY-CONTINUALLY or STUDY-REGULARLY. For the study of these three rules, data were gathered from 141 signers (132 Caucasian and nine African American signers). Other social variables included whether the signer was deaf (i.e., some signers were hearing, non-native signers), whether the signer's parents were deaf, the age at which sign language was learned, whether the signer attended college, and gender. Signers were shown examples of the linguistic variables in question and asked to indicate on a questionnaire whether they use the forms presented. The overall results showed that deaf signers who had learned to sign before age six and who had deaf parents used the form of the rules being investigated that more closely reflected ASL structure. Internal linguistic constraints are reported only for agent-beneficiary directionality: Woodward proposed a continuum of semantic features ranging from "extremely beneficial" to "extremely harmful" to account for the variation. His continuum predicts that signs such as GIVE (beneficial) will tend to show directionality, whereas signs such as HATE (harmful) will not.

DIACHRONIC VARIATION

Any review of research on variation in ASL must also include Frishberg's 1976 study of historical development in ASL signs. Frishberg compared signs from earlier stages of ASL and from French Sign Language with present-day usage in ASL to demonstrate that changes have occurred in sign formation. Although Frishberg's study is usually viewed as a historical study, it pertains directly to the study of variation in ASL for two related reasons, one general and one specific. The general reason is that historical change manifests itself first in the form of variation. That is, historical change does not occur from one day to the next. Rather, it normally begins as variation, that is, with "different ways of saying the same thing," and those ways may involve sounds, parts of signs, or grammatical structures coexisting within the language of an individual or community. As mentioned earlier, the focus of variation studies is what Weinreich et al. called "orderly heterogeneity" (i.e., a heterogeneity that is not random but rather is governed by internal and external constraints). Moreover, as James Milroy remarked, "In the study of linguistic change, this heterogeneity of language is of crucial importance, as change in progress can be detected in the study of variation" (1992, 1). In some cases, the variation may become stabilized and continue indefinitely, while in other cases it eventually gives way to the use of one form to the exclusion of the other (or others) in question. Viewed across the broad landscape of history, it may be difficult to see the variation that gives rise to large-scale historical changes, such as the change from Old English to Middle English to Modern English or the changes in Romance languages as they developed from Latin. However, a closer look reveals that change does not happen suddenly and that the transition from one period to the next is characterized by considerable synchronic variation. We expect this to be the case for sign languages as well. In addition, we suspect that the historical changes that Frishberg described first manifested themselves as synchronic variation.

The second reason for the pertinence of Frishberg's study to the study of variation is that the processes resulting in the historical change that Frishberg described are still operative in the language today. Therefore, an understanding of the processes involved in language change will help us predict what kind of variation we can expect to find in our data:

> Signs which were previously made in contact with the face using two hands now use one, whereas those which have changed from one-handed articulation to two-handed are made without contact on the face or head. Signs which use two hands tend to become symmetrical with respect to the shape and movement of the two hands. . . . As part of a general trend away from more "gross" movement and hand-shapes toward finer articulation, we find the introduction of new movement distinctions in particular signs, the reduction of compound forms to single sign units, a decreased reliance on the face, eyes, mouth, and body as articulators, and a new context-dependent definition of "neutral" orientation. (1976, xvii)

Frishberg also found that (1) the signs that change from two hands to one are also typically displaced (i.e., change their location from the center of the face and or from contact with the sense organs to the periphery of the face); and (2) signs that change from one hand to two hands tend to centralize by moving toward what Frishberg called the *line of bilateral symmetry* (an imaginary line that runs vertically down the center of the signer's head and torso) and up toward the hollow of the neck. These findings help direct our analysis and determine what to look for. They are also important because they are described as examples of historical change in ASL. The examples of historical change are particularly relevant to the research described in this volume because our data reveal variation between two-handed and one-handed versions of signs, between centralized and noncentralized versions, and between displaced and nondisplaced versions. It appears that some aspects of what Frishberg characterized as historical change, implying perhaps that the change was complete, may be better characterized as change in progress.

Recent Research on Variation in ASL

In recent years the amount of research on variation in ASL and other sign languages has increased substantially. This body of work includes studies of variation at all linguistic levels, from features of individual segments to discourse units. Here we discuss representative studies of variation focusing on different linguistic levels.

LEXICAL VARIATION

The work on lexical variation in ASL is quite extensive. In addition to general studies of lexical variation such as that by Shroyer and Shroyer discussed in the previous section, the literature contains small-scale studies of various social and occupational categories, most of which were undertaken in the 1990s. Researchers have looked at gender differences (Mansfield 1993), differences in the use of signs for sexual behavior and drug use (Woodward 1979, 1980; Bridges 1993), variation related to socioeconomic status (Shapiro 1993), and lexical variation in the signing produced by interpreters for deaf-blind people (Collins and Petronio 1998). (Readers should note that lexical variation has been explored in sign languages other than ASL—see for example Deuchar 1984, Woll 1981, and Kyle and Woll 1985 on British Sign Language; Collins-Ahlgren 1991 on New Zealand Sign Language; Schermer 1990 on Dutch Sign Language; Boyes-Braem 1985 on Swiss German Sign Language and

Swiss French Sign Language; Radutzky 1992 on Italian Sign Language; LeMaster 1990 on Irish Sign Language; Yau and He 1990 on Chinese Sign Language; and Campos 1994 on Brazilian Sign Language).

PHONOLOGICAL VARIATION

Variation at the phonological level has received considerable attention in recent years. Metzger (1993), for example, looked at variation in the handshape of second- and third-person pronouns, which can be produced either with the index finger or with an S handshape with the thumb extended. Metzger's data yielded one example of the thumb variant and one unexpected variant—the fingerspelled pronoun s-h-e. There is some indication that the sign that precedes the thumb variant, AGO, with its extended thumb, may play a role in the occurrence of the thumb variant.

Lucas (1995) studied variation in location in DEAF. In its citation form (that is, the form of the sign that appears in sign language dictionaries and is most commonly taught to second-language learners), the 1 handshape moves from a location just below the ear to a location on the lower cheek near the mouth. However, this sign is commonly produced with movement from the chin location to the ear location or simply with one contact on the lower cheek. Observation might suggest that the final location of the sign (chin or ear) would be governed by the location of the preceding or following sign, so that DEAF in the phrase DEAF FATHER might be signed from chin to ear because the location of the following sign is the forehead, higher than the ear. Similarly, in DEAF PRIDE, one might expect that DEAF would be signed from ear to chin because the sign that follows DEAF begins below the chin.

Contrary to what we might expect, Lucas's analysis (based on 486 examples produced by native signers in both formal and informal settings) using the VARBRUL statistical program (described in chapter 2) indicated that the location of the following and preceding signs did not have a significant effect on the choice of a variant of DEAF. Rather, the key factor is the syntactic function of the sign itself, with adjectives being most commonly signed from chin to ear or as a simple contact on the cheek, and predicates and nouns being signed from ear to chin. Lucas's 1995 study is the foundation for the analysis of DEAF in chapter 4.

Pinky extension formed the subject of a recent investigation by Hoopes (1998), who studied in detail the signing of one native signer.

Some signs that in citation form have a handshape in which the pinky is closed and not extended variably allow the extension of the pinky. Examples include THINK, LAZY, and CONTINUE. Hoopes found that pinky extension seems to cooccur with the prosodic features of ASL that indicate stress. Specifically, in Hoopes's study, pinky extension tended to occur with signs often repeated throughout a topic, before pauses, and with signs lengthened to almost twice their usual duration. Neither topic nor the handshape of the preceding or following sign seemed to have a bearing on the occurrence of pinky extension. This finding parallels Lucas's conclusion about the relative lack of importance of the location of the preceding or following sign. In both cases the phonological factors that one might assume are playing a role—location in the case of DEAF and handshape in the case of pinky extension—in fact do not seem to be conditioning the variation. This is an observation that bears reexamination.

The final recent study of phonological variation we discuss here is Kleinfeld and Warner's (1996) examination of ASL signs used to denote gay, lesbian, and bisexual persons. Thirteen hearing interpreters and 12 deaf ASL users participated in the study. Kleinfeld and Warner focused on 11 lexical items and provided detailed analysis of phonological variation in two signs, LESBIAN and GAY. The analysis showed that the variation can be correlated to some extent with external constraints such as the signer's sexual identity (straight or gay/lesbian).

THE ALTERNATION OF FINGERSPELLING AND LEXICAL SIGNS

Blattberg et al. (1995) examined a subset of the data from the project described in this book. Specifically, they compared middle-class groups aged 15–25 and 55 and up from Frederick, Maryland, and Boston (see data from the project described in this book). They found that both groups of adolescents used fingerspelling in either full or lexicalized forms and that fingerspelling was produced in the area below the shoulder generally used for fingerspelling. The adolescents used fingerspelling primarily for proper nouns and for English terms that do not have ASL equivalents. The adults also used fingerspelling for these purposes, but their use of it also resembled the use of locative signs. In addition, Maryland adults and adolescents used fingerspelling much more frequently than their counterparts in Massachusetts.

Recently scholars have begun to investigate variation in ASL discourse. Haas, Fleetwood, and Ernest (1995) examined back channeling, turn-taking strategies, and question forms in conversations between Deaf-Blind individuals, comparing them to the same features in sighted ASL signing. They found that "in the tactile mode, Deaf-Blind signers use remarkably similar turn-taking and turn-yielding shift regulators as Deaf-sighted signers" (130). Touch is often substituted for eye-gaze, and "turn-yielding often uses a combination of dominant and nondominant hands in yielding to the addressee. The dominant hand rests and the non-dominant hand moves to 'read' the signer's dominant hand. Turn-claiming occurs with the dominant hand of the addressee repeatedly touching or tapping the nondominant hand of the signer until the signer yields and moves their nondominant hand to the 'reading' position." In this particular study, none of the question forms found seemed unique to tactile ASL. Collins and Petronio (1998) found that for yes/no questions, non-manual signals that in sighted ASL include the raising of the eyebrows in Deaf-Blind signing are conveyed manually as either an outward movement of the signs or a drawn question mark.

Malloy and Doner (1995) examined variation in cohesive devices in ASL discourse and explored gender differences in the use of these devices. Specifically, they looked at reiteration and expectancy chains. *Reiteration* is one type of lexical cohesion that "involves the repetition of a lexical item, at one end of the scale; and a number of things in between—the use of a synonym, near-synonym, or superordinate" (Halliday and Hasan 1976, 278). *Expectancy chains* have to do with the fact that, in discourse, certain words or phrases are expected to follow certain others. The predictability of their order creates cohesion. In their analysis of the use of reiteration and expectancy chains in the retelling of a story by two native signers (one male and one female), Malloy and Doner found that the male signer used reiteration more frequently than the female signer but that the signers were similar in their use of expectancy chains.

RESEARCH ON AFRICAN AMERICAN SIGNING

African American signing has been the object of several recent investigations. Studies include Aramburo (1989), Guggenheim (1993), Lewis, Palmer, and Williams (1995), and Lewis (1996). Aramburo and Guggenheim observed lexical variation during the course of structured but informal interviews. Lewis et al. (1995) studied the existence of and attitudes toward African American varieties. Specifically, they described the differences in body movement, mouth movement, and the use of space in the signing of one African American signer who codeswitched during the course of a monologue. In addition, they explored how interpreters handled the codeswitching in spoken language from Standard English to African American Vernacular English (AAVE). Lewis (1996) continued the examination of African American signing styles in his paper on the parallels between communication styles of hearing and deaf African Americans. His investigation took its departure from two observations: first, ASL users recognize the existence of what is often referred to as "Black signing" but have difficulty in explaining what makes it Black; second, uniquely Black or "ebonic" (Asante 1990) kinesic and nonverbal features exist, and these features occur in the communication of both hearing and Deaf African Americans. His investigation described some of these kinesic and nonverbal features—specifically, body postures and rhythmic patterns accompanying the production of signs—in the language that a deaf adult African American woman used. The frequently articulated perspective that African American signing differs markedly from Caucasian signing in all areas of structure—and not just lexically—is thus beginning to be explored.

Perspectives on the Structure of Sign Languages

To understand variation in ASL, we also need to consider the changing perspectives on the basic structure of ASL and of sign languages in general. Current thinking about the linguistic structure of sign languages sheds new light on some of the earlier studies. At the same time, advances in our understanding of sign languages raise important issues for the analysis of the data we describe in this book. For example, the perspective on the fundamental structure of signs has changed dramatically since the earliest studies of variation. Stokoe's perspective, which shaped sign language studies from 1960 until fairly recently, held that signs are composed of three basic parts or *parameters* (the location at which the sign is produced, the handshape, and the movement of the sign) and that, unlike the sequentially produced segments of spoken languages, these parts are produced simultaneously. In a more recent perspective developed by Liddell (1984) and Liddell and Johnson (1989), signs are viewed as composed of movement and hold segments, sequentially produced, somewhat analogous to the consonants and vowels of spoken languages.

In this model, the handshape, location, orientation, and nonmanual signals constitute a bundle of articulatory features that are a part of each movement or hold segment. Currently there is considerable debate about the nature of the segments in question (see e.g., Coulter 1992, Sandler 1992, and Perlmutter 1992). We have chosen to work within the Liddell-Johnson framework because, as Liddell (1992) amply demonstrates, it allows not only for an accurate account of the description of any individual sign but also for an accurate account of phonological processes such as assimilation, metathesis, epenthesis, and segment deletion, processes that play central roles in variation.

Naturally, a central concern of any variation study is to define clearly the linguistic variables under examination and to ensure that they are indeed variable. Current thinking about the linguistic structure of sign languages and about data collection methodology (we address the latter in chapter 2) has implications for the identification of variables in the earlier studies of sign language variation. It is not clear, for example, that the rules of negative incorporation, agent-beneficiary directionality, and verb reduplication in Woodward's (1973b, 1973c, 1974) studies are actually variable in native signer ASL. The apparent variability of these rules merits reexamination because the variability observed may simply have been an artifact of combining data from native and non-native signers. For example, in terms of the semantic continuum proposed for agent-beneficiary directionality (from signs that have "beneficial" connotations to those that have "harmful" connotations), directionality may be obligatory in most of the verbs in question and unrelated to semantic considerations. It is basically the way in which agreement is shown with the subject and the object of the verb and is not optional. Failure to use space properly in these verbs would seem to result not in a variable form but in an ungrammatical one. Although the semantic categorization does seem to work for some verbs (e.g., "beneficial" for GIVE and "harmful" for HATE), it does not work at all for others. For example, it is not clear at all why FINGERSPELL would be labeled as "harmful." It may be that at the time of the study, FINGERSPELL as an agreement verb was an innovation and hence not widely attested, placing it at the "less frequent use of directionality" end of the continuum. But FINGERSPELL cannot therefore be said to have a semantic characteristic of "harmful," the researchers' account of this end of the continuum that they set up.

In summary, research undertaken since the 1960s has provided us with a great deal of information about variable phenomena in ASL and other sign languages, and advances in our understanding of sign language structure have enabled us to define variable forms in a more precise manner. We have gained some idea of the geographic distribution of lexical items and the ways in which social factors such as ethnicity and sexual orientation are likely to influence a signer's choice of a lexical variant. The literature also contains a number of detailed studies of variation at different linguistic levels. As we have noted, however, most of the studies undertaken to date have been rather small-scale, and, aside from Lucas (1995), not many have taken full advantage of the methods and theoretical insights that quantitative sociolinguistics offers, in some cases simply because these methods and insights were not available for earlier studies. The result is that, although we have sufficient evidence to suggest that variation in ASL and other sign languages is systematic and subject to multiple internal and external constraints, we lack a sufficient basis for comparing variation in spoken and sign languages or for comparing variation in ASL as used by signers of diverse social categories in different regions. This study draws upon previous work on the sociolinguistics of sign languages as well as recent theoretical proposals about the nature of sign language structure that have a direct bearing on the identification and description of variables and constraints. These two strands of research, combined with the extensive body of work on variation in spoken languages, inform the current study, which systematically examines variation in ASL as used in representative Deaf communities in seven regions of the United States.

In the following section we consider in more detail the nature of linguistic variables and constraints in both spoken and sign languages.

VARIABLES AND CONSTRAINTS

In this section we first summarize current knowledge about variables and constraints in spoken languages. We begin by describing the kinds of units that can vary in spoken languages.

Linguists generally accept that spoken languages are composed of segments of sound produced by the vocal apparatus and that these segments are themselves composed of a variety of features. In spoken languages whole segments or features of segments may be variable. For example, a final voiced consonant in a word may be devoiced, a non-nasal vowel may acquire the feature of nasalization, and vowels may vary from their canonical position and be raised or lowered within the vowel space.

A new segment may also be created from the features of other segments, as often happens in palatalization. Individual segments may be variably added or deleted, and syllables (i.e., groups of segments) can be added or deleted. Parts of segments, whole segments, or groups of segments can also be variably rearranged, as we see with metathesis in English. It is also important to note that variable whole segments may be bound morphemes. For example, the sound [t] that can be variably deleted when it occurs in word-final consonant clusters, as in the word "missed" [mist], is also a past-tense morpheme. What is variably deleted in this case is not simply a segment, but a morphemic segment.

Word-sized combinations of segments and combinations of words are also variable. With lexical variation we see variation in word-sized segments, where separate morphemes denote the same concept, and use of these separate morphemes correlates with region, ethnicity, gender, and other nonlinguistic categories. But we may also see syntactic variation characterized by the deletion of whole morphemes or by the variable position of whole morphemes.

We also see variation in units of discourse (i.e., units consisting of many words), as in variation in text type or in lists used in narratives (Schiffrin 1994). We see, then, that what varies in spoken languages may range from the features of a segment to a discourse unit that consists of many segments, from the very smallest unit we can identify to the largest.

We can then talk about the kinds of processes that are involved in spoken language variation. Our discussion here takes its departure from Wolfram's (1991b) work on variation in spoken languages. One set of processes involved in variation has to do with the phonological component of a language. For example, variation may be the result of the process of assimilation, such as vowel nasalization or consonant gemination. Variation may result from weakening, as in vowel or consonant deletion. We may see variation resulting from the processes of substitution or addition of elements, as with *coalescence* (the creation of a new segment from two other segments), *metathesis* (the rearranging of the order of segments or features of segments), or *epenthesis* (the addition of a segment). Variation may result from analogy, as in the generalization of third-person singular –s to all present-tense forms of an English verb, or conversely, the deletion of third-person singular –s by analogy with all other verb forms in a given paradigm.

Other processes involved with variation may have to do with the morphosyntactic structure of a language. For example, variation may have to do with the process of the cooccurrence of items in syntactic structure. Negative concord in English is one example, whereby some varieties allow the cooccurrence of more than one negative element while other varieties disallow such cooccurrence. Another process involved in variation at the syntactic level concerns the permutation of items within sentences. The variable placement of English adverbs is a well-known example.

This brings us to a consideration of the internal constraints on spoken-language variation. Recall that internal constraints on variation are features within the immediate linguistic environment that may influence a language user's choice of one or another variable form. Wolfram (1991b) states that the internal constraints on variables may be compositional, sequential, functional, or the result of structural incorporation. *Compositional constraints* have to do with the linguistic nature of the variable itself. For example, Wolfram (1989) studied final nasal absence in the speech of three-year-old African American children. He found that final alveolar nasals were much more likely to be absent than either velar or bilabial nasals. A *sequential constraint* has to do with the role of an element occurring in the same sequence as the variable, either preceding or following it. For example, the final consonant in a word-final consonant cluster is more likely to be deleted if the following segment is another consonant than if it is a vowel. *Functional constraints,* also known as *grammatical category constraints,* relate to the linguistic function of the variable. For example, as explained in the preceding paragraph, the final consonant in a word-final consonant cluster may function as a past-tense morpheme. Finally, the constraint of *structural incorporation* has to do with the syntactic environment in which a variable occurs. For example, copula deletion in AAVE is more likely in a construction with *gonna* (e.g., *He's gonna do it/He Ø gonna do it*) than in one in which the copula is followed by a noun phrase (e.g., *He's my brother/He Ø my brother.*)

External constraints on variation include demographic factors such as region, age, race, gender, and socioeconomic level, all factors that have been shown to covary with linguistic factors. *Covariance* here means that a correlation can be observed between the behavior of a linguistic factor and social factors. For example, working-class speakers may exhibit a greater incidence of the use of a variable than middle-class speakers. African American speakers may use a particular variable less frequently than Caucasian speakers. These correlations capture the sociolinguistic nature of the variation. Earlier studies of both spoken and sign languages focused on a fairly limited inventory of demographic factors such as those listed earlier. However, as Wolfram points out, more recent studies have focused on the nature of communication networks (L. Milroy 1980), the dynamics of situational context (Biber and Finegan 1993), and the projection of social identity (LePage and Tabouret-Keller 1985) "in an effort to describe more authentically the social reality of dialect in society" (Wolfram 1997, 116). That is, researchers have realized that the external constraints on variation are more complex than they thought. There may be more discrete factors such as region and socioeconomic level, but other factors such as who a person interacts with on a daily basis and a person's desire to project a particular identity to others may also play a central role in constraining variation.

WHAT WE EXPECTED TO FIND BASED ON WHAT WE KNEW

We can now turn our attention to what we expected to find in our analysis of the data based on what we knew about variation in both spoken and sign languages. First we consider the kinds of linguistic units we expect to be variable in sign languages.

Table 1.1 provides a comparison of variability in spoken and sign languages. We can see that, at this point, we can expect to find the same kinds of variability in sign languages that pertain to spoken languages. Specifically, the features of the individual segments of signs can vary. In spoken languages, a vowel may become nasalized or a consonant may be devoiced, for example. In sign languages, the handshape, the location, and the palm orientation may vary. Pinky extension and thumb extension in 1 handshape signs (PRO.1 'I,' BLACK, FUNNY) are examples of handshape variation, while signs such as KNOW and SUPPOSE provide examples of location variation because they can be produced at points below the forehead. Individual segments may be deleted or added. Spoken languages do this with consonant cluster reduction at the ends of words such as *west* or *find,* pronounced as *wes'* and *fin'.* In sign languages, movement segments may be added between holds (as in the

TABLE 1.1 *Variability in Spoken and Sign Languages*

	Example	
Variable Unit	Spoken Languages	Sign Languages
Features of individual segments	Final consonant devoicing, vowel nasalization, vowel raising and lowering	Change in location, movement, orientation, handshape in one or more segments of a sign
Individual segments deleted or added	-*t,d* deletion, -*s* deletion, epenthetic vowels and consonants	Hold deletion, movement epenthesis, hold epenthesis
Syllables (i.e., groups of segments) added or deleted	Aphesis, apocope, syncope	First or second element of a compound deleted
Part of segment, segments, or syllables rearranged	Metathesis	Metathesis
Variation in word-sized morphemes or combinations of word-sized morphemes (i.e., syntactic variation)	Copula deletion, negative concord, *avoir/être* alternation, lexical variation	Null pronoun variation, lexical variation
Variation in discourse units	Text types, lists	Repetition, expectancy chains, deaf/blind discourse, turn taking, back channeling, questions

phrase MOTHER STUDY), or hold segments may be deleted between movements (as in the phrase GOOD IDEA). Groups of segments (i.e., syllables) can be deleted. The English words *because* and *supposed (to)* are sometimes pronounced as *'cause* and *'posed to*. The first element of a sign compound, such as WHITE in the compound sign WHITE⌐FALL ('snow') is often deleted. In fact, many signers are not even aware that the first element is part of the standard form.

Other processes are also involved in variation. Parts of segments, segments, or syllables can be rearranged. English speakers sometimes pronounce the word *hundred* as *hunderd,* for example. In sign languages this same process can be seen in the location feature of DEAF. That is, the sign may begin at the ear and end at the chin or vice versa. Everything else about the sign is the same, but the location feature is rearranged. And there can of course be variation in word-sized morphemes, otherwise known as lexical variation, and in combinations of word-sized morphemes (i.e., syntactic variation). As mentioned, variation has also been described in bigger units, that is, in the units of discourse. The one kind of variation that we have not seen in sign languages yet is coalescence, whereby a new segment is created from the features of other segments. We see this in English, for example, when the sound *sh* is created by the interaction between *s* and *y* in the sentence 'I miss you.' Frequently in conversation, *sh* is created and the original segments disappear.

In addition, although we assumed that syntactic variation exists, we were not certain at the beginning of our study what it would look like. Woodward (described earlier) claimed that there was variation in three syntactic rules (what he referred to as agent-beneficiary agreement, verb reduplication, and negative incorporation). However, the data upon which the claim is based combine the signing of native and non-native signers. In our chapter on syntactic variation, we describe the syntactic variation that we see on the data tapes with a particular focus on variable subject presence with plain verbs. Variable subject presence is of particular interest because, in addition to the many verbs in ASL in which the pronominal information is incorporated into the structure of the verb (as in GIVE or FLATTER), there are many so-called plain verbs (Padden 1988) such as LIKE or KNOW that would seem to require the production of separate signs for subject and object. However, as mentioned earlier, ASL seems to be a *"pro-drop" language,* that is, the subject and object pronouns that accompany plain verbs seem to be variably deleted. We explore this deletion and try to discover what governs it.

Finally, in considering what kinds of units can be variable, we have noticed two kinds of variability that seem to be artifacts of a language produced with two identical articulators (i.e., two hands as opposed to one tongue). That is, sign languages allow the deletion, addition, or substitution of one of the two articulators. Two-handed signs become one-handed (CAT, COW), one-handed signs become two-handed (DIE), and a table, chair arm, or the signer's thigh may be substituted for the base hand in a two-handed sign with identical handshapes (RIGHT, SCHOOL). In addition, one-handed signs that the signer usually produces with the dominant hand (i.e., the right hand, if the signer is right-handed) can be signed with the nondominant hand. Variation is also allowed in the relationship between articulators, as in HELP, produced with an A handshape placed in the upward-turned palm of the base hand. Both hands can move forward as a unit, or the base hand can lightly tap the bottom of the A handshape hand.

Expectations of Variable Processes

Table 1.2 shows that the same kinds of processes that pertain to spoken language variation also pertain to sign language variation: assimilation, weakening, substitution and addition, and analogy. We see *assimilation,* for example, when a 1 handshape in PRO.1 (first-person pronoun, 'I') becomes an open 8 handshape in the phrase PRO.1 PREFER ('I prefer'). We see *weakening* when holds are deleted or when a two-handed sign becomes one-handed, as in CAT or COW. *Substitution* occurs when a table top or the signer's knee is substituted for the base hand of a two-handed sign or in the version of DEAF that begins at the chin and moves to the ear, as opposed to beginning at the ear and moving to the chin. *Addition* occurs when movements are added between holds. Finally, the process of *analogy* takes place when a one-handed sign becomes two-handed.

In terms of morphosyntactic variation, we expected to find variation in cooccurrence relations, as found in spoken languages. Recall the example of the cooccurrence of negative items for spoken English. In some varieties of American English, a sentence such as *Ain't nobody seen nothing like that before*, with three negative items cooccurring, is acceptable, while the sentence *No one has seen anything like that before*, with only one negative element, is preferable in other varieties. We are not exactly sure what variable cooccurrence relations might look like in ASL, but a possible candidate for investigation is the cooccurrence of nonmanual signals with lexical signs or with morphological or syntactic units. For example, must a given nonmanual signal such as the mouth configuration in NOT-YET cooccur with the manual sign? Is there any variation in the morphological and syntactic nonmanual signals that occur with manual adverbs and sentences? Another kind of morphosyntactic variation concerns the fact that certain items, such as adverbs in English, can occur in different positions in a sentence. The adverb *quickly,* for example, can occur as follows: *Quickly John ran to the door; John quickly ran to the door; John ran quickly to the door;*

TABLE 1.2. *Variable Processes in ASL: Expected Findings*

Process	Examples	
	Spoken	Signed
Assimilation	Vowel harmony, consonant harmony, gemination, nasalization	Assimilation in handshape, location, orientation
Weakening	Deletion: CC reduction, haplology aphesis, syncope, apocope; vowel reduction	Hold deletion; deletion of one articulator; deletion of first or second element of a compound
Substitution, addition	Coalescence, metathesis, epenthesis	Metathesis; epenthetic movement; substitute hand base
Analogy	3rd person sing. *-s*	Add second hand to one handed sign
Concerning morphosyntactic structures:		
Cooccurrence relations	Negative concord	Possibly nonmanual signals
Item permutation	Adverb placement	Possibly placement of interrogative words

John ran to the door quickly. Again, item permutation in ASL, and specifically the placement in sentences and the repetition of interrogative signs (WHO, WHERE, WHAT, WHEN, WHY, FOR-FOR), is an area that requires exploration.

Table 1.3 summarizes the internal constraints on variable units.

Earlier studies of variation in ASL focused on compositional constraints. That is, the variation was seen to be conditioned by some feature of the variable sign itself, as described earlier in Battison, Markowicz, and Woodward (1975). Sequential constraints are those that have to do with the immediate linguistic environment surrounding the variable, such as the handshape or palm orientation of the sign immediately preceding or following the variable sign, as we see with 1 handshape signs. Grammatical category constraints have to do with the role that the sign's grammatical category plays in the variation, as seen in Lucas (1995). The constraint of structural incorporation has to do with the preceding or following syntactic environment surrounding the variable. We will be considering structural incorporation as a constraint as we try to under-

TABLE 1.3. *Internal Constraints on Variable Units*

Constraint	Example Spoken	Example Signed
	Example	
Constraint	Spoken	Signed
Compositional	Phonetic features in nasal absence in child language	Other parts of sign in question (e.g., handshape, location, orientation)
Sequential	Following consonant, vowel, or feature thereof	Preceding or following sign or feature thereof
Functional	Morphological status of -s in Spanish -s deletion	Function of sign as noun, predicate, or adjective
Structural incorporation	Preceding or following syntactic environment for copula deletion	Syntactic environment for pronoun variation?
Pragmatic	Emphasis	Emphasis (e.g., pinky extension)

stand what conditions the variable subjects in plain verbs (e.g., PRO.1 LIKE vs. [PRO.1] LIKE). Finally, pragmatic features may act as constraints. Hoopes (1998), for example, found that the lengthening of a sign for emphasis played a role in the occurrence of pinky extension. Emphasis is a *pragmatic factor,* a feature chosen by the signer in a particular context to convey a particular meaning. It is not an inherent feature of the sign.

The results of Lucas's (1995) and Hoopes's (1998) studies of DEAF and of pinky extension show us that the analysis of internal constraints on variation in ASL needs to proceed with caution because the identification of such constraints is not always completely straightforward. Although casual observation might suggest the presence of phonological constraints, further examination might well reveal functional constraints (as in the case of DEAF) or pragmatic ones (as in the case of pinky extension). Furthermore, a possible fundamental difference between sign language variation and spoken language variation is emerging from the analysis of internal constraints. This difference relates to the fact that variation in spoken languages is for the most part a *boundary phenomenon*—that is, a phenomenon that affects linguistic segments that occur in sequence, segments occurring at the boundaries of larger units (i.e., words). And as Wolfram (1974) and Guy (1991a) have found, one constraint on -t,d deletion in English, for example, was whether the -t or -d in question was a past-tense morpheme, that is, an affix.

It is now beginning to be clear that sign languages make considerably less use of affixation than do languages such as English, Italian, or Spanish. In sign languages, deletable final segments may not be morphemes in the same way that they are in many spoken languages. The past-tense marking accomplished by the *-t* or *-d* in English is accomplished in different ways in ASL. Similarly, verb agreement is not accomplished by affixation as in many spoken languages. Rather, agreement is accomplished by a change in the location and/or palm orientation feature of one segment of a sign. There are many agreement verbs in ASL, and there are also *plain verbs* (i.e., verbs that do not allow agreement to be incorporated into the location or orientation feature of the verb and that require separate lexical signs for subject and object). There is some anecdotal evidence for plain and agreement variants of the same verb—for example, CALL-ON-TELEPHONE. But because verb agreement is not accomplished by the sequential affixation of morphemes, the internal constraints on such variation will have nothing to do with the sequential occurrence of morphemes, as it does in Caribbean Spanish, for example, with final *-s* aspiration or final *-s* deletion in verbs. Clearly, we will most likely have to search elsewhere in the linguistic environment for some of the internal constraints on variation.

In summary, based on our review of studies of variation in ASL and what we knew about variation in spoken languages, we expected to find variable linguistic units in ASL, parallel to the variable linguistic units in spoken languages. We also anticipated finding variable processes in ASL parallel to the variable processes in spoken languages, and we expected to find internal constraints on the variable units. However, we expected these constraints to reflect the structure of sign languages, different in fundamental ways from the structure of spoken languages, and indeed this turned out to be the case, as we show in chapters 4, 5, and 6. Not all internal constraints on sign language variables parallel the constraints on spoken language variables.

Finally, all aspects of the variation in our data—phonological, morphosyntactic, and lexical—are examined for correlation with external constraints such as region, age, gender, ethnicity, and socioeconomic status. This informs us as to gender, age, and regional differences and allows us to begin to construct the comprehensive picture of sociolinguistic variation in ASL that was the original goal of the project. It allows us to see how variation is distributed in the community and to begin to formulate an empirical response to the perceptions that "grassroots" Deaf people sign differently from middle-class Deaf people or that "Black ASL" differs from what is produced by White signers. Will noncitation 1 handshape (e.g., all fingers open) prove to be more prevalent among male signers than among female signers? Will the chin-to-ear variant of DEAF be more common among working-class signers than among middle-class signers? Will younger signers produce more pro-drop than older signers? Are these examples of stable variation, or is there change underway toward noncitation 1 handshape, chin-to-ear, and pro-drop? These are the kinds of questions that we hope to answer.

In addition, there may be external constraints unique to the Deaf community to which we need to pay attention. For example, we know that some ASL users are raised in deaf families as native users of the language, whereas many are raised in hearing families in which ASL may not be used. Family background may help us understand the variation we observe. Furthermore, the development of residential schools for deaf people and of policies of language use in those schools have had a direct impact on language use in the Deaf community. The history of these developments needs to be considered in any examination of sociolinguistic variation in ASL. We examine this history in chapter 3, but first we describe the methodology of the project that is the focus of this book.

Chapter 2

Collecting and Analyzing an ASL Corpus

The study of language variation requires that we collect and analyze data from a representative sample of the community whose language we are studying. In this chapter we describe how we accomplished these goals. Specifically, we describe the selection of the communities where the research was carried out, participant selection, the role of community-based contact people in data collection, and the procedures we used to gather data on ASL as it is used across the United States. We also discuss the selection of linguistic variables and the statistical procedures we used to analyze the data.

To examine sociolinguistic variation in ASL, we needed to create a large videotaped corpus representative of the language as it is used across the United States. The creation of a videotaped corpus immediately raises the question of what is representative of ASL use. The American Deaf population is linguistically diverse and comprised of numerous Deaf communities. However, as Croneberg pointed out in 1965, despite the diversity, there is definitely a shared sense of ASL as a language used by Deaf people all across the country. Accompanying this shared sense are shared perceptions that signing varies from region to region, that African American signers sign differently from Caucasian signers, and that there exists a "Black ASL" (Aramburo 1989; Lewis 1996). Many in the U.S. Deaf community also believe that younger signers sign differently from older signers, that men differ from women in their signing, and that working-class Deaf people sign differently from middle-class Deaf professionals as a function of social class. The challenge for the project, then, was to capture on videotape ASL signing that would be representative of the regional, ethnic, age, gender, and socioeconomic diversity within the American Deaf community.

COMMUNITIES, LOCAL CONTACTS, AND PARTICIPANTS

The Communities

To obtain a representative sample of regional variation, we selected seven sites: Staunton, Virginia; Frederick, Maryland; Boston, Massachusetts; Olathe, Kansas; New Orleans, Louisiana; Fremont, California; and Bellingham, Washington. The Kansas site included some signers from Kansas City, Missouri; the Fremont site included some signers from San Jose; and the Boston site included young signers at the Learning Center for Deaf Children in Framingham. All of these sites have thriving communities of ASL users. In addition, Staunton, Frederick, Boston, Fremont, and Olathe are the sites of residential schools for deaf children, all with long-established surrounding Deaf communities. A basic motivation in the selection of the sites was to represent major areas of the country—northeast, east, south, midwest, west, and northwest. Because Staunton and Frederick are within driving distance of Washington, D.C., the site of Gallaudet University, where the project was based, they served as the pilot sites. In the late summer and early fall of 1994, we tested and refined the data collection methodology before implementing it in the other five sites. Data were collected in Boston in January 1995; in Kansas City and Olathe in May 1995; in Fremont and Bellingham in June 1995; and in New Orleans in September 1995.

Participant Selection

It is well known that Deaf people in the United States have many different kinds of backgrounds. Because our focus is on sociolinguistic variation in ASL, we set out to recruit native or near-native ASL users, including deaf individuals from Deaf families who learned to sign natively in the home as well as deaf individuals who learned to sign before age 5 or 6 from their peers in residential schools. Because we wanted to control for the effects of late and second-language acquisition as much as possible, we did not recruit individuals who, while competent adult users of ASL, learned to sign as adolescents either because of lack of exposure to the language or because they were born hearing and were native speakers of English before being deafened.

Our sample included both Caucasian and African American signers in four sites: Boston, New Orleans, Kansas and Missouri, and California. The goal was to gather empirical evidence of the differences that signers feel exist between the signing of African Americans and Caucasian. Although Latino, Asian, and Native American Deaf communities can be found in various areas of the United States, we did not recruit participants from these communities for two reasons. The first reason is practical. The time for data collection was limited and did not allow us to

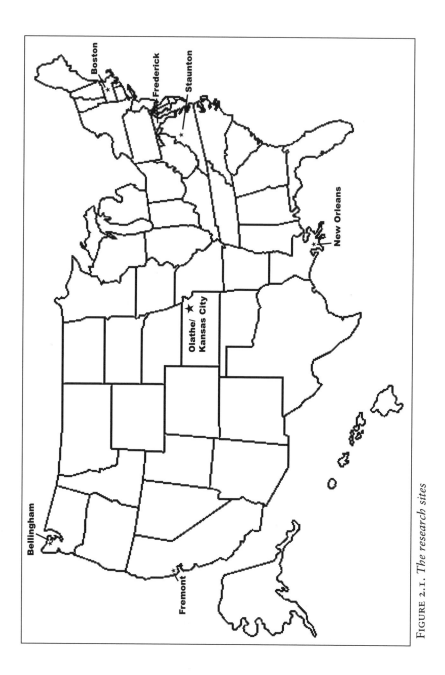

FIGURE 2.1. *The research sites*

collect representative data from all Deaf groups in the country. We hope that the project design and data analysis described here will provide a point of departure for research in other communities. The second reason concerns the sociolinguistic role of a third language in many communities. That is, we focus on deaf people who use ASL and English in their everyday lives, with special attention to variation in ASL. Latino, Asian, and Native American communities often have Spanish, Chinese, Vietnamese, Hmong, Navajo, or other spoken and sign languages in the picture (see e.g., Davis and Supalla 1995; Gerner de García 1995; Ramsey 2000). Clearly sociolinguistic research is warranted in these multilingual communities. However, the complexities of dealing with the effects of a third, fourth, or nth language simply exceeded the practical capabilities of the project.

Participants were recruited in three different age groups: 15–25, 26–54, and 55 and up. The division of participants into these age groups was motivated by developments in language policy in deaf education. Specifically, the early 1970s witnessed both the passage of Public Law 94–142 (the Education of All Handicapped Children Act of 1975, resulting in the implementation of mainstreaming policies) and the shift from purely oral methods of instruction to the philosophy of Total Communication (Denton 1976), which often results in the simultaneous use of speech and signing. The consequences for the acquisition of ASL are that children who previously might have been sent to residential schools and exposed to ASL by their peers (while oral methods dominated in the classroom) may now be mainstreamed with hearing children and may not be exposed to ASL until much later, if at all. Children in residential schools, while still using ASL among themselves, would now be exposed to Total Communication in the classroom. At the same time, ASL has been implemented as the medium of instruction in several locations since the mid-1980s, including at two of our sites (Fremont and Boston), and the recognition of ASL as a full-fledged language independent from English has increased dramatically in recent years. Participants in the 15–25 age group, then, could be expected to have been exposed to Total Communication, possibly to ASL as the medium of instruction, and to increased awareness of the status of ASL. Participants in the 26–54 group would have been exposed to oralism and would also have witnessed the change to Total Communication and the beginning of changes in attitudes about ASL resulting largely from Stokoe's pioneering work in the early 1960s. Finally, participants in the 55-and-up group would most likely have been educated in residential schools through the oral method and possibly also through fingerspelling, with ASL tolerated in the dormitories but certainly not allowed in the classroom. In fact, some project participants in this group told the familiar story of being physically punished for using ASL in class.

Gender has been a major focus of research on variation in spoken languages since the earliest sociolinguistic studies (Fischer 1958; Wolfram 1969; Trudgill 1974). Labov summed up the results of a large number of studies conducted in various cities throughout the world with two general principles:

(I)   In stable sociolinguistic stratification, men use a higher frequency of nonstandard forms than women.
(II) In the majority of linguistic changes, women use a higher frequency of the incoming forms than men. (1990, 205–6)

In recent years the number of studies of language and gender has expanded greatly. Scholars investigating the social patterning of linguistic variation have moved beyond viewing gender as a dichotomous variable and developed much more finely nuanced views of the relationships among language, gender, and identity (see e.g., Dubois and Horvath 1999; Eckert 1989, 2000; Galindo and Gonzales 1999; Hall and Bucholtz 1995; Romaine 1999; Wodak and Benke 1997). Sign language researchers have also begun to investigate gender differences (see e.g., Nowell 1989; Wulf 1998). We recruited both male and female participants in order to determine whether the principles that Labov (1990) summarized also applied to sign languages and to explore the complex interplay between gender and variable linguistic forms in Deaf communities.

Our sample also included both working-class and middle-class participants. Although social class has long been a major focus of sociolinguistic research on spoken languages, the relationship between linguistic variation and socioeconomic status has not been examined closely in ASL. To define social classes, we followed demographic studies of the Deaf community (see e.g., Schein 1987; Schein and Delk 1974). Working-class participants had not continued their education past high school (in some cases, not past elementary school or eighth grade) and worked in blue-collar, vocational-type jobs. In most cases, they also lived their entire lives in the places where they grew up and went to school. By contrast, middle-class participants had completed college (and in many cases had graduate degrees), were working in professional positions, and often had left their home areas to go to school but had since returned and settled. In all of the seven sites, we were able to recruit participants in all three age groups and at both socioeconomic levels, with one very striking exception: We were unable to recruit any middle-class African American participants in the 55-and-up age group. This is striking and sad evidence of the double discrimination confronting deaf African Americans of this generation.

Summaries of the demographic characteristics of the participants and of the project appear in table 2.1 and the boxed text.

The Project at a Glance

A seven-year project on sociolinguistic variation in ASL. (June 1, 1994–July 31, 2000)

OVERVIEW OF DATA COLLECTION:

Sites Visited:

1. Staunton, Va.
2. Frederick, Md.
3. Boston, Mass.
4. New Orleans, La.
5. Fremont, Calif.
6. Olathe, Kans./Kansas City, Mo.
7. Bellingham, Wash.

Twelve groups at each site, except for Virginia, Maryland, and Washington (only Caucasian groups)

African American Groups		Caucasian Groups	
Middle Class	Working Class	Middle Class	Working Class
15–25	15–25	15–25	15–25
26–54	26–54	26–54	26–54
(55+)	55+	55+	55+

A total of 207 ASL signers (Each group consisted of two to six signers)

OVERALL GOAL OF THE PROJECT:

A description of phonological, morphosyntactic, and lexical variation in ASL and the correlation of variation with external factors such as age, region, gender, ethnicity, and socioeconomic status

TABLE 2.1. *Signer Social and Demographic Characteristics*

Site	Age			Social Class		Gender		Ethnicity		Language Background	
	15–25	26–54	55+	WC	MC	M	F	AA	C	ASL	Other
Boston, Mass. (*n* = 30)	9	12	9	17	13	15	15	11	19	5	25
Frederick, Md. (*n* = 21)	7	6	8	11	10	11	10	—	21	6	15
Staunton, Va. (*n* = 26)	5	11	10	15	11	12	14	—	26	5	21
New Orleans, La. (*n* = 34)	7	15	12	20	14	17	17	13	21	8	26
Olathe, Kans.; Kansas City, Mo. (*n* = 42)	12	16	14	26	16	20	22	14	28	7	35
Fremont, Calif. (*n* = 34)	6	16	12	18	16	16	18	15	19	11	23
Bellingham, Wash. (*n* = 20)	6	7	7	9	11	12	8	—	20	3	17
Totals (*n* = 207)	52	83	72	116	91	103	104	53	154	45	162

Note: WC = working class; MC = middle class; AA = African American; C = Caucasian.

The Recruitment Process: The Contact People

The approach to the participants was guided by the work of Labov (1972a, 1984) and Milroy (1987). Each group interviewed consisted of two to seven individuals. Groups were assembled in each area by a contact person, a Deaf individual living in the area with a good knowledge of the community. These contact people were similar to the "brokers" described by Milroy, individuals who "have contacts with large numbers of individuals" in the community (1987, 70). At the four sites where we interviewed both Caucasian and African American signers, we had two contact people, one for each community. It was the responsibility of the contact people to identify fluent lifelong ASL users who had lived in the community for at least ten years.

Some potential participants expressed reluctance to the contact person about being videotaped and declined the invitation to participate. Some of the actual participants were asked about this reluctance and gave two reasons for it. The first concerned fear of being videotaped, with the knowledge that the tapes might be shown at large gatherings such as professional conferences. This reason is not surprising, given that sign language researchers depend on videotaped data but, as a result, simply cannot guarantee participants the anonymity enjoyed by participants in spoken language studies in which data are usually audiotaped.

The second reason related to a lack of awareness about the importance of this kind of research. This points to a lack of metalinguistic awareness and even to negative attitudes about ASL and variation. There is, for example, a very commonly expressed perception that phonological variation, such as signing a two-handed sign one-handed or signing a sign usually produced on the forehead at a lower location, is just "lazy" signing. Notwithstanding this reluctance of some potential participants, the contact people were able to recruit 207 people who met the criteria for the study. In some cases the contact people also participated in data collection activities.

Data Collection

The first part of each videotaped session consisted of approximately one hour of free conversation among the members of a particular group without the researchers present. In most cases the participants already knew each other, and it was very easy to get a conversation started. After this period of free conversation, two participants were selected from the group and interviewed in depth by the deaf researchers about their backgrounds, social networks, and patterns of language use. (In cases where there were only two participants, both were interviewed.)

It has been demonstrated that ASL signers tend to be very sensitive to the audiological and ethnic status of the interviewer (i.e., hearing or deaf, Caucasian or African American) (Lucas and Valli 1992). This sensitivity may be manifested by rapid switching from ASL to Signed English or contact signing in the presence of a hearing person. That is, many Deaf people tend to adjust their signing to bring it closer to what they perceive as the preference of their interlocutor, a phenomenon described by Beebe and Giles (1984) in relation to their accommodation theory. We clearly had to be very mindful of the Observer's Paradox articulated by Labov (1972a), which states that, in studies of the use of the vernacular, "our goal is to observe the way people use language when they are not being observed" (61). To ensure the consistent elicitation of ASL rather than Signed English or contact signing, the participants were never interviewed by a hearing researcher. In addition, all of the African American participants were interviewed by a Deaf African American research assistant. Caucasian researchers were not present during the African American groups' sessions and interviews.

Each data collection session concluded with the interviewees being shown the same set of 34 pictures and fingerspelled words (the latter in cases where an appropriate picture representing the target concept was not found) to elicit their signs for the objects or actions represented in the pictures or by the fingerspelling. Participants also provided general information about themselves on a one-page questionnaire and signed a consent form.

These data collection procedures, consisting of free conversation, an interview, and an elicitation task, were followed for 62 groups. Data were collected at community centers, at schools for deaf students, in private homes, and for three groups, at a public park. Two Panasonic S-VHS camcorders were used on tripods and with wide-angle lenses. In some cases one camera provided a panoramic view of the group while the other provided a close-up view of individuals; in other cases only one camera was used and provided a clear view of the whole group.

As soon as the data collection was completed for the first site, a cataloguing system was developed to provide easy access to the data tapes, and a computer database was developed to store a wide variety of information about the tapes. Information entered into the database about each group interviewed includes details about when and where the group was videotaped, who appears on each tape (names, ages, educational background, occupation, patterns of language use, and so forth), and detailed information about the phonological, syntactic, and lexical variation observed.

Three target phonological variables were identified early in the data-collection process. In selecting the variables, we followed the guidelines provided by Labov (1963) and Wolfram (1991b). That is, we selected variables that are sufficiently common in the data to allow for statistical analysis and that, judging from initial viewing of the data, appeared to be socially stratified on a number of different dimensions. The three target variables are as follows:

1. Signs produced with a 1 handshape (that is, in citation form, index finger extended and all other fingers and thumb closed). Many signs are produced with this handshape. Moreover, the 1 handshape is found with lexical signs, pronouns, and classifier predicates. There is also a wide range of variation with these signs, including, thumb open, all fingers and thumb open, and several other forms.

2. Signs produced in citation form on the side of the forehead, in the center of the forehead, or at the side of the eye and that allow downward movement, that is, the sign can be produced at a location lower than the citation location. These signs are exemplified by KNOW, SUPPOSE, and FOR.

3. DEAF, which in citation form is produced from ear to chin but which can also be produced from chin to ear or as a contact on the cheek (i.e., it shows variation in location). We should clarify that DEAF is representative of signs like it that are produced on the face and that move on the vertical plane between the chin and the ear. Other signs in this class include INDIAN, HOME, DORM, and YESTERDAY. We chose to focus on DEAF because it is the only one that clearly allows metathesis (INDIAN, DORM, and

YESTERDAY definitely do not—they move only from chin to ear; there are varying opinions about HOME. Liddell and Johnson (1989) claim that it allows metathesis, whereas there is disagreement among Deaf informants as to whether it does). DEAF also occurs frequently enough in discourse to allow for statistical analysis.

In our examination of syntactic variation, the focus was on the fact that in ASL, lexical verbs can be produced without an overt subject pronoun. For this reason ASL has been characterized as a pro-drop language. This absence of a subject pronoun is observed not only with verbs that indicate the subject and object in their morphological structure but also with so-called plain verbs (Padden 1988), verbs whose morphology does not include such subject and object marking and in theory require the production of an overt subject pronoun or noun phrase. The target variables for this part of the analysis were plain verbs with and without overt subjects, extracted from narratives that occurred in the data.

The focus for the analysis of lexical variation was the responses by the interviewees to the thirty-four pictorial and fingerspelled stimuli. In addition, we made note of phonological, syntactic, and lexical variation on the tapes for which there may have been only one or two examples, not enough for statistical analysis but nevertheless worth noting. In one case, for example, a participant substituted the table in front of him for the base hand in SCHOOL. In another case a signer used the chair arm as the base for IMPORTANT. Although not numerous, these examples show us the range of variation that occurred on the tapes.

The information entered into the database about phonological and lexical variation included the identification of the specific variable observed, a brief description of the nature of the variation, the code for the signer producing the example, and for the phonological examples, the syntactic context in which the variable occurred. An example from the database follows:

CONV PV Hdsp PRO.2 1 hdsp -cf; palm up, thumb extended, 234 relaxed (pause) PRO.2 BORN WHERE PRO.2 (pause) FIIT

This is an example of the 1 handshape (Hdsp; 1 Hdsp) target phonological variable (PV) that occurred in a conversation (Conv) as opposed to in a narrative and is not a citation form (-cf). This particular 1 hand-

shape is a second-person pronoun (PRO.2). Because the sign was produced with the palm up, the thumb extended, and with the middle, ring,
and pinky fingers relaxed (as opposed to tightly closed), this is considered an example of a noncitation form. The sentence in which this sign
occurred was (pause) PRO.2 born where PRO.2 (pause), "Where were you
born?" and is of interest also because of the occurrence of pronoun copy.
We note the occurrence of pauses because they may play some role in the
variation. Finally, this sentence was produced by FIIT, a 74-year-old
working-class Caucasian female from Fremont, hence "F," the IIT being
her individual code. The string of information shown in the example is
typical of the information entered in the database for each example extracted from the corpus.

MULTIVARIATE ANALYSIS WITH VARBRUL

The entry of data from the videotapes into the database leads to a discussion of variable rule analysis because the database was designed
specifically to facilitate the use of VARBRUL, the statistical package that
we used for analysis of the target phonological and syntactic variables.
Because variable rule analysis (VARBRUL) has not been commonly used
in sign linguistics, we briefly describe the program here.

The goal of the quantitative study of language variation is to understand linguistic phenomena and their relationship to social structure.
We want to be able to understand, for example, the direction of linguistic change or the relationship between the form and the grammatical function of a class of signs. We also want to be able to test hypotheses about the relationships between different linguistic and social
constraints, to compare alternative analyses, and to create models that
allow us to make predictions (Guy 1993, 235). To accomplish these
goals, we need to go beyond reporting percentages of occurrence or
nonoccurrence of linguistic forms and use statistical procedures that
enable us to model simultaneously the many potential influences on
variation.

The quantitative modeling of the correlations between language variation and the multiple contextual factors that promote or inhibit use of a
particular variant is no easy matter. In studies that relate variation to a
single contextual factor (e.g., the effect of the following sign on the
choice of a variant of DEAF), a simple statistical procedure such as

comparison of means with the help of a t-test might be adequate. However, such a model is inadequate when multiple influences are likely to be involved.

Analysis of variance is another technique that has been used in studies of spoken language variation (e.g., Tarone 1985) to relate variation to a single independent variable with multiple levels. In principle, it is possible to extend an analysis of variance to additional variables, but with the kind of data usually collected in studies of linguistic variation, this is hardly ever practicable. An example should help make clear why this is the case. Bayley (1994) originally hypothesized that variation in *-t,d* deletion in Tejano/Chicano English was influenced by 11 separate independent variables, each of which had theoretical and empirical support from previous studies. The 11 independent variables were all nominal (that is to say, they could be further subdivided into two or more categories) and were as follows:

> Morphological class: monomorpheme, semiweak verb (e.g., *left*),
> past tense or past participle, *-n't*
> Phonetic features of the preceding segment: /s/, nasal, stop, fricative,
> /r/, /l/
> Phonetic features of the following segment: consonant, /l/, /r/, glide,
> vowel, pause
> Syllable stress: unstressed, stressed
> Voicing agreement of the preceding and following segments:
> homovoicing, heterovoicing
> Cluster length: CCC, CC
> Speech style: conversation, reading continuous passage, word list
> Reported first language: English, Spanish
> Current home language: English, English and Spanish, Spanish
> Gender: male, female
> Age: 14–24, over 25

In this model there are thus 11 separate factor groups (independent variables) comprising a total of 34 separate factors (categories). The number of possible combinations of factors (also known as *cells*) is 82,944. This is an extremely large number of cells for a multiple analysis of variance (ANOVA). In addition, most cells are empty, although Bayley collected nearly 5,000 tokens of the dependent variable—final consonant clusters. This is because many combinations are linguistically impossible or highly unlikely, leaving more than 80,000 cells with missing data.

Moreover, the majority of the filled cells represent only one token of the dependent variable, presence or absence of final *-t,d*. Algorithms for calculating ANOVA normally require equal numbers of tokens in each cell and are clearly inapplicable to such a case. Even algorithms for calculating unbalanced ANOVAs will fail when faced with such extreme distributional imbalances. ANOVA is a statistical procedure designed to deal with the kind of balanced data that emerge from controlled experiments. It is inadequate to handle the kind of naturally occurring data that are collected in studies of sociolinguistic variation.

Modeling linguistic variation can be carried out by a number of commercial statistical software packages, usually under the name of logistic regression (e.g., Norušis and SPSS 1996). However, in sociolinguistics, the programs known as VARBRUL have been used most extensively because they have been deliberately designed to handle the kind of data obtained in studies of variation. They also provide heuristic tools that allow the investigator to modify hypotheses and reanalyze the data easily. The statistical bases for the VARBRUL programs are set out in Sankoff (1988), and the procedures for using the software are explained in Young and Bayley (1996) and in the documentation that accompanies the programs. The two most widely available versions are GoldVarb for the Macintosh (Rand and Sankoff 1990) and VARBRUL for the PC (Pintzuk 1988).

A full explanation of the steps involved in carrying out a multivariate analysis with VARBRUL is beyond the scope of this chapter. Here, we limit ourselves to addressing briefly several questions that arise early in a study, to the interpretation of results, and to the limitations inherent in the program. Readers who wish to pursue the topic in greater depth should consult the literature on the subject (e.g., Cedergren and Sankoff 1974; Guy 1980, 1988, 1993; Rousseau 1989; Rousseau and Sankoff 1978; Sankoff 1988; Sankoff and Labov 1979).

The first steps in a variable rule analysis are to define the variable and the envelope of variation. That is, what forms count as instances of the variable? Are the forms that vary indeed two ways of saying the same thing? In many studies, particularly of phonological variation, defining the envelope of variation is not a problem. For example, KNOW signed at the level of the temple and KNOW signed at the level of the cheek clearly have the same referential meaning. However, it becomes less obvious that variable forms meet the criterion of being two ways of signing the same thing at higher levels of linguistic structure, an issue that has been raised by Lavandera (1978).

The second issue that arises early in a study concerns specifying the factors that may potentially influence a signer's choice of a variant. In general, it is best to be liberal at this stage. Lucas (1995), for example, investigated the potential effects of eight separate factor groups on the choice of a variant of DEAF. As it turned out, most of these groups proved not to be statistically significant. However, the labor of coding for many factors was not in vain. The study demonstrated that Liddell and Johnson's (1989) claim that variation in the form of DEAF is influenced primarily by the location of the preceding sign is at best incomplete. Lucas also demonstrated the previously unsuspected influence on the choice of variant of the grammatical category to which DEAF belongs.

Once coding is complete and the data are entered into the program, VARBRUL estimates the factor values (or probabilities) for each contextual factor specified (e.g., the handshape of the preceding segment or the social class to which a signer belongs). The program provides a numerical measure of the strength of each factor's influence, relative to other factors in the same group, on the occurrence of the linguistic variable under investigation. Values range between 0 and 1.00. A factor value, or *weight,* between .50 and 1.00 indicates that the factor favors use of a variant relative to other factors in the same group. For example, Baugh's (1983) study of African American Vernacular English (AAVE), examined -t,d deletion, among other variables. VARBRUL results for the grammatical category of the word containing the -t,d cluster are shown in table 2.2.

Baugh's results show that, like speakers of other English dialects, speakers of AAVE are more likely to delete final -t,d when it does not carry any grammatical meaning, as is the case in monomorphemic words such as *just, mist,* and *past.* They are less likely to delete -t,d when it functions as a past-tense ending. Ambiguous, or semiweak verbs, which are

TABLE 2.2. *-t,d Deletion by Grammatical Class in African American Vernacular English (AAVE)*

Grammatical Function	VARBRUL Weight
No grammatical function, e.g., *past*	.683
Ambiguous function, e.g., *lost*	.523
Past tense function, e.g., *passed*	.353

Source: Baugh 1983, 98.

characterized by an internal vowel change and affixation of *-t,d* such as *lost* or *left,* have an intermediate value.

In addition to grammatical function, Baugh investigated the influence of a number of other factors, among them the type of speech event from which the tokens were extracted. He divided the speech events into four types, depending on the speakers' familiarity with one another and the extent to which they participated in African American vernacular culture. He hypothesized that participants in type-1 events, characterized by familiarity of the speakers and shared participation in African American vernacular culture, would favor use of vernacular forms, in this case, *-t,d* deletion. Conversely, he hypothesized that vernacular forms would be less likely to occur in type-4 events, where the speakers were not well acquainted and where AAVE was not common to all. The results for this factor group are shown in table 2.3.

The results for speech event all hover around .5 and show that, contrary to Baugh's hypothesis, *-t,d* deletion was *not* significantly affected by this factor.

In addition to calculating values or weights for each factor, VARBRUL also calculates the *input probability,* the overall likelihood that speakers/signers will choose the variant selected as the *application value* (the value that counts as an application of the "rule" being investigated). In Bayley's study of *-t,d* deletion in Tejano English, for example, the input probability was .469, indicating that there was a fairly high likelihood that *-t,d* would be deleted regardless of the presence or absence of any other factor in the environment. The program provides several measures of goodness of fit between the model and the data. These

TABLE 2.3. *-t,d Deletion by Speech Event Type in African American Vernacular English (AAVE)*

Speech Event	VARBRUL Weight
Type 1. Familiar participants, all of whom share AAVE	.482
Type 2. Participants are not well acquainted, but all share AAVE	.523
Type 3. Participants are well acquainted but do not share AAVE	.499
Type 4. Participants are not well acquainted, and AAVE is not common to all	.496

Source: Baugh 1983, 98.

include the total chi-square, the chi-square per cell, and the log likelihood. The total chi-square measures the degree of interaction among factors from different factor groups. The chi-square-per-cell figure is simply calculated by dividing the total chi-square by the number of cells. The lower the chi-square-per-cell figure, the less likely there is interaction among factors. The log likelihood also measures goodness of fit. In general, figures closer to zero represent better models than log likelihoods further removed from zero (see Young and Bayley 1996, 272–73). Finally, VARBRUL provides a means of testing whether a particular factor group contributes significantly to the model of variation by means of the step-up/step-down procedure, with the significance level set at .05. (See Young and Bayley 1996, 279–80, for information about how to test whether factors within a group differ significantly from one another.)

INTERPRETING THE RESULTS OF VARBRUL ANALYSIS

VARBRUL enables us to give precise and replicable measures of the strength of a wide range of contextual influences on a speaker or signer's choice among variable linguistic forms. However, simply reporting results such as those given earlier by Baugh is not sufficient. Rather, our goal as linguists is to understand why we achieve the results that we do. Take the effect of grammatical category on the likelihood of -t,d deletion as an example.

Many explanations have been proposed for the widely replicated pattern seen in table 2.2. At first glance, it appears as though the amount of functional load carried by final -t,d might provide an adequate explanation. Nothing is lost if a speaker says *jus' me* instead of *just me,* but it is not so easy to determine whether *I miss/Ø/ my friend* refers to a past appointment or to an ongoing emotional state. Guy (1980), however, showed that the rate of -t,d deletion from past participles (e.g., *she was miss/Ø/ by all*) did not differ significantly from the rate of deletion from past-tense forms, despite the fact that past participles carry a lighter functional load.

Guy's (1980) finding that -t,d is deleted from past participles and past-tense verbs at the same rate suggests that we must look beyond functionalism for an explanation. A number of possible explanations have been proposed. Guy (1993) and Bayley (1991), for example, observe that the grammatical categories that are subject to *-t,d* deletion are characterized by different internal morphological boundaries and that regular past-tense forms and past participles have the same internal structure. The results for grammatical category can thus be explained by a boundary constraint on *-t,d* deletion. A deletion rule applies freely when no internal boundary is present, as is the case with monomorphemes such as *past*. Deletion is inhibited somewhat by the formative boundary in semiweak verbs and strongly inhibited by the inflectional boundary in regular past-tense verbs and past participles.

Other explanations have also been advanced. Guy (1991a, 1991b) proposed an exponential model of constraints to explain the relationships observed in the grammatical category factor group, which related the retention of past-tense, semiweak, and monomorphemic clusters in the ratio of x: x^2: x^3. He explained this ratio as a result of a model of lexical phonology, whereby the three types of clusters are subject to one, two, or three passes of a deletion rule. More recently, Kiparsky (1994) suggested that the exponential relationship pointed out by Guy could be explained by an exploded optimality constraint.

Our point here is not to argue which of these explanations is correct.[1] Indeed, we want to emphasize that the results achieved by the use of VARBRUL—or any other statistical program—do not in and of themselves provide explanations about linguistic structure or the social distribution of linguistic variants. Rather, explanations must be sought in linguistic theory and in our understanding of the history and social structure of the communities we study.

METHODS: SUMMARY

To sum up, the project described in this volume relies on the methods of data collection and analysis developed by sociolinguists over the last four decades. That is, with the exception of data on lexical variation, the analysis relies on language samples collected in the community in settings designed to elicit informal signing. The study of sign languages requires more intrusive methods of observation than the study of spoken languages. That is, video cameras and the small size of many closely knit

---

1. See Labov (1997, 148–51) for a discussion of the theoretical models proposed to account for the constraints on *-t,d* deletion.

Deaf communities magnify the effects of the Observer's Paradox. We sought to counteract the effects of intrusive observation and participants' concerns about protecting anonymity by working with respected contact persons in each community, by videotaping groups without a researcher present, and by arranging for interviews to be conducted by a Deaf researcher of the same racial background as the interviewee. As the distribution of variants described in the following chapters suggests, although we cannot claim to have overcome all the effects of the Observer's Paradox, the procedures described in this chapter did result in the elicitation of a great deal of relatively informal signing.

The quantitative analysis, like variable selection and data elicitation, relies on methods that have long been used in variationist sociolinguistics. The logistic regression modules now available in statistical software packages such as SPSS might have served our purpose of discovering whether variation in ASL was indeed systematic (Young and Yandell 1999). However, we wished to compare our results with previous studies of variation in spoken languages, most of which have employed VARBRUL. The diversity of our sample, as well as the natural tendency of social factors to interact, necessitated that we recode many of the data files to deal with interactions. As described in the chapters on phonological and morphosyntactic variation, VARBRUL enabled us to perform this task and, in the process, uncover a number of surprising aspects of the social distribution of patterns of variation.

Chapter 3

The Sociohistorical Context for ASL Variation

In order to understand the nature of sociolinguistic variation in the American Deaf community, we need to understand the sociohistorical context in which it occurs, especially the parts of this context that concern the residential schools for deaf children and the social and political organizations formed by deaf people. Researching the historical language attitudes and policies in schools for deaf students can aid in our understanding of variation because we can better visualize how other people perceived and treated deaf people and how these perceptions may have shaped the language use in deaf communities. The following chapters discuss in more detail some of the similarities and differences that these covert and overt policies may have affected.

The first section of this chapter provides a brief historical sketch of the schools in each of the seven sites in the study and an account of their connection to the Hartford, Connecticut, school, the first U.S. school for the deaf. The second section discusses a repeated pattern in these sites, a transition from the exclusive use of signs to the use of a combined method and then to oralism. The chapter also explores how the residential schools participated directly in the creation of an ASL community across the United States.

It is well known that the majority of deaf children are born to hearing parents and therefore that most deaf children do not acquire ASL from their parents in the same way that hearing children acquire their native language from their parents. Overwhelmingly, it has been the case that deaf children have acquired ASL from their peers in residential school settings, peers who belong to the minority of deaf children born to deaf parents and who are thus native users of ASL. Lane, Hoffmeister, and Bahan explain:

> [R]esidential schools for the Deaf—large, centrally located schools providing education from preschool through high school (and, in some cases adult education)—were at one time the center of the DEAF-WORLD. However, starting in the 1860s, and especially after the Congress of Milan in 1880, oralists took control of the residential schools

in the U.S. and abroad, virtually eradicating the influence of the DEAF-WORLD. From then on, the teaching staff and administrators were hearing, instruction in almost all schools was oral throughout the elementary years, and the Deaf staff were relegated to nonacademic posts with less influence on academic achievement, posts such as dormitory supervisor, coach, shop instructor, and custodian. . . . As a result of these changes, the students acquired much of their information and, unless they had been born into the DEAF-WORLD, all of their language, from other Deaf students or the after-school staff. (1996, 241)[1]

Residential schools, then, have played central roles in the transmission of ASL and can be considered crucibles for the acquisition of language and culture. And residential schools play a continuing role in the lives of Deaf adults.

Residential schools have also played a central role in the transmission of ASL from one side of the country to the other. After the establishment in Hartford of the Connecticut Asylum for the Education and Instruction of Deaf and Dumb Persons in 1817 (now the American School for the Deaf), Laurent Clerc instructed the school's hearing teachers in the use of "manual French adapted to English" and also gave private lessons "to nearly a dozen hearing teachers from as many eastern cities" (Lane et al. 1996, 56). These teachers in turn founded schools in several states:

In America, as in France, the mother school sent its teachers and Deaf graduates throughout the country to teach in various Deaf schools and to found new ones. *As early as 1834, a single signed dialect was recognized in the schools for Deaf students in the U.S.* [emphasis added]. By the time of Clerc's death in 1869, over fifteen hundred pupils had graduated from the Hartford school, and there were some thirty residential schools in the United States with 3,246 pupils and 187 teachers, 42 percent of them Deaf. Most such pupils and teachers married other Deaf persons and had children. This, too, helped to disseminate ASL. (Lane et al. 1996, 58)

The history of residential schools for deaf children, then, is important for understanding sociolinguistic variation in ASL. We look at how the American School for the Deaf served as a "standard"—an institution

---

1. Lane (personal communication, 2000) notes that thirteen schools were founded by Deaf superintendents after 1880 (Gannon 1981, 18), some of which were later taken over by oralists.

that new schools look to as a model for development. Next we trace the paths of some of the early alumni from the American School and other residential schools to see how ASL made its way from coast to coast. Finally, we examine the language policies and attitudes that surface in the reports made by the residential schools to their governing bodies and how these perspectives on language may have affected variation in American Sign Language.

ROLE OF THE AMERICAN SCHOOL FOR THE DEAF

The American School for the Deaf (ASD; originally called The American Asylum for the Deaf and Dumb) in Hartford, Connecticut, was founded in response to the desire of community members to have their deaf children receive an education. In 1815, Dr. Mason F. Cogswell, whose daughter Alice was deaf, had a young neighbor by the name of Thomas Hopkins Gallaudet, a Yale College graduate, who was intrigued by the idea of working with Alice. Cogswell, with financial support from the community, sent Gallaudet to England so he could learn the methods of deaf education in use there and bring them back to the United States.[2]

Gallaudet traveled to England and inquired about working with the Braidwood family, among the best-known deaf educators of the period. Dr. Joseph Watson, Thomas Braidwood's nephew, told Gallaudet that he could observe for one month at the London asylum for the Deaf and Dumb if he would then agree to serve as an assistant for three years and promise not to use what he had learned for profit (Lane 1984, 186–88). Gallaudet did not agree to these terms and decided to seek help elsewhere. While still in London, he attended an exhibition given by the Abbé Sicard, the director of the Institute for Deaf Mutes in Paris, and two of his deaf students. Fascinated by the potential use of the "sign language" with deaf students, Gallaudet made arrangements to go back to Paris to study with Sicard and the other teachers at the Institute (Lane 1984, 187).

Before Gallaudet's training in the use of the manual method of education was finished, however, his funding began to run out, forcing him to make plans to return to the United States. Mindful that he was not ready

2. The history of the American School for the Deaf has been well documented. See, for example, Baynton (1996), Van Cleve and Crouch (1989), and Gannon (1981).

to run a school for deaf students by himself, Gallaudet contracted with Laurent Clerc, a graduate of and teacher at the Institute. In his shipboard diary, Gallaudet stated that the voyage to the United States provided the necessary time for him to learn more sign language from Clerc and for Clerc to continue learning English (Lane 1984).

Upon their arrival in Connecticut, Gallaudet and Clerc, with assistance from Cogswell, began an intensive effort to open a school. The American School for the Deaf opened in 1817 with seven pupils and funds from private investors in England. When the first year of school came to a close, thirty-two students were listed in the pupil roster (ASD 1844).

Because the American School for the Deaf was the first institute of its kind to gain permanence in the United States, others looked to it when making plans to set up schools for deaf students in their own states. This kind of influence most likely made an impact on how the administration (and in turn, the staff and students) viewed the use of "the natural language of signs" in the everyday life of the school. This section illustrates a few of the ways in which other young residential schools in the early-to mid-nineteenth century regarded the American School for the Deaf as a pedagogical guide.

To begin, it is important to show that the American School's perspective was on Deaf education and the use of sign language during its early years. One perspective on "the language of signs," as it was called, is evident in a statement made in ASD's second annual report in 1818. The report says that the students have "happy intercourse with each other — an intercourse, too, which has contributed in no small degree, to their improvement in the acquisition of language, by affording them frequent opportunities of conversation with their instructors and each other" (4). The same report also emphasizes the importance of written English for Deaf students for "the purposes of their common intercourse with mankind, most of whom know nothing of the manner in which thoughts can so easily be expressed by signs and gestures" (5).

Thus it is clear that in only the second year of the school's existence, the directors had already established that they had strong attitudes about language. According to the "self-reporting" seen in the preceding statements, the school administration felt that using sign language was important not only for communication with others at the school but also in helping the students acquire language. Furthermore, the directors acknowledged that the ability to communicate with the world outside the doors of the residential school was an important one, but they also spoke to the ease with which students could express themselves through sign and gesture. Clearly, the early directors at the American School had a very high opinion of sign language and the potential it held for the linguistic and social development of Deaf students.

From a pedagogical viewpoint, the directors of the American School felt that not only was sign language important for the students to use among themselves but also that an instructor at a school for Deaf students should "make himself master of that methodical system of signs, which the combined talents and experience of European instructors have been for years mastering" (ASD 1820, 4–5).

With teachers who were "masters" of sign, the school was able to carry out the mode of communication that it felt best served the students. In one of its earliest reports, the American School explained why sign language is preferable to articulation when working with Deaf students: "As sight is quicker than hearing, so ideas reaching the mind by the eye, are quicker, more striking and vivid, than those which reach the mind by the slow progress of sound" (ASD 1819, 6). The same report deals with the issue even more directly on the next page: "Articulation is not taught. It would require more time than the present occasion furnishes, to state the reasons which have induced the Principal of the Asylum and his associates not to waste their labour and that of their pupils upon this comparatively useless branch of the education of the deaf and dumb" (1819, 7). The report goes on to explain how the teaching of articulation can be given a "rank only a little higher than the art of training starlings and parrots" (1819, 8) and that the use of sign language allows its users to "unfold silently the latent capacities of the understanding; an effect which is not, like the other, palpable to sense, and of which but a few are able to either ascertain the existence, or to appreciate the value" (1819, 8).

This set of attitudes and beliefs about the importance of sign language in Deaf education formed a foundation for the American School that was passed on to other institutions as their representatives came to ASD for help. One such example is the Pennsylvania Institution for the Instruction of the Deaf and Dumb in Philadelphia, founded in 1820. Some of the early reports of the American School mention that Laurent Clerc was allowed to be "released, for a winter, from his duties in this Asylum, to afford that establishment the benefits of his experience and skill; in addition to which it has also obtained from this its present Principal, and two assistant teachers" (ASD 1827, 7). More evidence of the American School's willingness to act as a guiding force appears in the school's 14th report (1830), in which the authors document the opening of the Ohio School. The authors report that the principal of the Ohio School, the Rev. H. N. Hubbell, "spent some time" at the American School and that the school was more than happy to share "the benefits of our experience and course of instruction" (18) with the new administration there.

The authors of that same report make it clear that the opportunity to provide this kind of assistance was not something that the directors of the American School sought but that "their obligations to the public . . . and especially to the General Government, have strongly impelled them to wish to extend the benefits of their system of instruction as widely as possible" (7). It is reasonable to conclude that Thomas Gallaudet did not want others who were interested in Deaf education to face the same kinds of barriers that he encountered during his early, method-seeking voyage to Europe.

Aside from the more direct methods of sending instructors from the American School to provide training, or vice versa, the directors at the American School also realized that what they included in their annual reports could potentially exert some influence on what other schools did for Deaf people. One such example comes from the 29th Report (1845), in which Principal Lewis Weld commented on the idea of changing the mode of instruction from one that used "the natural language of signs" to one focused more on articulation and lip reading. He said, "I can then recommend no fundamental change in the system pursued in the institution with which I am connected, *or in the other American schools*" (120, italics added). He went on to say that he was not completely closed to the idea of using articulation with *some* students who became deaf after learning to speak or with those who had enough residual hearing to benefit from such methods. But the mere fact that he generalized his statement about the philosophy at the American School to what other institutions should do shows that the administrators at the American School had considerable influence in Deaf education at the time and that they were cognizant of that fact. This influence was reinforced by the fact that Edward Miner Gallaudet, youngest son of Thomas Hopkins Gallaudet, and the first president of what is now Gallaudet University, was president of the Conference of Principals of Institutions for the Deaf in the 1860s and had been reared in the environment of the Hartford school (Lane, personal communication 2000).

SCHOOLS ATTENDED BY THE STUDY PARTICIPANTS

Virginia School for the Deaf and Blind

Some of the study participants had attended the Virginia School for the Deaf and Blind (VSDB). An act of the state legislature established the Virginia School for the Deaf and Blind in 1839 in Staunton. One of the two parents who led the efforts to establish such a school was Dr. Lewis W. Chamberlayne of Richmond, who had two deaf sons (*VSDB* 1952). It seems that Dr. Chamberlayne placed such a high value on education for his children that he was willing (as were a number of other parents, in other communities) to send at least one of his sons to ASD. The school's 28th report (1844) lists Ed. Chamberlayne, from Richmond, Virginia, as a student from 1830 to 1834.

The Reverend Joseph D. Tyler, a late-deafened man who had been an assistant instructor at the American School, was the first superintendent. A former ASD student, Job Turner, was the school's first instructor.

Missouri School for the Deaf

Several of the participants from Kansas, including some of the African American participants from this site, were former students of the Missouri School for the Deaf, which was founded by an act of the Missouri Legislature in 1851 in Fulton, Missouri. Its first superintendent, William D. Kerr, had been a teacher at the Kentucky School for the Deaf, a school that had been established with the advice and support of instructors at ASD. Kerr's father was instrumental in setting up the Kentucky school and served as its first superintendent. Thus, a direct link can be traced from ASD to the Missouri school. The Missouri school found itself in a state with divided allegiances during the Civil War, and the school was closed between 1861 and 1863 when Union soldiers occupied Fulton, which was located in a county loyal to the Confederacy. In 1863 the troops withdrew from Fulton, and the school was reopened.

Louisiana School for the Deaf

Many of the participants from the New Orleans site had attended the Louisiana School for the Deaf (LSD). In 1852 an act of the Louisiana State Legislature established LSD, located in Baton Rouge. James S. Brown, who had been serving as the superintendent at the Indiana

School for the Deaf, was hired as the first superintendent. Eleven of the 13 pupils during the school's first year were natives of Louisiana; they had been attending the Kentucky School for the Deaf until a school could be founded in their home state. The school was open for only eight years before the board removed Superintendent Brown, and, subsequently, most of the teaching staff resigned (LSD 1899–1900). In addition, the Civil War began, and the number of students dropped from 77 to around 25 or 30 for the duration of the war. Union troops occupied LSD's campus for approximately three years and provided rations to the remaining students and staff when attempts to earn money through the sale of school-produced cakes and vegetables failed.

Louisiana State School for Deaf Negroes

Some of the African American participants from the New Orleans site had attended the Louisiana State School for Deaf Negroes. The school opened in Scotlandville, Louisiana, on the campus of Southern University in October 1938. During the school's first year of operation there were 44 students and 9 faculty members. By 1952 those numbers had increased to 94 students and 21 faculty and staff ("A Brief Summary" 1952).

Gannon (1981) notes that following the Civil War, some southern states began to open schools or departments for Black Deaf children within already-established schools. North Carolina was the first to establish a school for Black Deaf children in 1869; South Carolina followed in 1876 and Georgia in 1882. Thirteen states still had separate and segregated schools for Black Deaf children in the early 1950s, and as late as 1963, there remained eight states with such schools (Lane et al. 1996). No separate schools in the North admitted Blacks, but Baynton (1996) reports that the oral Clarke School in Northampton, Massachusetts, in 1908 affirmed a policy excluding Black students. What is also very interesting is that, according to Baynton, oral education was not extended equally to Black students and White students. By the early part of the twentieth century, when many white schools described themselves as having an "oral" or "combined" method, most of the Black schools described themselves as "manual" (1996, 46).

California School for the Deaf, Berkeley

Several of the participants had attended the California School for the Deaf (CSD), which was founded in 1860 in Berkeley (it is now located in

Fremont) by a group of women led by Pomeroy B. Clark (who had a deaf sister). Clark was the first principal. In 1862 a former teacher at the Louisiana School for the Deaf, Azel S. Roe Jr., became the principal instructor (CSD 1862). From the beginning, then, the school had some link to the ASD. That connection was strengthened in 1865, when Warring Wilkinson became the principal. Wilkinson had gotten his start in the field of deaf education as a result of observing classes at the American and New York schools for the deaf while visiting a cousin, who was an instructor at both schools. Wilkinson ultimately decided that teaching deaf students was something he also wanted to do. He stayed at CSD for forty-four years.

Kansas State School for the Deaf

The Kansas School for the Deaf in Olathe was founded in 1861 by Philip A. Emery, an alumnus of the Indiana School for the Deaf. After graduating from the Indiana school (also founded by a deaf man, ASD graduate William Willard), Emery taught there for four years before moving to Kansas to claim some land for himself and his wife. Emery moved to Kansas not only to stake a claim to land but also to possibly set up a central location for more Deaf people to come to and settle together (Liberman 1966). As it happened, Emery's new settlement was located near the homestead of the Kennedys, a family that had three deaf children. Mr. Kennedy approached Emery and convinced him to set up a school for deaf students, assuring him that there were more families in the area who would send their deaf children to such a school if only he would found it. Emery agreed and founded the Kansas School partly so the deaf could have "the Gospel preached in their silent yet expressive language" (Liberman 1966). The school's opening was delayed for two months, however, because no students showed up. When a student finally arrived, her father paid for her admission with ham, butter, eggs, and corn (Liberman 1966). The first year of school ended in 1862 with four students.

Maryland School for the Deaf

Some of the participants in the study were former students of the Maryland School for the Deaf (MDSD). In January 1867 an act of the state's general assembly founded the school, located in Frederick.

William D. Cooke, previously the principal of the North Carolina School for the Deaf at Raleigh, became the school's first principal. The school opened with 34 students; this number increased to 59 students by the end of the year. Only 34 of the students in the school's first year had received previous instruction; they most likely had been students at the Columbia Institution for the Deaf and Dumb in Washington, D.C. (now the Laurent Clerc National Deaf Education Center). From 1828 to 1865, deaf children from Maryland went to the Pennsylvania Institution in Philadelphia to receive an education. In 1865 the state of Maryland decided to send the children to Washington, D.C., and finally in 1868, the state passed a resolution that brought all Maryland residents back to the state to attend the newly opened school (Ely 1893). Charles M. Ely (formerly employed at the Ohio Institution for the Deaf and Dumb) was elected as principal of the school in 1870 and served in that role for the next thirty-two years (MDSD 1870).

Washington State School for the Deaf

The Territorial Legislature founded the Washington State School for the Deaf (WSD) in 1886 in Vancouver. From 1885 to 1886 the Rev. W. D. McFarland, a Presbyterian minister, taught a private class of deaf students in Tacoma. This group became part of WSD's first class of 17 students when the school officially opened its doors one year later, with McFarland as principal. He was assisted by a classroom teacher, George Layton, who was a graduate of VSDB at Staunton and the National Deaf-Mute College in Washington, D.C. (now known as Gallaudet University). Keeping in mind that ASD graduates and staff established and ran VSDB in its early years, the fact that a VSDB graduate found himself in Washington state illuminates one of the ways in which the ASD may have had an impact on ASL and language use in general, even in that (then) remote part of the country.

California School for the Deaf at Riverside

Some of the project participants attended the California School for the Deaf at Riverside, which opened in 1953 as a result of an act of the California State Legislature. Dr. Richard G. Brill, a hearing man working in the field of deaf education, became the school's first superintendent before the school ever officially opened its doors. It is interesting to note that Brill had worked at VSDB prior to coming to California.

ASD's Regional Influence

Not only are five of the study's Boston participants ASD alumni, but students from Boston and other areas of Massachusetts have attended the school since its inception. The school's 28th Annual Report (1844) provides a complete listing of students who had attended ASD since 1817, and 6 of the 32 students (one of whom was from Boston) in attendance during the first year were from Massachusetts. This trend continues throughout the roster and provides us with historical evidence that the American School has played a role in the Boston deaf community. Also of relevance to our project are three Massachusetts schools that study participants attended: the Clarke School, the Beverly School, and the Horace Mann School. The Clarke School was founded in 1867 and has always been exclusively oral. It was founded in Northampton, Massachusetts, by Mr. and Mrs. Gardiner Greene Hubbard, who wanted to provide oral education for their daughter, Mabel. While her parents searched for funding for the proposed school, Mabel attended oral institutions in Germany because none existed in the United States. After struggling for several years and failing to get the Massachusetts legislature to support the school, the Hubbards eventually received the funds from a man named John Clarke, who had experienced a gradual hearing loss and was willing to contribute $50,000. The Hubbards founded the school in 1867 and named it in honor of its benefactor. Alexander Graham Bell came to Clarke School to teach the methods of Visible Speech to the teachers there in 1871 and eventually served as a board member from 1898 to 1922 (Clarke School for the Deaf 2000).

By contrast, the Beverly School was founded in 1879 by William Swett, a deaf man who had two deaf daughters, Persis and Lucy Maria (who, to Bell's dismay, married his deaf pupil George Sanders). Swett also had a deaf wife and two deaf granddaughters (Lane, personal communication 2000; Lane, Pillard, and French 2000). A friend of Thomas Hopkins Gallaudet, Swett, an active member of the Deaf community in Massachusetts, founded the school because he was concerned with the lack of educational opportunity for deaf students in the area in which he lived.

Finally, the Horace Mann School opened in 1869 and was the first public day school for deaf students in the United States. Operating under the direction of the Boston school board, the school allowed deaf children to live at home. It is well known for using a purely oral approach, but since 1982 it has used the Total Communication approach, which incorporates sign language.

ASL: MAKING ITS WAY FROM COAST TO COAST

One of the key ways that a "standard" form of ASL may have made its way across the country was through ASD graduates who accepted positions at various schools for deaf students. Figure 3.1 summarizes the connections between the American School for the Deaf in Hartford and schools in the seven project sites. From this figure we can see how ASL moved from Hartford to points as distant as Washington state and Louisiana. We also see clear evidence of the role of residential schools in this movement.

One of the earliest graduates of ASD was Abigail Dillingham, who left the school in 1821 and went to Philadelphia to become an instructor at the newly founded Pennsylvania Institution (ASD 1844). She taught there until her death in 1824, at which time another ASD graduate, George Comstock, took her place (ASD 1844; Braddock 1975). Thus not only was Laurent Clerc brought to the Pennsylvania Institution as a "consultant" in its first few months, but ASD graduates held teaching positions there as well, bringing with them the experience of an education provided to them in a language they could clearly understand.

As more schools sprang up, other ASD alumni moved west to fill the demand for qualified teachers. A prime example of this is William Willard, who was a student at ASD from 1824 to 1829 and taught at the Ohio School for the Deaf until 1841 (ASD 1844). Sometime between 1841 and 1843, he moved to Indiana to start a private school for deaf students there. Arriving in Indiana, he discovered that the state legislature was already in the process of establishing a deaf school, and in 1844 Willard became its first principal. However, according to Braddock (1975), "the intention of the legislature from the first had been to find a Principal who could hear and speak" (17). As a result, Willard was demoted to assistant principal two years after his appointment and then later to a regular teaching position. His loyalty to the school remained strong, however, and he continued as a teacher until his retirement in 1864.

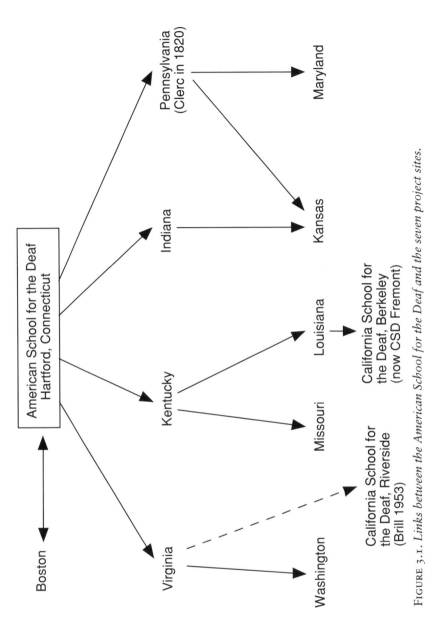

FIGURE 3.1. *Links between the American School for the Deaf and the seven project sites.*

ASD graduates also moved to the south as more and more schools for deaf students came into being there. An ASD student, Richard C. Springs, attended ASD from 1831 to 1833 and was thereafter listed in one of the school's annual reports as a teacher in the South Carolina Institute for Deaf and Dumb (ASD 1857).

The case of the Rev. Job Turner provides a more in-depth example of movement south and around the United States. Turner was an ASD student from 1833 to 1839. In 1839 an ASD teacher was appointed as the principal of the (new) Virginia School for the Deaf and Blind (VSDB) in Staunton. The teacher, Rev. Joseph Tyler, determined that he needed at least one teacher for the school's first year and asked Turner to accompany him to Virginia. Interestingly, Turner's family had moved to Staunton nine years earlier; Braddock (1975) speculates that "this is possibly how the School for the Deaf happens to be situated in that Virginia city" (140).

Turner remained at VSDB as a teacher for thirty-five years (VSDB 1839–1874). A few years after his retirement, Turner was reacquainted with the Rev. Thomas Gallaudet, oldest son of Thomas Hopkins Gallaudet, during a visit to Massachusetts. The Rev. Gallaudet had a deaf ministry in New York City, and his meeting with Turner resulted in Turner's desire to become a minister to the deaf community. From 1877 until his death in 1903, Turner traveled across North America, preaching to groups of Deaf people wherever he went. Not only is it plausible that his travels exposed people as far north as Canada and as far west as Portland, Oregon, to the variety of ASL that Turner initially acquired at ASD, but Turner was also apparently exposed to other sign languages. Braddock (1975) mentions that after Turner's sixth trip to the school for deaf people in Mexico City, Turner reported that "there were sixteen pupils under seven teachers, and that they used a different sign language system from ours" (141).

ASL made its way from east to west also through the help of George Layton, one of the first teachers hired to teach at the Washington State School for the Deaf when it opened in 1886 (Brelje and Tibbs 1986). As we mentioned earlier, George Layton was a Deaf man who graduated first from VSDB and then from the National Deaf-Mute College in Washington, D.C. (now Gallaudet University). These kinds of links may help to explain some of the similarities in the data from Washington and Virginia (e.g., why both Washington and Virginia participants similarly disfavor a low, -cf location when producing certain lexical items). At first it may seem extremely difficult to explain consistencies found in language use from one side of the country to the other. However, if we consider that Layton was educated at institutions with direct links to the prominent American School for the Deaf and that he traveled to Washington state to share what he had learned with other Deaf students, then the connections become more acceptable.

LANGUAGE ATTITUDES AT THE SCHOOLS FOR THE DEAF

It is important to look at language attitudes in a study of variation because the attitudes and beliefs about language may have influenced language use, especially as a standard variety of ASL was developing throughout the United States. For example, considering the high regard for ASD in the early days of deaf education may help us to understand why all of the Massachusetts participants are so conservative (i.e., prefer ear-to-chin production) in their productions of DEAF. We may never be able to come to any definitive conclusion about exactly how this preference developed, but using what we know about the external constraints involved aids us in forming a better overall picture of the situation.

Language Policies and Attitudes at VSDB

One of the earliest reports from VSDB (1846) included a statement made by the principal, the Rev. Joseph D. Tyler, saying that the school did not teach articulation. Not surprisingly, the reasons he gives are the same as those given by the directors at ASD—that deaf students cannot profit from articulation, that the natural language of signs is clearer and quicker, that articulation becomes the focus of education instead of a means to an end, and so on. Just six years later, however, Tyler passed away, and the principal of the blind department became the principal of the deaf department as well. That year's report mentions four students who were being taught articulation (VSDB 1852). The following year's report discussed an emphasis on the English language and the "natural sign language" (VSDB 1853). These fluctuations were indicators of a trend throughout the residential schools: When the administration changed, the policies often changed as well.

Twenty years later, however, the annual report cited the fact that although articulation was gaining in national popularity, the school administration decided that it was not worth the effort needed to begin using it because the school already used sign language (VSDB 1872). Job Turner, the school's first teacher, resigned in 1874 because of failing health. For the next six years, the language attitudes and policies remained relatively stable: Articulation was used with "semi-mutes" (students who had some hearing) who might benefit from it but was not used with deaf students.

Sociohistorical Context for ASL Variation : 65

The Second International Congress on Education of the Deaf—now referred to as the Milan Conference—convened in 1880, and educators of deaf people gathered there from all over the world to discuss the relative merits of using sign language or articulation. The following year, the annual report contained much discussion about the different methods of instruction used around the world. The report included the opinions of a variety of prominent educators of the time (Edward Miner Gallaudet; Harvey Peet of the New York Institution; and Job Williams, ASD's president at the time) and showed only one side of the story. Although a vast majority of the educators at the Milan Conference supported articulation as the best method for working with deaf students, the American delegates were initially hesitant. That hesitancy is evident in the following quote from the end of the conference report:

> These are the opinions of men in every way competent to judge of this subject; their extensive knowledge and observation has brought them to the same conclusion to which my meagre knowledge and limited observation has led me, and I am, as I said above, satisfied that the pure oral or articulation system of instruction for deaf-mutes will never amount to any very great deal except to those who, although classified as deaf-mutes, are really only semi-mute or semi-deaf, and to a very few of the true, congenital mutes. And I am also satisfied that as much is being done in this direction by the Virginia Institution, according to its means, as by any other of a like character in the country. (VSDB 1881, 10)

Another interesting pattern that occurs in this statement and in the annual reports of various schools was the concept of "keeping pace" with other schools. So although the administration at VSDB was confident in their decision to keep the use of articulation and oral training to a minimum, they still felt obliged to note that their efforts were similar to those of other institutions at the time.

The administration's seemingly strong stance changed significantly the very next year and included statements *supporting* articulation for students born completely deaf, saying that any such students are not necessarily dumb as well. One of the arguments mentioned the fact that France had now begun to accept articulation: "Is it in the nature of things that France, the birthplace of the sign-system, should accept the oral method unless led to do so by overpowering evidence in its favor?"

(1882, 7). Later in the report the VSDB's principal mentioned that "Mrs. Joanna Ross has entered upon her duties in this department of the school [teaching articulation] with flattering prospects of her success. Twenty-one pupils, congenital and semi-mutes, are now under her daily instruction, and it is indeed gratifying to notice the interest manifested by them so early in the session" (1882, 8).

Finally, around the turn of the century, VSDB's reports adopted a much more sophisticated format—they included many pictures of students and grounds and began to look like a brochure or a handbook for parents. Nevertheless, the reports still show that the change of method that began in the early 1880s had become solidified in the school's course of instruction by 1912:

> Our instruction in the Deaf Department is by the combined method—i.e., partly by signs, partly by manual spelling, and partly by the oral method. We are giving to all new pupils, however, an opportunity to learn speech and lip-reading, and where the pupil shows any aptitude for the work he is retained in the articulation or oral class. Otherwise he is put into a manual class where the instruction is by manual or finger spelling signs, written languages, etc. (VSDB 1911–1913, 19)

This shift in VSDB's method of instruction was representative of the shifts that other residential schools made during the same period. Indeed, this new perspective on deaf education would remain in many schools throughout most of the rest of the twentieth century.

Language Policies and Attitudes at the Missouri School for the Deaf

The language attitudes and policies evidenced in the early reports of the Missouri School for the Deaf (MSD) are strikingly similar to those found in the reports from VSDB. In a report issued just four years after the school opened, the school commissioners made this statement about the use of articulation:

> Articulation, as an instrument of instruction, proves to be entirely abortive, with a large majority of deaf persons. A few of the most gifted of those who could once hear, and still retain the faculty of speech to some extent, may acquire some fluency in spoken language.

It is admitted by all that the ability to read on the lip, is an art of the greatest refinement and delicacy, and can only be acquired by years of patient toil, and then often laid aside, when the pupil is removed from the instructor. (MSD 1857, 13)

This attitude about instructional method is almost identical to that held by the administrators at the American and Virginia schools. In fact, the commissioners at the Missouri School may have even unwittingly foreshadowed part of the future of deaf education—that when articulation becomes the focus, many deaf students will "lay it aside" when not in the teacher's presence.

In the same report the commissioners alluded to the experience of the Missouri School's principal as a teacher at the Kentucky School for the Deaf, where he was able to compare the results of each method. They spoke of a group of students who had previously been taught at another school using the articulation method that had "through the medium of signs, made greater attainments in three months than during a period of from one to two years before" (14).

Finally, the section on the "Mode of Instructing Deaf Mutes" closed with an encouragement to parents: "Every parent of deaf children should cultivate sign language, and stimulate them to communicate their wants, &c. It is no difficult thing to invent a sign for visible objects and actions" (15). Again the school commissioners seemed to be foreshadowing a current trend in Deaf education, that of parent involvement at every level.

The 1863–1864 report of the Missouri School included another statement that showed a very positive attitude: "Those more gifted become rapidly proficient in the use of their vernacular, that beautiful but silent language, so simple yet powerfully eloquent. It is through this language of signs that deaf mutes acquire a knowledge and use of written language" (8). In the 11th Biennial Report, the superintendent reported that although articulation had proved successful in many cases, the school was not ready to abandon sign language for oralism (1876, 20–21). Here we see the same hesitancy to change methods that the reports of VSDB exhibited.

Like VSDB and others, however, the Missouri School gradually shifted away from using sign language in favor of articulation. A section of the school's 14th Biennial Report (1881–1882) provides evidence of this shift and of the external pressures the school's administration faced:

"A growing belief in the importance of instruction in articulation and the increasing desires of parents and friends to have pupils acquire this art made the classes in articulation so large that another teacher was needed" (17).

Our final comments about language come from the 29th Biennial Report (1912), which shows both a shift in methodology and the concern that sign language use may undermine language training and development:

[The sign language] is a great aid and time saver in classes where it is necessary to explain difficult parts of a lesson. Our objection to it is that because of the facility with which the deaf use it, they are liable to fall into the habit of making use of the sign language when they should spell with the fingers or write out complete syntactical sentences for the practice it gives in language. The sign-language has little or no syntax and the continued use of it in communication while at school, to the neglect of written language (or spoken if there is that ability), is detrimental to progress in language expression. (22)

A note about racial attitudes is necessary in the discussion of the Missouri School, which we studied because some of the African American participants from Kansas reported that they attended the school during a time when the Kansas School did not admit Black students. The reports from the Missouri School give us some startling insights into the attitudes held by the institution as a whole. The first mention of "colored" pupils occurred in the 17th Biennial Report (1888), when, in the interest of following suit with state laws and in order to formulate a policy that "will not be repugnant to [the school's] white patrons," the school made the decision to segregate students. The Commissioner said that "we respectfully submit, that, in our opinion, both races will be better satisfied, more naturally adjusted, and more progressive under a separation" (18). The report also says that the standards of education would be the same for both groups of students, but the fact remains that the school administration decided to separate black and white students.

Finally, one incident mentioned in the school's reports is unique in the literature: The 29th Biennial Report (1912), the included an account of a survey of former students. One area of the survey pertained to ideas for improvements. The superintendent asked, "Have you any helpful suggestions as to the manner the Missouri School for the Deaf might be made better, scholastically, industrially or physically?" (29–30). Of the twenty responses he received, four related to language issues at the school. One alumnus said that classes should be taught using sign language and that those who can be taught to speak should receive oral training but only for one hour a day. Another respondent said, "Do away with pure oralism" (30), while another said that the superintendent should have the final say over parents about placing students in either the oral or manual department. The fourth language-related comment was that "more language should be used in the shops by foremen in teaching trades" (30).

The fact that these former students responded to a question about improving the school through changes in language use shows us that language attitudes and policies were salient issues in the Deaf community ninety years ago and that Deaf people were aware of the instructional options and outcomes. This was certainly true after 1880—120 years ago—and from 1880 until fairly recently. Aware of these outcomes, Deaf alumni may have made a point to foster the language that may have been denied them during their school years.

Language Policies and Attitudes at the Louisiana School for the Deaf

We can glean only a little information about language attitudes and policies from the first 10 reports of the Louisiana School for the Deaf. According to the first report, the school's first 11 students had studied at the Kentucky School before the Louisiana school opened in 1852. The Eighth Annual Report (1860) briefly mentioned a proposal to print a "Dictionary of Signs for the Deaf and Dumb" (7). Other than these brief references, however, we found no in-depth information about the language attitudes at the school in its earliest reports.

In 1861 the school board removed the school's superintendent, J. S. Brown, and fired two teachers; the rest of the teachers resigned (LSD 1861). As a result, the school was forced to close 2 months earlier than scheduled for the summer, and most of the students returned to their homes.

Following the internal tumult at the school was a period of inactivity brought on by the Civil War and the occupation of LSD by Union troops. When the school reopened and published another report in 1867, each of the school's two departments, "Mute" and "Blind," had only one teacher (LSD 1867).

In discussing the difficulties that the students had faced as a result of the school's troubles, the authors of the 1869 Annual Report made one of the first comments about language attitudes in the reports thus far:

> Bright and able pupils, of several years' experience in school, have fallen back till half their labor of learning must be passed over again. This is hard, also, from the fact that, with increasing years, the mind becomes less pliable in adapting itself to the rigid, uncompromising forms of language. Their natural language of signs is utterly devoid of law or system, except that its pantomime must be true to nature. System in it is only a product of taste and cultivation. System in spoken language is an inherent principle. (17)

Thus we can see that as the school was reestablishing itself, strong language attitudes remained intact. It is difficult to discern exactly what this segment from the school report means, however. It could mean that the sign language, being "utterly devoid of law or system," was regarded as actually facilitating learning; on the other hand, it may also mean that the potential for student progress was seen as in peril because their use of communication without a system (the natural language of signs) hinders the development of communication with a system (spoken language).

Just one year later, however, the school's annual report gave evidence of a more balanced perspective on language and teaching methodology. The report mentioned that "[articulation] has the advantage of a fascinating possibility of teaching the deaf to speak and understand language from the lips of others, but the serious objection of impracticability in a very large majority of cases" (1870, 24). The report went on to say that even though a small number of students had found much success under the articulation method, this small number "led to the wise provision in the larger institutions for educating by this method in any case believed to be best for the pupil," while at the same time "there is room for regret that so much precious time has been spent in this tremendous work of attaining an accomplishment which is almost sure soon to lapse into disuse" (24).

In 1872 the wish to be competitive with other schools in terms of educational methods was not lost on the Louisiana School. Its annual report said that the school was keeping "abreast with all improvements in deaf-mute instruction if it is possible to secure the means" (20).

Two years later the school's report gave evidence of a more positive language attitude with regard to using sign language with deaf students.

The Annual Report (1874) stated that articulation was appropriate for "semi-mutes" and for students who became deaf later in life. It concluded by saying that, for those whose articulation would be "gibberish," the school should "educate them to the highest possible achievement of knowledge, culture, and refinement, by a sure and rapid means of communication [sign language], and secure to them the highest possible attainments in written language" (15). Thus the school, in a matter of five years, exhibited three very different language philosophies. This serves as a testament to the potentially volatile area of language methodology in the history of deaf education. Major changes in language policy and instruction were not mentioned in the reports of the Louisiana school after 1880, as they were in other schools, but the Biennial Report of 1889–1890 did say that an oral class had been established. The overall trend at LSD seems to have been to give all students the opportunity to learn how to speak. If no success was evident (as the administrators seemed to expect, based on their comments about the viability of articulation), these students were then moved to manual classes.

A report published not long after the turn of the century mentioned visiting sign language lecturers as well as a sign language course, referring to sign language as the " 'Mother tongue' of the deaf and to which all deaf persons resort when freest and most vivid expression is desired" (1906–1908, 14). At this time, at least, the school administration exhibited a very positive attitude about sign language and made various attempts to provide students with exposure to skilled sign language users.

Language Policies and Attitudes at the California School for the Deaf

The California School for the Deaf has been representative of the constantly shifting language attitudes and policies present in American schools for deaf students. As we mentioned earlier, CSD was led, in its earliest years, by a man who could be considered one of the earliest sign language linguists. Warring M. Wilkinson became principal in 1865 and started making positive statements about sign language from the very beginning of his tenure:

Words are arbitrary signs of ideas, settled and understood by usage. A sign of the hand is no more arbitrary, and may be as suggestive, when agreed upon by a community to represent a definite idea. Upon this fact the sign-language has been devised, whereby the eye is made to do the office of the ear, the hand becomes the vicar of the tongue. (CSD 1866, 11)[3]

Wilkinson touched upon one of the main findings of the current project: Deaf people with different backgrounds and experiences can end up having different signs for the same thing. The fact that Wilkinson gave this much thought to the development of sign language among the deaf students at CSD shows him to be a skilled observer of "the sign language." His comments in the school's reports also show that he was confident about the role of sign language in deaf education:

What part articulation may play hereafter in American schools for the deaf and dumb, is still a question, but that it will ever supercede signs as a method of instruction is not believed by any intelligent teacher who knows, by practical experience and use, the value of the sign language. . . . It is, therefore, my firm belief—a belief based on twenty-five years of careful observation and investigation—that the sign language will hold its preeminence in American institutions. (CSD 1882, 14)

Wilkinson's attitude about the "preeminence" of sign language in deaf education wavered slightly six years later, when he said that "articulation and lip-reading are acknowledged to be legitimate branches of a deaf mute's education, and no school for the deaf is complete that does not offer facilities for the acquiring of speech" (CSD 1888–1890, 10). This statement is not unlike those made by other principals at schools for deaf students and hints at the attempt to keep pace with other institutions that we have noted in many of the schools studied thus far. Clearly, however, two years later Wilkinson completely embraced articulation at CSD:

Whenever and wherever the use of a man is considered more important than the man himself, then and there that system of training will prevail which is supposed to increase his commercial value. Whenever and wherever a man is considered superior to any use he may be put to, then and there education will be based on broader grounds and

3. This perspective is representative of Wilkinson's attitude about sign language. Ten years after he took over as principal of CSD, Wilkinson made some of the only early comments about variation in sign language, as cited in chapter 1.

tend to develop manhood and character rather than handcraft and mechanics (CSD 1888–1890, 8)

In 1909 Wilkinson resigned from his post as CSD principal, and Douglas Keith took his place (CSD 1908–1910). Keith's reports do not say much about language use but instead focus on the importance of vocational training for deaf students. Three years later, however, L. E. Milligan became principal and brought a significant change in language policy with his new administration.

In the 31st Annual Report, Milligan stated that "in the early school life of the deaf child it is highly advisable that he be taught the speech habit and to think in English. After he has acquired these two accomplishments signs will do him no harm" (1912–1914, 17). Milligan went on to acknowledge that signs could be of use for the moral development of deaf children, but his educational methodology was clearly different from that of his predecessors.

After Milligan's death in 1920, William A. Caldwell served as principal until 1928. During this time the school's annual reports reflected yet another shift in language policy: Caldwell placed the highest priority on English. In the First Biennial Report he said that "As signs become more and more [the student's] mode of thought, English becomes more and more a foreign language to him and in his attempt to understand and use it he first has to go through the cumbrous process of translation" (1922–1924, 11). Caldwell did recognize that the students would inevitably learn "signs" from one another, but he saw regular use of sign language as an impediment to learning English.

Finally, Elwood A. Stevenson, the son of deaf parents and an administrator with experience at a wide variety of schools for deaf students, was appointed as CSD's principal in 1928. Stevenson had very positive attitudes toward sign language, which were likely a result of his experience with deaf parents and his years at various residential schools. As before, the new administrator brought a new perspective on language. Stevenson kept certain instructional policies intact: He made it clear that all students would start in oral classes until it was proven that they were not succeeding. Stevenson saw signs as something that students would naturally learn among themselves and not as something acceptable for use during instruction. Stevenson's new (or revived) ideas were the notions that "the main objective, however, is an educated mind" (CSD 1934–1936, 20) and that "when properly used, signs prove a great asset in mental development, in social growth, in general happiness, in better and more wholesome discipline, and finally in a more normal later adjustment as an adult" (21). Stevenson's thirty-two-year administration was important in changing language attitudes at CSD. In one of his last reports, Stevenson included a list of recommendations for the school's future, one of which was: "Consider the revolutionary step of starting a beginning class as non-oral" (CSD 1958–1960, 14).

Language Policies and Attitudes at the Kansas School for the Deaf

The Kansas School for the Deaf (KSD) is one of a small number of schools for deaf students in the United States that deaf individuals themselves have founded. Not only was the school's founder (Philip A. Emery) deaf, but the school's first three superintendents were deaf as well. It would be interesting to see whether a school founded and initially run by deaf people exhibits a perspective on the value of using sign language that differs from that taken by other schools for deaf students founded during the same time. However, the school's reports made almost no mention of language until 1871, by which time the school had a hearing administrator, Louis H. Jenkins. Jenkins had this to say about sign language:

> The education of the deaf and dumb is carried on by means of the sign language. This language has reached such a state of perfection that by it can be expressed the most delicate shades of thought. To the casual observer, this language appears to be without system or method. On the contrary, it is based on scientific principles, which elevate it to a high position among the languages of mankind. By means of it, the deaf and dumb are enabled to converse as rapidly as we can in our own vernacular, and, what is still more wonderful, can be taught to use the English language with facility (KSD 1871, 20).

Although it seems as though this sentiment appears in many of the school reports studied thus far, it is unique in that Principal Jenkins elevates sign language to a level near that of spoken languages. Of the schools in this study, the only other person to have advanced the concept of sign language as having rules and being on a par with spoken language was Warring Wilkinson, who made his comments during roughly the same time period.

Five years later a new attitude about sign language began surfacing at the school, concurrent with the school board's decision that the school needed a new principal. The new principal, Theodore C. Bowles, said that,

> Signs are only used as stepping-stones, or a medium by which to conduct the pupil to a knowledge of established language. The sign language may be compared to a scaffolding or wooden arch temporarily constructed to receive a more substantial superstructure, which may be torn down or left to waste away when it has served its temporary purpose (KSD 1876, 16).

Over the course of just five years, then, the school's prevailing attitude went from one in which sign language was seen as "based on scientific principles, which elevate it to a high position among the languages of mankind" (20) to one where sign language was seen as "a scaffolding or wooden arch temporarily constructed to receive a more substantial superstructure, which may be torn down or left to waste away when it has served its temporary purpose" (16).

In addition, it is interesting to note that in the 11th report, an attempt was made to show the "desultory construction of the language of signs" (17) by writing down the Lord's Prayer as it was signed by teachers. However, the ensuing sign "transcription" had been *very* meticulously cut out, possibly in an attempt to "save face" for a language that is transmitted in a three-dimensional visual, and not a written, mode.

The pendulum of language attitude and policy swung back once again under a new superintendent, S. T. Walker. The school's 1886 report mentions a monthly course in sign language, in which lectures were "prepared with care, and special design to instruct and interest the pupils" (KSD 1886, 15). Four years later, under the same superintendent, an enumeration of the desired skills of teachers at the school showed that knowledge of sign language was deemed important:

> A knowledge of this kind means more than ability to spell with the fingers. . . . But the ability to take any subject, whether original or from the speaker's lips, and translate the living thoughts into vivid air-pictures, capable of being read by scores of upturned silent faces, or to unravel the mysterious technical language of the school or college text-book so that the deaf may "read between the lines," is the kind of skill which we look for in the most experienced teachers of the deaf. (KSD 1890, 13)

Following the turn of the century, the school reports became strikingly similar to those of other schools not only in physical production (they were more technically produced, with many pictures) but also in content. The Kansas School continued to shift back and forth between a positive attitude about the use of signs among students or for educational purposes and a viewpoint in which signs were at best a rudimentary means to an end.

Language Policies and Attitudes at the Maryland School for the Deaf

The Maryland School for the Deaf followed the same methodological path set forth by other schools for deaf students in the United States— that of using the combined method (both sign language and oral instruction) to varying degrees with different students. Charles M. Ely, principal from 1870 to 1912, published a brief history of the school and summarized the language policy up to that point as "the combined or eclectic method, which prevails in most American schools for the deaf" (1893, 7). He explained that sign language was used to clarify concepts and other material for students, while the opportunity to learn articulation and speechreading was given to every student at the school.

Earlier in the school's development, we see the beginnings of this overall language policy taking place: In the school's third annual report, Ely mentioned that he felt pressure to have articulation classes because most people saw these classes "as essential in all first-class institutions" (1871, 3). In 1873 Ely expressed some hesitation about the efficacy of teaching articulation and mentioned that, although the articulation class had been running smoothly, two years is not enough time in which to render a verdict about the value of one methodology over another (MDSD 1873).

One year later Ely mentioned the addition of another teacher of articulation and reported that all students "are placed in the oral classes and whether bright or dull are taught faithfully through the first year" (MDSD 1874, 10). He explained that any students who had not made progress in the articulation classes after the first year of instruction were subsequently dropped from the class. Interestingly, Ely also remarked that "any deaf-mute of average intelligence can be taught to make articulate sounds and to speak some words" (11). Although this idea is not a new one to those familiar with the history of U.S. deaf education, the way in which Ely phrased this concept provides us with insight into a strong language attitude; Ely did not mention sign language but instead made a powerful statement about the value of speech and the English language for students at the Maryland School.

In 1883 Ely commented on the role that signs played in the school's overall agenda. He said that "written language is the key to knowledge, and to intercourse with others" and that "to gain a knowledge of this, the language of signs is employed. Signs are used simply as the instrument. Proficiency in their use is not education, yet some seem to suppose that it is to learn signs that deaf mutes are sent to school" (MDSD 1881–1883, 14–15). He further remarked on the "convenience" of signs for assemblies of deaf students (e.g., church and public meetings). Clearly, Ely saw sign language as a tool for facilitating knowledge of English, but he ended his statement about signs by saying that "We do not encourage the parents or friends of deaf mutes to learn signs, considering it preferable that they should rely upon language written or spoken" (15).

Ely's perspectives about using the combined method (but always starting out with articulation) did not change much over the years, but it seems as though the concept of using signs in deaf education did gain some merit in his mind. In 1889 he stated, "If we were compelled to use one method for all pupils, we should, having regard for the greatest good of the greatest number, be obliged to choose the sign language" (MDSD 1889, 10). Ely's reasoning for this position was that through sign language, "all [students], whatever their mental or physical defects, can be reached," but he concluded by saying that, fortunately, deaf education had not been reduced to the use of sign language alone.

Ely's foundational principle of Deaf education, one that ran throughout all of the school reports during his tenure at the Maryland School, was this: "Mental and moral training stand first" (MDSD 1897, 10). Although he certainly had specific views about the relative merits of using articulation versus using sign language, his primary goal was to develop the students' mental and moral character by using whichever method best suited their individual needs.

Language Policies and Attitudes at the Washington State School for the Deaf

One of the earliest reports at the Washington School mentioned the use of the combined method and emphasized the concept that signs were used sparingly, only as a means to an end—education in general, skill in English in particular (WSD 1887–1889). Two years after the school reported using a combined method, George Layton, a graduate of VSDB and the National Deaf-Mute College, was appointed as an instructor. This is significant because VSDB was run in its early years by staff and former students of ASD, and it is possible that ASD's pro-sign language attitudes strongly influenced VSDB. In turn, Layton was most likely exposed to some of the beliefs upon which VSDB was founded, and these attitudes may have shaped his views toward language.

The school's 1908 report mentions a policy about education that is exactly like those at other schools: Put all new students in oral classes first. The students who "can not learn to talk" were then moved to classes "carried on by silent methods under equally well trained specialists in those methods" (WSD 1906–1908, 5). Although this statement seems to show that the school regarded both oral and manual classes as having equal status, manual classes were still regarded as a "default" option for students unable to learn to speak. However, a few years later, the school was leaning more toward the combined method of instruction: "Our rule is that adopted by the American Instructors of the Deaf in convention assembled. 'Any method for good results. All methods, and wedded to none' " (WSD 1910–1912, 11–12).

SUMMARY AND CONCLUSIONS

From our investigation of the language attitudes and policies in effect at the schools for deaf students involved in this study, several patterns emerge. One of these is that many of the schools founded in the 1820s and 1830s looked to the American School for the Deaf for assistance. Sometimes this assistance came via personnel, as was the case with Laurent Clerc, who went to the Pennsylvania Institution to help get the school running. At other times ASD provided assistance by example; by virtue of its being the first school of its kind in the United States, ASD was a role model for other schools in determining the most effective way of educating deaf children.

A second pattern was that schools for deaf people as a whole began as staunch supporters of sign language in the early- to mid-1800s and gradually shifted to become supporters of articulation beginning around 1880. One of the primary reasons for the shift was that educators at the 1880 Milan conference so strongly supported oralism in deaf education. But other factors were also at work; Baynton suggests that an overall shift in what American society considered valuable may have facilitated the swing from sign language to oralism at the end of the nineteenth century. He summarizes this shift by saying, "While manualists went on extolling the glories of ancient Rome, oralists were more in tune with the current status of foreign nations in America. The nation most in favor [in the late nineteenth century] was not ancient Rome but modern Germany, the undisputed leader in both science and education" (1996, 106).

Another pattern across the schools we studied was that as administrators came and went, so did language policies. Different principals brought different experiences and perspectives about how best to educate Deaf children. For example, Elwood A. Stevenson, at the California School for the Deaf, was a child of deaf adults (CODA). Although practices that were popular during his tenure in the first half of the twentieth century (e.g., starting students in oral classes to see whether they would make progress, then transferring those who were not successful) influenced his attitudes about language, he also believed that using signs was one key to the development of a healthy mind for deaf students (CSD 1934–1936), an idea not widely held during his time.

Finally, we must note that social organizations also played key roles in the transmission and maintenance of ASL. Lane et al. (1996) mention the importance of the residential school alumni associations, starting with the one for the Hartford school, and point out that residential schools have important ties with Deaf clubs and athletic organizations such as the American Athletic Association of the Deaf, founded in 1945:

> Some Deaf people attend athletic tournaments to play, of course, but they and many more are there for another reason: to be with other members of the DEAF-WORLD . . . and to see old friends who have become separated after graduation or marriage or a move to a new job. Athletics in Deaf culture also serve linguistic and political functions. ASL is a truly national language, in part because of the co-mingling of Deaf people in the residential schools, in the clubs and in regional and national athletics. (131)

Chapter 4

Phonological Variation 1:

Variation in Handshape

This chapter presents the quantitative analyses of the first of three target phonological variables: signs produced with a 1 handshape. We explain how the data were coded and present the results of the quantitative analyses of linguistic and social factors. Overall, the analyses presented here and in the following chapter show that phonological variation in ASL is largely systematic. Like variation in spoken languages, it is subject to both linguistic and social constraints. The results of quantitative analyses also suggest, however, that social factors particular to the Deaf community influence signers' choices among variable linguistic forms. Of particular note is the fact that grammatical function strongly constrains variation in 1 handshape signs as well as in the two variables considered in the following chapter, DEAF and the location of a class of signs represented by the verb KNOW.

A DISTINCTIVE-FEATURE MODEL OF ASL

As discussed in chapter 1, earlier studies of variation in ASL were based on simultaneous rather than sequential models of sign language structure. Recently, however, sequential models have been developed. These models appear far more suitable for the study of variation than earlier simultaneous models. One challenge for our study, then, was to define the variable and the linguistic constraints within a sequential distinctive-feature model. This section summarizes the aspects of a distinctive-feature model of ASL sign structure and handshape articulation that are relevant to this study, that of Liddell and Johnson (Liddell and Johnson 1989).

In Liddell and Johnson's autosegmental model, signs consist of sequentially ordered units (Liddell 1984). Each unit is defined by whether the hands are static (hold segments) or dynamic (movement segments). Each segment is an articulatory bundle that includes the features of handshape, location, palm orientation, and nonmanual signals (facial expressions). States of the hands, location, palm orientation, and finger configuration (or handshape) are thus described as articulatory features attaching to hold or movement segments. We focus here on the features that describe handshapes. In ASL the thumb and fingers move independently of one another, so distinctive-feature models specify how the thumb and each finger are positioned in any handshape. For example, as table 4.1 shows, to describe the 1 handshape variable, we looked at three kinds of features that define the position of the fingers.

The position of the thumb also varies in sign production. Table 4.2 shows three kinds of features that specify the position of the thumb during articulation of a sign.

TABLE 4.1. *Features of the Fingers that Describe ASL Handshapes*

Feature Type	Description
1. Selected fingers	These features specify which of the four fingers are selected, that is, which fingers are salient in the handshape: [+/− index selected], [+/− middle selected], [+/− ring selected], [+/− pinky selected].
2. Selected fingers up	These features specify whether the selected fingers are up or down, that is, pointing away from the palm or curled into the palm.
3. Finger joint alignment	These features specify whether the fingers are bent or straight at any particular joint.

TABLE 4.2. *Features of the Thumb that Describe ASL Handshapes*

Feature Type	Description
1. Thumb opposed	This feature specifies whether the thumb is aligned with the fingers or positioned so its pad faces the palm: [+/−opposed].
2. Align with fingers	These features specify whether the thumb is on the same plane as the palm or out of alignment with the palm.
3. Thumb joint alignment	These features specify which joints of the thumb are bent or are straight.

To show how these features combine to form part of the definition of a segment, a picture of the sign ONE is shown in figure 4.1. ONE has the 1 handshape that is our focus; this handshape appears in many other signs unrelated to numbers, such as FOR, THINK, and DISCUSS.

We explain first the configuration of the segmental tier and then the distinctive features, which are important for understanding the 1 handshape variable. Figure 4.1 shows an ASL sign—ONE—that consists of a single phonetic segment. On the segmental tier, the segment is designated as a hold segment. This means that the hand does not move during the production of this sign. Further, the handshape does not change during the production of this sign. Note that the features of the handshape are one cluster of features that define the segment. Also parts of the segment are features of the location and palm orientation of the hand. The nature of the 1 handshape variable, then, is not a whole phonological unit but a cluster of features within the segment. The level of structure that is variable is similar to that in vowel nasalization before word-final nasals. In vowel nasalization only one feature changes its value. In handshape variation many features may change their values, but the crucial similarity is that the variation occurs on a single tier of features.

In Liddell and Johnson's model, fingers are selected if they are most salient in the sign or if they contact the body or point. In the case of a 1 handshape, only the index finger is selected because it is the only finger that is salient in the production of the sign. In signs other than our example sign, the index finger contacts the body, or, in indexical signs, the tip of the index finger is aimed at the referent. In Liddell and Johnson's model, selected fingers are "up" if their fingertips are pointing away from the palm. Finger joint aligned means that the joint in question is tensed so that the finger is straight at that point. In the following analyses we call this posture of the finger straight. If distal finger joints are not aligned, this creates a hooking of the finger. Note also in figure 4.1 that

FIGURE 4.1. *The sign for* ONE

the middle, ring, and pinky fingers are closed against the palm. In Liddell and Johnson's model, this means that they are unselected and thus not salient or important in the phonotactics of that sign. The thumb may be either opposed to the fingers or unopposed. If the thumb is [+opposed] but [–aligned], the thumb is neutral. This means that the thumb is not salient in the articulation of this sign.

The I Handshape Variable

The 1 handshape variable consists of all the various handshapes that occur in signs lexically specified for the features just discussed—the combination of features that specify the handshape as in ONE. Many signs are produced with the handshape shown in figure 4.1, the 1 handshape, and include lexical signs such as TO-SIGN, GO, CANCEL, BLACK, and LONG, pronouns, glossed as PRO.1, PRO.2, and PRO.3, classifier predicates such as LONG-THIN-THING-LYING DOWN, *wh*-words, and some grammatical function words, such as FOR. The 1 handshape variation thus satisfies the criteria for selecting linguistic variables set forth by Labov in his study of Martha's Vineyard:

> First, we want an item that is frequent, which occurs so often in the course of undirected natural conversation that its behavior can be charted from unstructured contexts and brief interviews. Secondly, it should be structural: the more the item is integrated into a larger system of functioning units, the greater will be the intrinsic linguistic interest. . . . Third, the distribution of the feature should be highly stratified: that is, our preliminary explorations should suggest an asymmetric distribution over a wide range of age levels or other ordered strata of society. (1972a, 8)

The 1 handshape variable occurs often enough to be amenable to large-scale statistical analysis. Moreover, as the preceding examples illustrate, it is widely distributed across a range of different grammatical categories. In addition, preliminary examination suggested that preferred forms differed considerably according to a variety of social factors.

VARIANTS OF THE I HANDSHAPE
The variants of the 1-handshape that are seen in actual production diverge greatly from the citation form. The index finger may be hooked instead of straight. Any of the other three fingers may be selected and

FIGURE 4.2. *Variants of 1 handshape signs*

arranged in any of the possible patterns seen in ASL handshapes. The thumb may be open from its neutral position and extended to the side of the hand or point up in alignment with the radial side of the hand. Figure 4.2 shows two variants of the 1 handshape seen in our database.

Phonologists working on ASL have recognized more than 100 contrastive handshapes (Liddell and Johnson 1995), many of which appear where we might expect a 1 handshape citation form. This fact presents a problem for variable rule analysis because even the multinomial version of VARBRUL, MVARB (Pintzuk 1988), is limited to five variants. Moreover, many of the variants are infrequent and hence not suitable for quantitative analysis. Although we have not investigated exactly how many of these handshapes appear in 1 handshape signs, we know that the number is much higher than five. Faced with the relative rarity of some variants, our task was not only to define the variants to retain the most salient aspects of their variability but also to allow for maximum distinctness among them. At the beginning of our coding process, we felt that we could not reduce the number of our variants to fewer than six. Thus, we have not coded all possible variants. However, three variants comprise 95 percent of a representative sample of more than 5,000 tokens.[1]

1. The problem of reducing multiple phonetic realizations of a variable to a manageable number is not unique to sign language studies. Wolfram (1974, 1993), for example, identified a number of subvariants of the morpheme-final /θ/ in words such as *tooth* and *both* and proposed ten different phonological rules to account for the observed patterns. Wolfram (1993) also notes that studies of -*t,d* deletion in English dialects normally deal only with presence or absence, although variants of -*t,d* may also include a glottal stop or a flap.

Next we define the three main variants as well as three others that occur less frequently. The definitions are based on a reduction of the features from Liddell and Johnson's model to the salient ones that define a 1 handshape. To define the variable, we treat the hand as having an index finger, a thumb, and a combination of three other fingers rather than having a thumb and four independent fingers. Each of these three parts — thumb, index, or other fingers — can be open or closed, giving us three sets of binary features. The salient elements of the 1 handshape that led us to divide these features in this way are as follows:

The index finger is the only finger selected. The middle, ring, and pinky fingers are unselected, or closed.

The index finger's joints are aligned; that is, the finger itself is extended, or straight.

The thumb is in a neutral position, opposed, joints bent, and aligned with the tip of the selected finger, or closed around the nonselected fingers.

The index finger is the most salient element of this handshape, and our division of variants treats this finger as having two possible values:

straight: The finger is selected, and the distal joints are straight.

hooked: The finger is selected or not selected, but the distal joints are bent.

Treating each of the fingers other than the index finger as a separate unit would lead to many possible variants. Therefore, we grouped these three fingers as a unit, as fingers other than the index finger, and treated them as if they behaved as a unit. We defined two possible values for these fingers:

open: One or more of the fingers are selected, and their distal joints are straight.

closed: None of these fingers is selected, and their distal joints are bent, or hooked.

The thumb postures were also defined with respect to the 1 handshape citation form. In the citation form of one, for example, the thumb is neutral. We defined the possible values that the thumb could have as either neutral or not neutral:

open: The thumb is not in a neutral position. It may be opposed or unopposed, but its joints are extended so that the thumb is not closed on the palm or unselected fingers.

TABLE 4.3. *Variants of 1 Handshape Signs*

Variant	Description
+cf	Citation form: thumb closed, fingers closed, index straight
–cf 1	L handshape: thumb open, fingers closed, index straight. Includes handshapes [21, G, L]
–cf 2	open hand: thumb open, fingers open, index straight or hooked. Includes handshapes 5, 9, 8, 7, ILY, Y, 3, 6, and others
–cf 3	4 handshape: thumb closed, fingers open, index straight or hooked includes handshapes 4, hooked 4
–cf 4	X handshape: thumb closed, fingers closed, index hooked
–cf 5	thumb open, fingers closed, index hooked (includes where sign points with thumb)

closed: The thumb is in a neutral position, opposed to the fingers, but its joints are bent so that the thumb is closed.

Assuming that thumb, fingers, and the index finger act independently of one another, this combination of binary features for each unit gives us nine possible variants. However, with the phonotactic consideration that bending of joints applies to all selected fingers, we could combine the variants into six. These are defined in table 4.3.

Coding

LINGUISTIC CONSTRAINTS

We coded for three linguistic constraints that are well known from studies of phonological variation in spoken languages: (1) the grammatical category of the word as used in the token sentence; (2) the preceding phonological environment; and (3) the following phonological environment. Each of these is discussed in some detail in the following section. Because research has shown that involved narratives of personal experience tend to promote the production of vernacular forms (Labov 1972b), we also coded for a fourth linguistic constraint, the genre of the text in which the token occurred, defined as either a conversational turn or a narrative.

Grammatical category.
We coded for the grammatical category of the sign in which the handshape in question occurred. Factors in this group, shown with examples, were as follows:

PRO.1 'I'

PRO.2 'You'

PRO.3 'He,' 'She,' 'It'

wh-word (e.g., Where, When)

Grammatical function word (e.g., For)

Adverb (e.g., Really)

Verb (e.g., Go, Cancel)

Adjective (e.g., Black, Long)

Noun (e.g., Week, Month)

Classifier predicates were not included in the analysis because the 1 handshapes in these signs are separate morphemes with independent meaning, unlike the lexical signs and pronouns in which the handshape has no independent meaning.

Phonological constraints.
The coding system for phonological factors was designed to test Liddell and Johnson's claim that the 1 handshape is subject to processes of assimilation in pronouns and possibly in other signs as well:

> There are numerous instances of assimilation in ASL. For example, the hand configuration of the sign ME typically assimilates to that of a contiguous predicate in the same clause. . . . The extent to which signs other than ME assimilate to the hand configuration of another sign . . . appears to be considerably more limited. (1989, 250)

We assumed that only the handshape features of the preceding or following phonological segments would have an effect on variable features of the handshape of the target sign. Therefore, rather than coding for preceding location, orientation, and handshape, we limited our definition of the preceding and following environments to the preceding and following handshape.

The first step in coding for features of the phonological environment was to code for whether the variable was preceded or followed by a segment or a pause. We then coded preceding and following segments for relevant features of the thumb, index finger, and fingers 234. Features were selected because the variable as defined here does not constitute a

TABLE 4.4. *Coding the 1 Handshape Variable: Features of the Preceding and Following Segments*

	Thumb	Fingers	Index
Preceding segment	+/−	+/−	Straight/hooked
Following segment	+/−	+/−	Straight/hooked

Note: +, feature selected; −, feature not selected.

whole linguistic unit, or segment, but a cluster of features that defines only the handshape in the formation of the sign. In the same way, the handshape of the segments preceding or following the 1 handshape sign is simply a bundle of features. Recall that our definitions of the variants of the 1 handshape variable incorporated a notion of the three units of that handshape, which combined to define the handshape itself: the index finger, the thumb, and a combination of the middle, ring, and pinky fingers. Each of these elements of the handshape could be categorized as having one of two binary features: open or closed, in the case of the thumb or fingers, and straight or hooked, in the case of the index finger. Our analysis treated each of the elements of the handshape of the preceding or following environment in a separate factor group. Table 4.4 shows how we coded for the features of the preceding (and following) segments in three binary factor groups.

SOCIAL CONSTRAINTS

Given the size of the corpus, comprising many hours of conversation from more than 200 signers, and the pervasiveness of the 1 handshape, it was neither possible nor necessary to code all examples of the variable that appeared on tape in order to understand the constraints on variation. Rather than code all possible examples, we settled on a sample of least 25 tokens per signer, resulting in 5,356 tokens, more than sufficient for VARBRUL analysis. All of these tokens were extracted from the spontaneous conversation portion of each videotaped session. The tokens were divided between lexical 1 handshape signs, *wh*-words, grammatical function words, and pronouns. For each example, the features of the variant were described and the syntactic context in which the variable occurred was recorded.

The decision to code data from each of the signers represented in the corpus allowed us to test the effect of the main social constraints that we had earlier identified as potential influences on variation: age (15–25,

26–54, 55+), gender, social class, ethnicity (African American or Caucasian), parents' audiological status (Deaf or hearing), and region where the signer resided.

Exclusion from Quantitative Analysis

When examining the contexts in which the thumb-only variant (–cf 5) was used, the coders concluded that the use of this variant was constrained not only by the potentially relevant linguistic and social factors but also by the physical location of second- and third-person referents in the conversation. For example, if the pronoun referred to the person sitting to the immediate right of the signer, the signer would be more likely to use this thumb-only variant to refer to that person rather than switch hands to use a citation-form pronoun. Because the thumb-only variant was thus potentially constrained by the physical position of interlocutors rather than by factors having to do with the linguistic system, tokens were excluded from quantitative analysis. This exclusion is in line with the conclusion reached by Metzger (1993), who suggested that it is an open question as to whether the thumb variant is best treated as an instance of phonological variation or as a separate lexical item and hence as an example of lexical variation.

RESULTS

Of the 5,195 tokens remaining after the exclusion of the thumb-only variant, 95 percent were examples of one of three variants: citation form (+cf); noncitation form 1, the L handshape variant (thumb open, fingers closed, index straight); noncitation form 2, the open hand variant (thumb and fingers open, index straight or hooked). The remaining 5 percent were divided between two noncitation forms: the 4 handshape variant and the X handshape variant. The distribution of variants is similar to that in other recent studies of variation in ASL (Bayley et al. 2000), in which noncitation forms are more common than citation forms. In other words, handshapes other than '1' in these signs are more common than the 1 handshape for which the sign is specified. The citation form occurred in 40 percent of the tokens coded, and other handshapes occurred in the other 60 percent. In this section we summarize the distribution of variants by linguistic and social factors. We then present the results of variable rule analysis.

Overall results indicate that variation in 1 handshape signs is systematic and constrained by a rich array of linguistic and social factors. Among the linguistic factor groups, grammatical category, the preceding thumb, fingers, and index, and the following thumb and fingers all constrained signer's choices of one or another 1 handshape variant. Among the social factors, age, social class, ethnicity, region, and parents' audiological status were all selected as significant in at least one VARBRUL analysis. Discourse type (narrative, conversation), the position of the index finger in the following segment, and gender failed to reach significance in any of the variable rule analyses and will not be discussed further. The choice of a 1 handshape variant also failed to be affected significantly by the presence or absence of a preceding segment. That is, signers were just as likely to use one of the noncitations forms following or preceding a pause. Numbers and percentages of occurrence for each factor that had a statistically significant effect on the choice of at least one variant are shown in table 4.5. In addition, for the sake of completeness, we have included the percentages and numbers of variants in the environment of preceding and following segments and pauses as well as percentages and numbers of the less common variants.

Looking first at the grammatical category factor group, we see that first-person pronouns are not the only signs in ASL to vary from the citation form. In fact, all categories of lexical signs take handshapes whose phonetic shapes vary greatly from the citation form. Even for nouns and adjectives, the grammatical classes with the greatest percentage of citation forms, signers chose noncitation variants 32 percent of the time. Turning to the features of the preceding and following segments, we note two general principles. First, if the preceding or following thumb or fingers are selected, they tend also to be selected in the 1 handshape variant. That is, even judging from the percentages, we see evidence of progressive and regressive assimilation. Second, despite the general tendency of the preceding and following handshapes to favor 1 handshape variants with the same features selected, none of the phonological (or other) factors we have coded for always results in the choice of one or another 1 handshape variant. For example, as table 4.5 shows, if the preceding sign is produced with a closed thumb, 55 percent of the 1 handshape signs in this environment are in citation form (i.e., produced with a closed thumb). Forty percent of the 1 handshape signs in the environment, however, are noncitation forms produced with the thumb open, whether in the L handshape or the open hand variant.

Variable Rule Analysis: I Handshape

Multivariate analyses with VARBRUL confirmed our impressions of the effects of the different factors suggested by the percentages of occurrence of different variants shown in table 4.5. Here we report on three separate analyses—with the citation form, the L handshape variant, and the open hand variant respectively defined as the *application value*. Note that we have assumed here that the citation form is the underlying form. However, unlike the case of DEAF, which we report on in the next chapter, we do not suggest a model of rule ordering to produce each of the surface variants. In our corpus DEAF has only three variants, and the relationships among them are generally transparent. As we have noted, however, 1 handshape has many variants, although the three we report on in this section are by far the most common. Here, then, we conceptualized the choice of a 1 handshape variant as an unordered series of binomial choices (i.e., +cf vs. all other forms, L handshape vs. all other forms, and open hand vs. all other forms). In the following sections we report the results of all three analyses by factor group.

GRAMMATICAL CATEGORY

Contrary to what previous arguments about variation in the handshape of PRO.1 (Liddell and Johnson 1989) might lead us to expect, phonological constraints did not exert the strongest influences on the choice of the +cf variant. Rather, the grammatical category proved to the first-order linguistic constraint in two of the three VARBRUL analyses, with +cf and the open hand variant defined as the application value. Grammatical category also significantly constrained signers' choice of the L handshape variant. Results for this factor group are shown in table 4.6.[2] We have also included the input value for each run, an overall measure of the tendency of signers to choose the application value and the chi-square per cell, a measure of the goodness of fit. Since these later figures are the same for all the other factor groups, they are only reported here.

---

2. In table 4.6 and elsewhere we have combined factors within groups that did not differ significantly from one another in cases in which there was linguistic or social justification for doing so.

TABLE 4-5. *Variation in 1 Handshape Signs: Distribution of Variants by Factor Group*

Factor Group	Factor	+cf		-cf, L Handshape		-cf, Open Hand		-cf, 4 Handshape		-cf, X Handshape		Total
		%	n	%	n	%	n	%	n	%	n	n
Grammatical category	Noun, adjective	68	287	20	85	8	35	2	9	1	3	419
	Verb, adverb	59	730	29	358	10	118	2	20	1	12	1238
	Gr. function word	52	262	31	157	13	64	2	11	1	7	501
	wh-word	48	48	40	40	11	11	2	2	0	0	101
	PRO.3	45	195	34	150	19	81	2	9	0	0	435
	PRO.2	34	163	39	186	23	112	4	18	1	3	482
	PRO.1	19	382	29	580	44	898	6	124	2	35	2019
Preceding environment	Segment	41	1693	31	1276	24	1007	4	155	1	43	4174
	Pause	37	374	27	280	31	312	4	38	2	17	1021
Preceding thumb	Closed	55	799	23	333	17	244	4	60	2	25	1461
	Open	33	894	35	943	28	763	4	95	1	18	2713
Preceding fingers	Closed	49	870	33	577	15	265	2	34	1	25	1771
	Open	34	823	29	699	31	742	5	121	1	18	2403
Preceding index	Straight	41	1258	30	928	24	740	4	117	1	28	3071
	Hooked	39	435	32	348	24	267	3	38	1	15	1103
Following environment	Segment	39	1774	29	1347	27	1223	4	181	1	53	4578
	Pause	47	293	34	209	16	96	2	12	1	7	617
Following thumb	Closed	51	907	23	407	18	311	6	108	2	29	1762
	Open	31	867	33	940	32	912	3	73	1	24	2816

Factor Group	Factor	+cf		-cf, L Handshape		-cf, Open Hand		-cf, 4 Handshape		-cf, X Handshape		Total
		%	n	%	n	%	n	%	n	%	n	n
Following fingers	Closed	47	887	33	633	16	300	3	48	1	24	1896
	Open	33	887	27	714	34	923	5	133	1	29	1762
Age	55+	39	680	33	586	23	410	3	56	2	29	1761
	26–54	43	890	28	573	24	483	4	83	1	17	2046
	15–25	36	497	29	397	31	426	4	54	1	14	1388
Class	WC	41	1225	30	920	24	736	4	107	1	32	3020
	MC	39	842	29	636	27	583	4	86	1	28	2175
Ethnicity	AA	50	735	22	323	22	330	5	73	1	15	1476
	C	36	1332	33	1233	27	989	3	120	1	45	3719
Region	Mass.	50	425	20	169	22	188	7	58	2	16	856
	Calif.	49	455	23	212	23	218	3	29	2	14	928
	Kans./Mo.	49	507	24	254	23	234	4	37	0	5	1037
	La.	42	332	27	215	23	182	6	47	2	19	795
	Md.	25	135	44	241	30	163	1	7	0	1	547
	Va.	18	105	47	267	33	186	2	11	1	3	572
	Wash.	23	108	43	198	32	148	1	4	0	2	460
Language background	Other	40	1608	30	1208	24	975	4	158	1	47	3996
	ASL	38	459	29	348	29	344	3	35	1	13	1199
Total		40	2067	30	1556	25	1319	4	193	1	60	5195

Note: All factor groups except preceding and following environment (segment, pause) significant for one or more variants.

TABLE 4.6. *Variation in 1 Handshape Signs: Grammatical Category*

Factor	+cf, One Hand Weight	%	−cf, L Handshape Weight	%	−cf, Open Hand Weight	%
Noun, adjective	.838	68	.351	20	.219	8
Verb, adverb	.727	59	.474	29	.275	10
Grammatical function word	.708	52	.492	31	.306	13
wh-word	.647	48	.581	40	.275	11
PRO.3	.583	45	{.568}	{.37}	.439	19
PRO.2	.482	34			.505	23
PRO.1	.223	19	.515	29	.761	44
Input	.344	40	.281	30	.192	25

Note: +cf, χ^2 /cell = 1.0653; L handshape, χ^2 /cell = 1.1159; open hand, χ^2 /cell = 1.1241.

As table 4.6 shows, nouns and adjectives (p = .838), verbs and adverbs (p = .727), grammatical function words (p = .708), *wh*-words (p = .647) and PRO.3 (p = .583) favor the citation form. However, PRO.1 and PRO.2 (p = .482, .223) disfavor this form and are more likely to be realized as some other handshape. For the L handshape variant, the situation is nearly the reverse. Signers are more likely to choose the L handshape variant for *wh*-words (p = .581) and PRO.2 and PRO.3 (p = .568), which do not differ significantly from one another, than for verbs and adverbs (p = .474) or nouns and adjectives (p = .351). For this variant, grammatical function words (p = .492) and PRO.1 (p = .515) are relatively neutral in their effect, as can also be seen by the fact that the percentage of use of the L handshape variant for these categories differs by only 1 percent of the overall percentage in the data set. Turning to the open hand variant, we again see a pattern that is nearly the reverse of the pattern for +cf. Nouns and adjectives (p = .219), verbs and adverbs (p = .275), *wh*-words (p = .270), and grammatical function words (p = .306) all strongly disfavor the open hand variant. PRO.3 (p = .439) also disfavors the choice of this variant, while PRO.2 (p = .505) was neutral. In contrast, PRO.1 (p = .761) strongly favors the open hand variant, the form that differs most greatly from the citation form.

In formulating the coding scheme used here, we expected that features in the surrounding handshapes—previous or following environments—would favor like features in the target sign. The multivariate analyses show that this is indeed the case. Thus, a closed thumb in the preceding segment favors +cf (p =.635), as does a closed thumb in the following segment (p = .628). Similarly, closed fingers in the preceding segment (p = .551) and in the following segment also favor +cf (p = .532). A hooked index finger in the preceding sign slightly disfavors +cf (p = .468). These results suggest that assimilation is at work in handshape variation. As table 4.7 shows, the results of the analyses with L handshape and open hand defined as the application values bear out the suggestion. Note also that the preceding and following thumb and fingers are clearly the most important features involved. In contrast to the preceding index, which was significant only in the analysis with +cf defined as the application value, the positions of the preceding and following thumb and fingers were significant in all three analyses.

The hypothesis that features in the preceding and following handshapes would favor like features in the target variable was tested in several further analyses. In the first analysis +cf was selected as the application value, and the six factor groups specifying whether the preceding and following thumb and fingers were selected and whether the preced-

TABLE 4.7. *Variation in 1 Handshape Signs: Phonological Factors*

Factor Group	Factor	+cf		−cf, L Handshape		−cf, Open Hand	
		Weight	%	Weight	%	Weight	%
Preceding thumb	Closed	.635	55	.390	23	.440	17
	Open	.426	33	.560	35	.532	28
Preceding fingers	Closed	.551	49	.573	33	.385	15
	Open	.463	34	.446	29	.585	31
Preceding index	Straight	.512	41	ns	30	ns	24
	Hooked	.468	39	ns	32	ns	24
Following thumb	Closed	.628	51	.389	23	.429	18
	Open	.419	31	.570	33	.545	32
Following fingers	Closed	.532	47	.597	33	.375	16
	Open	.477	33	.431	28	.590	34

ing and following environments consisted of segments or pauses were combined into a single-factor group, with factors defined according to the number of features they share with the citation form. Tokens preceded or followed by a pause were coded as nonapplicable to this stage of the analysis. Recall that +cf was defined as –thumb, –fingers (i.e., the thumb and the fingers are closed in the citation form of the sign). Thus, considering only these two features, the preceding and following segments may share from zero to four features with the target sign. In this scheme, cases in which the thumb and fingers of the preceding and following segments were both selected were recoded as zero. That is, with respect to the position of the thumb and fingers, they share no features with the +cf form of the 1 handshape variable. Cases in which neither the thumb nor the fingers of the preceding or following segments were selected were recoded as 4. That is, they share four features with the target variable.

The results for the phonological factors from the analysis that combined the preceding and following thumb and fingers into a single factor group, defined according to the number of shared features with the +cf variant, are shown in table 4.8. Other than the features of the preceding and following segments, the analysis included all the factors included in the original analysis. The ordering of all other factor groups remained the same as in the original analysis. However, the preceding index factor group, which showed only a weak, if significant, effect in the original analysis, failed to reach significance in the alternative analysis.

The results shown in table 4.8 provide additional evidence to support the generalization that features of the preceding and following segments

TABLE 4.8. *Variation in 1 Handshape Signs: +cf by Shared Features of Preceding and Following Thumb and Fingers*

Shared Features	Weight	%	n
0, 1	.353	27	1731
2	.565	45	1163
3	.641	52	441
4	.824	71	318
Total/input	.349	40	3653

Note: χ^2 /cell = 1.3546; n = number of tokens that could share between from 0 to 4 features with the preceding and following signs. Tokens with preceding or following pauses were coded as not applicable.

favor like features in the target variable, in this case +cf. That is, the more features shared with the +cf form by the preceding and following segments, the more likely a signer is to choose that variant. Thus, the +cf form is disfavored when the preceding and following segments share no features or only one feature of the thumb and fingers with the +cf form ($p = .353$). The +cf form is favored, however, when the preceding and/or following segments share two features with the +cf form ($p = .565$). It is more strongly favored when the preceding and following segments share three features with the +cf form ($p = .641$) and very strongly favored when four features of both the preceding and following thumb and fingers are shared with the +cf form of the target variable ($p = .824$).[3]

If we were dealing with a binary variable, the analysis presented so far would be sufficient to demonstrate fully the relationship between the position of the preceding and following thumb and fingers and the target variable because the results for –cf would simply be the reverse of +cf. However, in this case, –cf represents two main variants and several minor ones. Moreover, the two main variants differ from one another and from the +cf form in whether the thumb and fingers are selected. To further test the generalization that features of the handshapes of the preceding and following segments favor like features in the target variable, we conducted two additional variable rule analyses, with the L handshape and open hand variants defined as the application values. In the case of the L handshape variant (thumb open, fingers closed), this involved again recoding the data to combine the binary factor groups specifying whether the preceding and following fingers were selected into a single factor group. As in the previous analysis, we defined factors ac-

---

3. Superficially, the results reported in this section might appear to constitute a violation of the Obligatory Contour Principle (OCP), which prohibits adjacent identical segments (McCarthy 1986; Yip 1988). Guy and Boberg (1997) have recently extended the OCP to provide a unified account of categorical and variable processes in spoken languages. However, our results are not germane to the status of the OCP. Recall that our focus in the examination of 1 handshape variation is on variation in the form of the handshape (i.e., we focus on only one of the parameters that comprise the phonetic description of a sign). Even in cases in which the handshape of the target variable assimilates to the handshape of the preceding and/or following segment, the result is not a geminate. The 1 handshape variant may still differ from the preceding and/or following handshape in other features such as location or orientation.

cording to the number of features they shared with the target variable, in this case the L handshape. For example, tokens of the L handshape variant preceded and followed by segments formed with closed thumb and open fingers were coded as having zero relevant shared features. Tokens preceded and followed by segments formed with open thumb and closed fingers were coded as having four relevant shared features. Recoding for the open hand variant, of course, was much simpler because the relevant features—the preceding and following thumb and fingers—are simply the opposite of their position in the +cf form.

The results of the additional analyses with the L handshape and open hand variants selected as the application values show clearly that the principle that features in the surrounding phonological environment favor like features in the target variable applies to –cf and well as to +cf variants. Table 4.9 shows the results of variable rule analyses with L handshape and open hand respectively selected as the application value. Figure 4.3 shows the results for all three variants graphically.

The Relationship between Grammatical and Phonological Factors

Signers' choices of a 1 handshape variant are clearly influenced by the features of the preceding and following segments. However, this influence works together with the influence of the grammatical category to

TABLE 4.9. *Variation in 1 Handshape Signs: L Handshape and Open Hand Variants by Shared Features of Preceding and Following Thumb and Fingers*

Shared Features	L Handshape Variant			Open Hand Variant		
	Weight	%	n	Weight	%	n
0	.331	16	63	.198	8	318
1	.400	22	537	.333	14	441
2	.451	25	2162	.428	19	1163
3	.658	45	750	.556	28	846
4	.807	66	141	.734	43	885
Total/input	.282	30	3653	.196	25	3653

Note: For L handshape, χ^2/cell = 1.1811; for open hand, χ^2/cell = 1.1911. n = number of tokens that could share between from 0 to 4 features with the preceding and following signs. Tokens with preceding or following pauses were coded as not applicable.

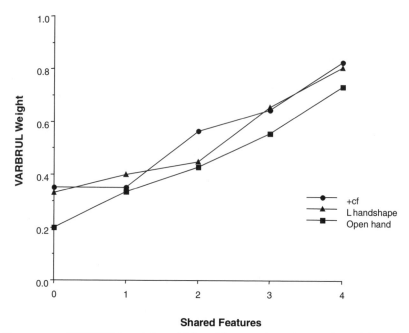

FIGURE 4.3. *VARBRUL weights of 1 handshape variants by number of shared features with preceding and following thumb and fingers*

which the 1 handshape sign belongs, as well as with a number of social factors reported on in the following section. For example, as table 4.10 shows, when the thumb and fingers are selected in the preceding and following segments, that is, when these segments do not share relevant features, or when they share only one feature, with the +cf form, signers chose this form of PRO.1 only 7 percent of the time. When two features are shared, the percentage of +cf forms of PRO.1 increases to 23 percent. The percentage increases to 26 percent when three features are shared and to 51 percent when four features are shared with the +cf form.

A similar pattern may be seen with nouns and adjectives, the grammatical category most favorable to the use of the +cf form. When no relevant features or only one feature is shared with the +cf forms, signers select this form for 57 percent of the tokens. With two shared features, the rate of +cf usage increases to 66 percent, and with three shared features, to 87 percent. When four features are shared, that is, when neither the thumb nor the fingers of the preceding or following handshape is selected, signers use the +cf variant for 100 percent of the nouns and adjectives formed with a 1 handshape.

TABLE 4.10. *Variation in 1 Handshape Signs, +cf: Grammatical Category by Number of Features Shared with the Preceding and Following Handshapes*

	0, 1		2		3		4		Total	
	%	n	%	n	%	n	%	n	%	n
PRO.1	7	668	23	438	26	159	51	114	18	1379
PRO.2	22	127	38	71	33	21	64	22	32	165
PRO.3	27	153	59	74	50	28	73	26	42	119
wh-word	44	27	43	23	71	7	67	3	48	60
Grammatical function	38	192	59	123	71	42	87	23	51	380
Verb, adv	45	408	62	327	68	139	84	100	58	974
Noun, adj	57	156	66	107	87	45	100	30	68	338
Total	27	1731	45	1163	52	441	71	318	40	3653

SOCIAL FACTORS

In addition to the linguistic factors examined in the preceding section, our initial analysis showed that signers' choices among 1 handshape variants are also constrained by a range of social factors: age, social class, ethnicity, and the region of the country where the signer resides. Table 4.11 shows the results from the initial analysis.

The regional differences comprise the most striking result shown in table 4.11. When signers in Massachusetts use a 1 handshape sign, they choose the +cf variant 50 percent of the time (*p* = .642). Signers in Virginia, however, use the +cf variant only 18 percent of the time (*p* = .226). Moreover, the results by region exhibit two general groupings. Signers in California, Kansas/Missouri, Louisiana, and Massachusetts all favor the +cf variant and disfavor both –cf forms considered here. In contrast, signers in Maryland, Virginia, and Washington all disfavor the +cf form and favor the –cf forms.

Our initial attempt to understand the regional clustering focused on the ethnic composition of the populations in our research sites. Recall that very few Deaf African Americans reside in Frederick, Maryland; Staunton, Virginia; or Washington. Hence, our samples in those areas were comprised of only Caucasian signers. Given previous claims in the literature that African American signers tend to favor older forms (Woodward 1976), we suspected that the regional differences might be attributable to the presence of African Americans in the samples from the sites that favored the +cf variant. To test the hypothesis that the regional groupings were a consequence of the ethnic distribution of the sample, we ran separate analyses for the sites that included African Americans and those that did not. Results from the analyses of sites that included African Americans, however, showed that ethnicity was not significant. We conclude, then, that the ethnic difference shown in table 4.11 is a reflection of regional differences. That is, the combined results for all regions show that African Americans tend to use a higher percentage of +cf variants than Caucasians because only the latter are included in the data from the regions that strongly disfavor the +cf form.

The results of the separate analyses by high and low +cf regional groupings raised additional questions for the analysis of social factors. With respect to social class, in Maryland, Virginia, and Washington,

TABLE 4.11. *Variation in 1 Handshape Signs: Age, Class, Ethnicity, and Region*

Factor Group	Factor	+cf, One Hand Weight	%	−cf, L Handshape Weight	%	−cf, Open Hand Weight	%
Age	15–25	.468	36	{.484}	{28}	.481	23
	26–54	.531	43			{.551}	{31}
	55+	.489	39	.530	33		
Class	WC	.518	41	ns	30	ns	24
	MC	.475	39	ns	29	ns	27
Ethnicity	AA	.535	50	ns	22	ns	22
	C	.486	36	ns	33	ns	27
Region	Mass.	.642	50	.389	20	.412	22
	Calif.	.626	49	.419	23	.470	23
	Kans./Mo.	.608	49	.445	24	.461	23
	La.	.549	42	.475	27	.447	23
	Md.	.301	25			.581	30
	Wash.	.284	23	{.653}	{45}	.627	32
	Va.	.226	18			.638	33
Language background	ASL	ns	40	ns	30	.487	24
	Other	ns	38	ns	29	.542	29

Note: Ethnicity is not significant when sites in which only Caucasian signers were interviewed are excluded from analysis.

middle-class signers used more +cf forms than working-class signers. In the other sites the situation was reversed, with working-class signers using more +cf forms than middle-class signers. In addition, Maryland, Virginia, and Washington differed from other sites in the distribution of +cf forms by age group. Tables 4.12 and 4.13 show the results for class and age, broken down by regional groupings. Note that the percentages do not always add up to 100 because only the three most common variants were selected as application values.

The results for social class by regional grouping illustrate striking differences. In California, Kansas/Missouri, Louisiana, and Massachusetts, working-class signers favor +cf ($p = .569$) and disfavor both –cf variants. The results for middle-class signers in these sites, of course, are the reverse. In Maryland, Virginia, and Washington, however, we see quite a different pattern. Working-class signers strongly disfavor the +cf form

TABLE 4.12. *Variation in 1 Handshape Signs: Social Class by Region*

Variant	Social Class	Calif., La., Kans./Mo., Mass.		Md., Va., Wash.	
		Weight	%	Weight	%
+cf	WC	.569	52	.352	12
	MC	.369	41	.672	34
L handshape	WC	.465	21	.579	54
	MC	.553	27	.407	34
Open hand	WC	.463	21	ns	33
	MC	.555	25	ns	29

TABLE 4.13. *Variation in 1 Handshape Signs: Age by Region*

Variant	Age	Calif., La., Kans./Mo., Mass.		Md., Va., Wash.	
		Weight	%	Weight	%
+cf	15–25	.534	47	.286	10
	26–54	.513	49	.607	30
	55+	.456	46	.563	24
L handshape	15–25	.425	19	.548	50
	26–54	.522	25	.427	36
	55+	.535	25	.536	49
Open hand	15–25	ns	27	.593	40
	26–54	ns	21	.510	34
	55+	ns	22	.422	21

and select this variant only 12 percent of the time; middle-class signers in these three areas favor +cf ($p = .672$). The results for middle-class signers, however, need to be interpreted in light of the low overall use of the +cf form in Maryland, Virginia, and Washington, which ranges from a low of 18 percent in Virginia to 25 percent in Maryland. Note that the rate of +cf use by middle-class signers in the three low +cf sites is only 34 percent. That is, even though middle-class signers in these regions favor the +cf variant in comparison to working-class signers in the same regions, they use a lower percentage of +cf forms than middle-class signers in other areas. Finally, we note that among working-class signers in Maryland, Virginia, and Washington, the L handshape variant is the most common form, used 54 percent of the time. In contrast, in other sites, working-class signers select the +cf variant for the majority of 1 handshape signs.

The results shown in table 4.13 also reveal a number of age differences between the two regional groupings. In California, Kansas/Missouri, Louisiana, and Massachusetts, signers aged 15–25 and 26–54 favor +cf, although not strongly ($p = .534, .513$), whereas older signers disfavor +cf ($p = .456$) but again, not strongly. The L handshape variant, in contrast, is disfavored by the youngest signers ($p = .425$) and slightly favored by the two older groups ($p = .522, .535$). Age does not reach statistical significance when the open hand variant is selected as the application value. In contrast to the patterns in the other areas, in Maryland, Virginia, and Washington, young people are very unlikely to use a +cf form, whereas both older groups favor +cf. Furthermore, in these areas, young people favor either the L handshape or the open hand variant. Signers aged 26 to 55 disfavor the L handshape variant and are neutral with respect to the open hand variant. Signers in the oldest group disfavor the open hand form and favor the L handshape, although not strongly.

A further difference between the two regional groupings can be seen in the magnitude of the effect of age on choice of a 1 handshape variant. Age has a much stronger effect among signers in Maryland, Virginia, and Washington than in other regions. Thus, for signers in these three states, factor weights with +cf as the application value range from a low of .286 for the youngest signers to .607 for signers aged 26 to 54. The difference is .321. Expressed differently, in Maryland, Virginia, and Washington, the difference between the age group most likely to use the +cf variant and the group least likely to use it is 20 percent. In contrast, in other regions, the difference between the age group most likely and the group least likely to use the +cf form is only 3 percent. As table 4.13 shows, similar differences in the magnitude of the age effect may be seen in the results when one or the other of the –cf variants is selected as the application value.

Finally, signers' language backgrounds proved to significantly affect use of the open hand variant but not use of the other variants, both in the overall analysis and in the separate analysis for California, Kansas/Missouri, Louisiana, and Massachusetts. In these four areas, signers from non-ASL-using families disfavored and signers from ASL-using families favored the open hand variant. It was not significant for the separate analysis that included only Maryland, Virginia, and Washington.

REGION AND LINGUISTIC FACTORS: ASL USERS AS A SPEECH COMMUNITY

The results just presented show clear differences between regional groupings in the effect of social class and age on the choice of a 1 handshape variant. However, a question remains: Do the linguistic constraints on variation in 1 handshape signs remain constant across regions, or do they differ in their effects as well? This question is important in deciding whether, despite regional differences, we can consider ASL users as a single *speech community:*

> The speech community is not defined by any marked agreement in the use of language elements, so much as by participation in a set of shared norms: these norms may be observed in overt types of evaluative behavior, and by the uniformity of abstract patterns of variation which are invariant in respect to particular levels of usage. (Labov 1972a, 120–21)

Thus, members of a single community may exhibit a wide range of use of a particular variant. For example, the fact that young signers in Maryland, Virginia, and Washington use the +cf form for the 1 handshape at a rate of only 10 percent, compared to a rate of 47 percent for signers from other regions, does not in and of itself constitute evidence that we are dealing with two different speech communities. Rather, the critical tests concern whether signers share norms in judging language production and whether the abstract patterns, expressed here in terms of VARBRUL weights, remain relatively constant regardless of region.

Labov and others evaluated shared norms by looking at variation across a stylistic continuum, ranging from the informality of an exchange with someone well known to the speaker to the formality of a list of minimal pairs. They hypothesized that speakers would pay the least attention to form in the former type of exchange and the greatest attention to form when reading a decontextualized list of minimal pairs. As Labov (1966, 1972a), Trudgill (1974), and others amply demonstrated, speakers did indeed use standard forms at a higher rate as they moved from the most informal to the most formal styles. However, the relative ranking of abstract constraints on variation did not change as speakers moved from one style to another.

The data collection for this project was not designed to elicit the full range of styles that characterized early sociolinguistic studies. Indeed such an undertaking is not possible with ASL. Labov (1966) defined five styles. The first two were based on different types of speech events: an informal exchange with a familiar person other than the interviewer and responding to questions during a sociolinguistic interview. Three were based on different types of reading tasks: a continuous passage; a word list; and a list of minimal pairs. Because ASL has no commonly agreed upon writing system, it was impossible to replicate continuous reading. Thus, the most we can say at this point is that all signers, when asked for the sign for a lexical item made with a 1 handshape or a pronoun, normally provide the +cf form. That is, in at least one sense, the signers in our study share a linguistic norm.

Although we are limited at this point in what we can say about signers' adherence to a shared set of linguistic norms, we have much more evidence when we turn to the second criterion for membership in the same community, the "uniformity of abstract patterns of variation." In this respect, in every case except one, the linguistic factors have very similar effects, regardless of region. Looking first at the phonological factors, we find that a closed thumb and closed fingers in the preceding and following segments favor the +cf form. Phonological constraints operate in a similar way when either the L handshape or open hand variant is selected as the application value. That is, in all regions, features of the preceding and following handshapes favor like features in the target variable. In some cases, however, factor groups that had significant but not strong effects in the combined analysis failed to reach significance in the separate analyses as a result of the smaller number of tokens.

When we turn to the relationship between grammatical category and regional grouping, we find a somewhat more complex picture. Figures 4.4a, 4.4b, and 4.4c show the results of separate analyses of the effect of

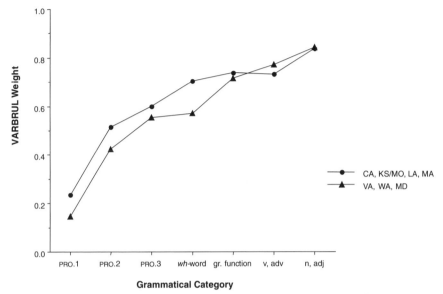

FIGURE 4.4A. *Variation of 1 handshape: +cf by region and grammatical category*

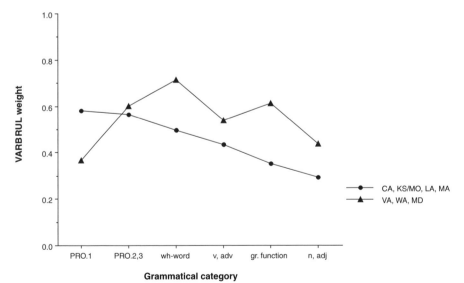

FIGURE 4.4B. *Variation of 1 handshape: L handshape variant by region and grammatical category*

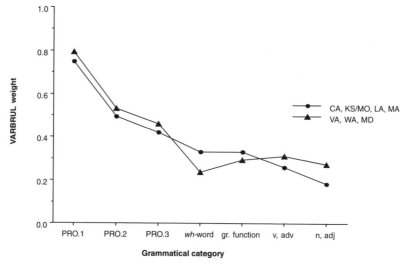

FIGURE 4.4C. *Variation of 1 handshape: Open hand variant by region and grammatical category*

TABLE 4.14. *Variation in 1 Handshape Signs: Grammatical Category by Region*

Variant	Grammatical Category	Calif., La., Kans./ Mo., Mass.		Md., Va., Wash.	
		Weight	%	Weight	%
+cf	PRO.1	.234	24	.146	4
	PRO.2	.513	45	.424	14
	PRO.3	.600	55	.555	18
	wh-word	.703	63	.572	21
	Gr. function	.737	68	.715	29
	V, adv	.732	70	.770	36
	N, adj	.836	79	.842	50
L handshape	PRO.1	.583	28	.368	32
	PRO.2, 3	.556	28	.602	54
	wh-word	.496	24	.715	66
	Gr. function	.352	15	.612	55
	V, adv	.434	20	.539	49
	N, adj	.293	11	.438	37
Open hand	PRO.1	.749	39	.793	60
	PRO.2	.494	19	.532	30
	PRO.3	.422	16	.460	27
	wh-word	.330	11	.238	11
	Gr. function	.330	11	.293	15
	V, adv	.259	7	.311	15
	N, adj	.183	6	.274	13

grammatical category by regional grouping, with +cf, L handshape, and open hand selected as application values.

These results show that, with very minor fluctuations, the effect of the grammatical category of the 1 handshape sign remains constant across regional groupings when +cf and the open hand variants are selected as the application values.[4] However, we see a very considerable divergence between the two groupings when the L handshape variant is selected as the application value. Detailed results for the effect of grammatical category within each regional grouping are shown in table 4.14.

A full account of the regional differences shown in table 4.14, particularly with respect to the L handshape variant, awaits further research. However, we can suggest two alternative ways of viewing the results for L handshape. First, the L handshape is an intermediate category between the two variables that occupy the ends of a continuum from a closed hand, with only the index finger extended (+cf), to an open hand. The L handshape results may therefore represent a kind of transition zone, and some of the regional differences may be epiphenomenona that result from small fluctuations at both ends of the closed- to open hand continuum.[5] Alternatively, the results for the L handshape also suggest the possibility that grammaticalization is at work (see Hopper and Traugott 1993). At least among signers in Maryland, Virginia, and Washington, the data suggest that signers make a distinction between PRO.1 on one side and PRO.2 and 3 on the other. Note that in these sites, the +cf form is only rarely used for PRO.1. Rather, the open hand variant is the preferred form for PRO.1, being used for 60 percent of all first-person pronouns. In Maryland, Virginia, and Washington, the +cf variant is also used relatively infrequently for PRO.2 and PRO.3. Only 14 percent of the PRO.2 tokens and 18 percent of the PRO.3 tokens in these sites are +cf. Rather than using the open hand variant for PRO.2 and PRO.3, however, signers in these areas are likely to use the L handshape variant.

To return to the question with which we began this section, we can

4. In figure 4.4c we see that for signers from Maryland, Virginia, and Washington, wh-words are least likely to be realized as the open hand variant, whereas for signers in other regions, nouns and adjectives are least likely to be realized as 'open hand.' Note, however, that the token count for wh-words is very low. Only 101 wh-words, or approximately one for every two signers, were included in the database. Thus, it is not surprising to see some fluctuation for words in this category.

5. We thank Gregory Guy for this suggestion.

say that for the most part users of ASL, regardless of region, form a community in Labov's sense of the term. That is, with respect to all except one of the linguistic factors examined here, the abstract patterns across regional clusters are identical or highly similar, although the overall rate of use of particular variants differs considerably. Thus, where they reach significance when the data are broken down by regional groupings, salient features of the preceding and following segments have the same effect. Moreover, the effect of the grammatical category to which a sign belongs has a similar effect on signers' choices of the +cf or open hand variants. That is, although we can identify a number of clear regional and social differences in varieties of ASL used in the U.S. Deaf community, the near uniformity of constraint effects across regional and social groups reinforces the perceptions of many Deaf people that ASL users constitute a single language community.

VARIATION IN 1 HANDSHAPE SIGNS: SUMMARY

The analyses presented here have shown that variation in the use of signs whose citation form requires a 1 handshape is highly systematic, at least with respect to the three most frequently observed variants: +cf, L [handshape, and open hand]. Significant constraints on signers' choice of a 1 handshape variant include the grammatical category to which the sign belongs and features of the preceding and following segments, as well as age, social class, and geographical region. The effect of the grammatical category will be treated more fully in chapter 6. For now, however, we suggest two possible and complementary explanations for the effect of grammatical class.

First, variation appears to be influenced by a cline of indexicality. Pronouns thus allow greater phonetic divergence from the citation form of the sign than lexical signs, in which the handshape carries some of the semantic burden. Second, as we shall see in chapter 7, the use of manual pronouns is highly variable. In ASL, even the subjects of plain verbs, which carry no information on the verb to indicate subject or object, are often realized as null. Moreover, PRO.1, the grammatical category that is most likely to diverge from citation form, is also most likely to be realized as null. Furthermore, the effect of the phonological factors found to be statistically significant clearly illustrates the processes of *progressive* and *regressive assimilation*. That is, signers tend to use a

1 handshape variant whose most important features, the thumb and fingers 234, match the features of the preceding and following handshapes.

Turning to nonlinguistic factors, we find that the region of the country where the signer resides has the greatest effect on the choice among 1 handshape variants. Further, the seven sites where the data were collected can be divided into two general groups. Although in no site do signers use more than 50 percent +cf forms, signers in California, Kansas/Missouri, Louisiana, and Massachusetts are far more likely to use the +cf variant than signers in Maryland, Virginia, and Washington. Moreover, age and social class have different effects on the choice of a 1 handshape variant in the two regional groupings.

Chapter 5

Phonological Variation 2:

Variation in Location

In this chapter we turn our attention to variation in the location of signs and examine two additional variables: the sign DEAF and a class of signs represented by the verb KNOW.

THE DEAF VARIABLE

As we explained in chapter 2, DEAF is representative of signs produced on a vertical plane on the face and that move from the chin to the ear. DEAF can be produced by moving the forefinger from ear to chin, from chin to ear, or by contacting the lower cheek.[1] DEAF, which consists of a hold, a movement, and a hold, has a 1 handshape, and the palm is generally oriented inward. In citation form, the sign begins just below the ear and ends near the corner of the mouth. It thus has two locations. A second variant begins at the corner of the mouth and moves upward to the ear. A third variant simply contacts the lower cheek. Figure 5.1 illustrates the three variants.

The ear-to-chin version of the sign is the citation form. The chin-to-ear version shows the process of *metathesis,* whereby the locations of the

---

1. We are aware, of course, that a variety of signs that are unrelated phonologically to the three variants considered here may also be glossed as DEAF (e.g., the form that consists of an A handshape opening to a 5 handshape at the ear or the form often seen in formal situations: index finger moving from the ear to neutral space where both handshapes are B handshapes, palms down, contacting each other on the side of the index fingers). However, these signs are distinct in meaning from the three variants we are examining. Our focus is on different ways of signing the same thing. Although our three variants differ phonologically, they are identical in meaning.

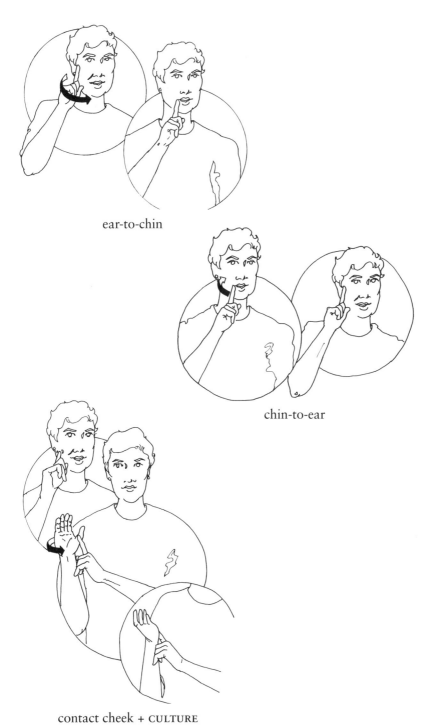

ear-to-chin

chin-to-ear

contact cheek + CULTURE

FIGURE 5.1. *Three variants of* DEAF

two hold segments are inverted. The contact-cheek version consists of a hold (H). The issue is what promotes the production of a particular variant. The ear-to-chin variant and the chin-to-ear variant each have two locations and, because what varies is indeed the location, it is logical to suppose that something in the environment having to do with location constrains signers' choices between these two hold-movement-hold (HMH) variants. Indeed, Liddell and Johnson, in their discussion of metathesis, argued that the choice between the ear-to-chin and chin-to-ear variants of DEAF involves a purely phonological process, which is conditioned by the location of the preceding sign:

> A number of signs exchange the initial sequence of segments with a sequence of final segments in certain contexts that appear to be purely phonological. The sign DEAF is typical of such metathesizing signs. [The ear-to-chin] form of the sign typically occurs immediately following signs produced in higher facial areas. . . . However, if DEAF is immediately preceded by a sign in the lower facial regions (and perhaps other lower areas), the initial two segments are exchanged with the final two segments. (1989, 244–45)

Here we use multivariate analysis to test the claim that variation in the form of DEAF is constrained by "purely phonological" factors. Data consist of all tokens of DEAF in the interviews and conversations, a total of 1,618 tokens.

Coding: DEAF

As with the 1 handshape variable, tokens were coded to test the possible effects of a broad range of sociodemographic and linguistic factors. Sociodemographic factors included the same ones coded for the 1 handshape variable: region, age, gender, ethnicity, social class, and language background. With respect to the linguistic factors, our coding scheme was designed to test the effect of grammatical function, which Lucas's (1995) pilot study found to be the first-order linguistic constraint on variation in the form of DEAF. In addition, as we have noted, we also wished to test previous claims about the effects of the location of the surrounding phonological environment. Finally, because sociolinguistic research has shown that highly involved narratives of personal experience tend to favor the use of the vernacular (Labov 1972b), we also coded the discourse genre in which DEAF appears. In addition to the dependent variable and the sociodemographic factors, we coded for fourteen linguistic factors, divided into four factor groups:

1. Grammatical function of DEAF:
   noun (e.g., DEAF UNDERSTAND ['deaf people understand'])
   adjective (e.g., DEAF CAT)
   predicate adjective (e.g., PRO.1 DEAF ['I am deaf'])
   compound (e.g., DEAF⌢WORLD, DEAF⌢CULTURE)[2]
2. Location of the preceding segment: high (at ear or above), middle (between ear and chin), low (chin or below), pause.
3. Location of the following segment: high, middle, low, pause.
4. Genre of text in which DEAF occurs: conversation, narrative.

Results for DEAF

Results of VARBRUL analysis of 1,618 tokens indicate that variation in the form of DEAF is systematic and conditioned by multiple linguistic and social factors, including grammatical function, the location of the following segment, discourse genre, age, and region. The results confirm the earlier finding of Lucas (1995), who showed that the grammatical function of DEAF, rather than the features of the preceding or following sign, is the main linguistic constraint on variation. For the choice between citation and noncitation form, only grammatical function and discourse genre proved to be statistically significant at the .05 level. For the choice between the two noncitation forms, both the grammatical function of DEAF and the location of the following segment proved significant. Among the social factors, only age and region contributed significantly to the observed variation. The other nonlinguistic factors—ethnicity, gender, language background, and social class—failed to reach statistical significance and will not be discussed further.

For this variable, as for the 1 handshape variable, noncitation forms were far more common than citation forms. Of the 1,618 tokens of DEAF

---

2. It may be argued that DEAF as used in compounds such as DEAF⌢WORLD and DEAF⌢CULTURE is also an adjective. However, terms such as DEAF⌢WORLD and DEAF⌢CULTURE, which are particularly salient in the Deaf community, have come to be regarded by ASL natives as single lexical items, such as English 'breakfast.'

analyzed in this study, only 500, or 31 percent, were in citation form, while 889 tokens, or 55 percent, were chin-to-ear, and 229, or 14 percent, were contact-cheek. We now turn to the VARBRUL analyses, with particular attention to the relationship of the three variants to one another.

Citation vs. Noncitation Form

In the initial quantitative analysis, the two –cf variants (chin-to-ear, contact-cheek) were collapsed and –cf defined as the application value. Among the linguistic factors considered in this study, only grammatical function and discourse genre significantly constrained signers' choices between citation and noncitation forms. VARBRUL results are shown in table 5.1.

Compounds favored –cf (p = .660) and predicate adjectives disfavored –cf (p = .370). Nouns and other adjectives, because they comprise the great majority of tokens, constituted the nearly neutral reference point in this factor group (p = .515).

The results showing that compounds favor and predicate adjectives disfavor –cf may be readily accounted for. As discussed in more detail in the following section, compounds strongly favored one –cf variant, the reduced form contact-cheek, a consequence of the compounding process. As for predicate adjectives, these forms may be subject to a discourse constraint. Predicate adjectives are normally the final sign in an utterance, an emphatic position that seems to favor the +cf variant.

Turning to the discourse genre, noncitation forms were favored in narratives (p = .628). Conversation, however, with over 90 percent of the data, was the nearly neutral reference point. (p = .489). Although the

TABLE 5.1. *VARBRUL Analysis of* DEAF, *+cf vs. –cf: Linguistic Factors (Application Value: –cf)*

Factor group	Factor	Weight	%	n
Grammatical	Noun, adjective	.515	71	1063
function	Predicate adjective	.370	58	361
	Compound	.660	81	194
Discourse genre	Conversation	.489	69	1489
	Narrative	.628	74	129
Total	Input/p_0	.743	69	1618

Note: χ^2/cell = 1.2952, all factor groups significant at p < .05.

difference between the effect of conversation and narrative discourse on signers' choice of variant was significant, this finding should be treated with caution because of the higher unequal distribution of tokens. Such a highly unequal distribution suggests that the results may not be fully reliable because there is too great an overlap between one factor, conversation in this case, and the input probability (Guy 1988). Finally, as in Lucas's (1995) study, neither the location of the preceding nor of the following sign significantly affected signers' choice between citation and noncitation.

Among the social factors, the results for age and region reveal a complex pattern. In the initial analysis, we treated the three age groups and the seven sites where the data were collected as separate factor groups. However, as is often the case with social factors (Sankoff 1988; Young and Bayley 1996), the results of the initial runs revealed considerable interaction between age and region. A closer examination of the data showed that in some regions, the oldest signers used the highest percentage of citation forms, whereas the youngest used the lowest percentage. In other regions signers aged 26 to 54 were most likely to use citation forms, while the oldest and the youngest signers used a correspondingly greater percentage of noncitation forms. In order to capture the variability by age and region and to better understand the direction of change within regions, we recoded the data and created a combined factor group with each age group within a region treated as a separate factor. This procedure accounted for all of the interactions and resulted in an acceptable chi-square-per-cell of 1.2952 for the model including the recoded age and region group, grammatical function, and discourse genre.

Although the substitution of a single age by region factor group for two groups in which age and region were analyzed separately proved successful in dealing with interactions, the results reported in table 5.2 do not illustrate an obvious general direction of change or a cohort effect, nor do they fall into clear patterns that show similarities between nearby regions. For example, in Massachusetts, signers aged 55 and older were very unlikely to use noncitation forms of DEAF (p = .097). Although noncitation forms were also disfavored by Massachusetts signers aged 15 to 25 and 26 to 54, both of these age groups were considerably more likely to choose noncitation forms than the oldest Massachusetts signers. In contrast to Massachusetts, among Maryland signers the likelihood of use of noncitation forms decreased with age. The youngest

Maryland signers were most similar to the oldest Massachusetts signers. Nearby Virginia illustrates yet another pattern. Although the Virginia results for signers aged 26 to 54 and 55 and older agree with the Maryland results in showing that signers in the middle age group were less likely than the oldest signers to choose noncitation forms, the results for the youngest group illustrate a sharp difference. In contrast to Maryland, where the youngest signers were very unlikely to use noncitation forms, the youngest Virginia signers favored such forms. Finally, the West Coast results exhibit the same pattern. In both northern California and Washington, noncitation forms were disfavored by signers in the 26 to 54 age group and favored by signers in the 15-to-25 and over-55 groups.

As might be expected in a factor group containing more than 20 factors, the results of the age and region group are complex. However, the results do allow us to identify one predominant pattern shared by four sites and three other patterns that each characterize only one site. In California, Louisiana, Virginia, and Washington, signers in the 26-to-54-year-old group are less likely to choose noncitation forms than either the youngest or the oldest signers. Figure 5.2 illustrates the most common pattern.

In contrast to the pattern shown in figure 5.2, among Kansas/Missouri signers, 26-to-54-year-olds were more likely to use a noncitation form of DEAF than either their younger or older counterparts. Finally, as we have seen, the oldest signers in Massachusetts and the youngest signers in Maryland were least likely to use noncitation forms of the variable.

We have identified a number of patterns in the data and established what appears to be a predominant pattern for the use of citation and noncitation forms. In chapter 6 we return to an explanation of the age and region results.

The Choice between Two Noncitation Forms

In the second stage of the analysis, we examined the choice between two noncitation forms of DEAF, chin-to-ear and contact-cheek, again using the coding scheme outlined earlier. As in the analysis of citation vs. noncitation forms, the grammatical category proved to be the first-order linguistic constraint in the analysis of the chin-to-ear and contact-cheek variants. The contact-cheek variant was strongly favored in compounds ($p = .850$) and disfavored in predicate adjectives ($p = .338$), with nouns and other adjectives having intermediate values. Table 5.3 shows the

TABLE 5.2. *VARBRUL Analysis of* DEAF, *+cf vs. –cf: Age by Region (Application Value, –cf)*

	15–25			26–54			55+			Total	
	Weight	%	n	Weight	%	n	Weight	%	n	%	n
Mass.	.264	54	63	.281	46	169	.097	24	80	41	312
Md.	.108	27	26	.458	71	48	.678	83	30	66	104
Va.	.656	86	22	.499	74	27	.874	96	48	85	97
La.	.794	90	52	.415	68	158	.547	76	51	74	261
Kans./Mo.	.573	78	122	.830	93	138	.641	82	87	85	347
Calif.	.597	82	55	.253	48	183	.776	90	101	66	339
Wash.	.779	92	59	.306	55	47	.815	92	52	81	128
Total		69	399		62	770		76	449	69	1618

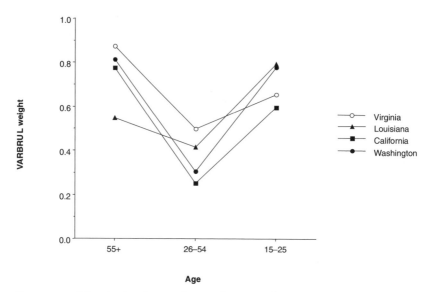

FIGURE 5.2. *Noncitation forms of* DEAF *by age and region: Dominant pattern*

TABLE 5.3. *VARBRUL Analysis of* DEAF, *Chin-to-Ear vs. Contact-Cheek: Linguistic Factors (Application Value: Contact-Cheek)*

Factor group	Factor	Weight	%	n
Grammatical	Noun	.490	17	411
category	Adjective	.403	10	191
	Predicate adjective	.338	12	299
	Compound	.850	56	151
Following sign	Low	.579	25	756
	Middle	.273	7	134
	High	.590	18	51
	Pause	.240	5	111
Total	Input/p_o	.142	20	1052

Note: χ^2/cell = 1.0294; all factor groups significant at $p<.05$.

VARBRUL results for the linguistic factors in the analysis of the two −cf forms, with contact-cheek defined as the application value.

Unlike the analysis of citation vs. noncitation forms, the analysis that included only the two noncitation variants did select a significant phonological constraint. The location of the following sign significantly affected signers' choice between the chin-to-ear and contact-cheek variants. When the following sign was between the ear and chin (middle) or null (a pause), contact-cheek was disfavored. When the following sign was at the ear or above or at the level of the chin or below, contact-cheek was favored. These results may best be explained by the need to maintain a distinction between DEAF and the following sign. Thus, the contact-cheek variant may be freely used if the location of the following sign is at the ear or below or at the chin or above (i.e., if the location of the following sign is somewhere other than at the cheek).

As Gregory Guy has pointed out, these results seem to represent a textbook case of the Obligatory Contour Principle (OCP) effect, in contrast to the results for the analyses of variants of 1 handshape signs by the number of features shared with the preceding and following signs discussed in the previous chapter (see Guy and Boberg 1997 for a review of the literature on the OCP). However, the analyses, both here and in the preceding chapter, are concerned with variation within a single parameter of the features that define a sign: handshape in the case of 1 handshape signs and location in the cases of DEAF and the class of signs represented by KNOW. It is premature to attempt to offer a full explanation as to why similar features favor like features in the case of handshape variation, whereas the location of the following sign disfavors an identical location in the case of location variation. However, we suspect that the fact that the location of a sign represents a grosser distinction than sometimes minor variations in the form of the handshape may provide a partial explanation for the results we see here.

Turning to the nonlinguistic factors, the same factor groups, age and region, reached statistical significance in the analysis of the two –cf forms as in the analysis that included both +cf and –cf forms. However, as in the earlier analysis, it was necessary to create a combined factor group including both age and region in order to compensate for the interactions between these two nonlinguistic factors. And, as in the earlier analysis of +cf vs. –cf forms, the results by age and region of the analysis of the two –cf forms did not show a clear direction of change that transcends different regions. In Massachusetts, for example, the oldest signers were very unlikely to use a –cf form of DEAF. However, when they did choose a –cf form, in our data they categorically chose the contact-cheek variant. Massachusetts signers aged 26 to 54 also showed a preference for the contact-cheek variant when choosing between the two –cf variants ($p = .806$); however, their use of the contact-cheek form was not categorical.

In contrast, the youngest Massachusetts participants disfavored the contact-cheek variant (p = .284).

The patterns of variation in Maryland and Virginia again differed from one another and from Massachusetts and other sites. In Maryland, signers aged 26–54 were most likely to choose the contact-cheek variant. In Virginia, the youngest signers were most likely to use the contact-cheek variant. In both Maryland and Virginia, in contrast to Massachusetts, the oldest signers strongly disfavored the contact-cheek variant. Our second southern site, Louisiana, showed still another pattern. In Louisiana, the contact-cheek variant was categorically absent among the youngest signers and favored by the two older groups. When we move farther west, we find yet other patterns. In Kansas, Missouri, and Washington, signers in the 26-to-54 age group were the least likely to use the contact-cheek variant of DEAF. In California, signers in this age group were the most likely to use the contact-cheek variant. Table 5.4 shows the results for age and region for the analysis that included only the two –cf forms.

Issues in the Analysis of DEAF

In our analysis of the 1 handshape variable, we assumed that the citation form was the underlying form. Given the number of variants that appeared in the data, even though the great majority could be reduced to the citation form and two noncitation forms, we decided that the best solution at this point would be to treat the variation as a series of binary choices (i.e., +cf vs. all other variants, L handshape vs. all other variants, open hand vs. all other variants). In the case of DEAF, however, the problem is somewhat simpler. Although a number of scenarios is possible, depending on our analytical decisions, since there are only three variants, the number is much less than in the case of 1 handshape variation. In this section, then, we deal with a problem that has arisen in our analysis of DEAF but that may potentially arise in any study where the variable under investigation has three or more surface alternates (cf. Guy and Bayley 1995, 158–59). With binary rules consisting of an input and an output, how do we get three surface forms?

The first decision concerns which of the three forms is basic or underlying. In the case of DEAF, it is possible to postulate any of the three surface alternants or some abstract lexical alternative, giving four starting points for the analysis. (Contact-cheek, the least frequently occurring variant, is admittedly an unlikely candidate, if only on the grounds of its

TABLE 5.4. *VARBRUL Analysis of DEAF, Chin-to-Ear vs. Contact-Cheek: Age by Region (Application Value: Contact-Cheek)*

	15–25			26–54			55+			Total	
	Weight	%	n	Weight	%	n	Weight	%	n	%	n
Mass.	.284	12	34	.806	36	74	—	100	(19)	29	108
Md.	.526	29	7	.586	29	34	.221	4	25	20	66
Va.	.617	37	19	.552	20	20	.105	2	46	12	85
La.	—	0	(47)	.568	23	108	.596	23	39	23	147
Kans./Mo.	.684	33	95	.368	14	129	.424	11	71	19	295
Calif.	.400	16	45	.600	22	87	.521	15	91	18	223
Wash.	.548	22	54	.147	4	26	.574	21	48	18	128
Total		25	254		22	478		13	320	20	1052

Note: To avoid knockouts, numbers in parentheses were not included in the VARBRUL analysis, nor were they included in the token totals or percentages.

rather limited distribution.) The next step is to decide whether the rules are to be ordered, with some forms serving as intermediate steps in the derivation of other forms, or unordered (cf. the models in Sankoff and Rousseau 1989). Table 5.5 shows some possible models for the derivation of the different forms of DEAF.

With these options, as well as others we might list, how do we conduct the analysis? If we postulate +cf (ear-to-chin) as the underlying form and a series of ordered rules as in table 5.5a, below the analysis we have just reported would seem to be correct. That is, our first step involves a binomial choice between +cf and –cf, whether the –cf alternative eventually surfaces as chin-to-ear or contact-cheek. In the second stage, however, +cf forms are no longer involved. Rather, we again have a binomial choice, this time between the two –cf variants. The ordered set of rules in table 5.5b implies a similar set of binomial choices. However, if we were to postulate chin-to-ear as the underlying form, perhaps on the grounds of its greater frequency of occurrence, our results would be substantially different. The first stage would involve a choice between the –cf form chin-to-ear on one side and –cf contact-cheek and +cf ear-to-chin on the other. In the second stage, all occurrences of chin-to-ear would be excluded, and the choice would be between contact-cheek and ear-to-chin. As table 5.5 suggests, still other scenarios are possible, and these imply other types of analysis. The unordered rules in table 5.5c and 5.5d, for example, might best be tested in a one-stage trinomial analysis.

Given these scenarios, all of which may be tried using the analytical tools that have long been available in sociolinguistics, which should we

TABLE 5.5. *Derivation of* DEAF: *Possible Models of Ordered and Unordered Rules*

Ordered Rules	Unordered Rules

a. Underlying form: ear-to-chin
  1. Ear-to-chin → chin-to-ear
  2. Chin-to-ear → contact-cheek
	c. Underlying form: ear-to-chin
	  1. Ear-to-chin → chin-to-ear
	  2. Ear-to-chin → contact-cheek

b. Underlying form: chin-to-ear
  1. Chin-to-ear → ear-to-chin
  2. Ear-to-chin → contact-cheek
	d. Underlying form: DEAF
	  1. [DEAF] → ear-to-chin
	  2. [DEAF] → chin-to-ear
	  3. [DEAF] → contact-cheek

choose? We are tempted to offer a quantitative answer in line with the research tradition that goes back to Labov's (1969) copula study. However, a quantitative answer alone will not suffice. The various rule possibilities to arrive at the three variants of DEAF all imply different theoretical models. In the analysis of DEAF, we assumed +cf is the underlying form, both because +cf is the form normally offered by ASL native signers when asked for the sign for DEAF and because +cf is more widely distributed across linguistic environments for signers of all ages in all regions of the United States. For example, when they chose a –cf variant, in our data Massachusetts signers over 55 always chose contact-cheek rather than chin-to-ear. Conversely, when the young Louisiana signers in our sample chose a –cf variant, they always chose chin-to-ear rather than contact-cheek. However, both older Massachusetts signers and young Louisianans sometimes used the +cf variant.

Additional evidence for the choice of +cf, ear-to-chin, as the underlying form comes from historical sources. For example, in French Sign Language, which forms one of the main sources of ASL, we find in Sicard's dictionary of the early nineteenth century that the form of the compound sign *sourd-muet* (deaf-mute) was ear-to-chin (1808, 331–32). From the early twentieth century, we have both print and filmed evidence that the ear-to-chin variant (or in some early cases, ear-to-mouth) was the preferred form of DEAF in ASL. In an early twentieth-century manual of signs, for example, J. Schuyler Long, head teacher of the Council Bluffs, Iowa, school for deaf pupils, described how DEAF should be signed: "Place the end of the forefinger of the right 'G' hand at the right ear and then carry it around and place it against the mouth" (1910, 142). Filmed evidence dating back to 1910 is also abundant because the U.S. National Association for the Deaf (NAD) was quick to take advantage of the possibilities offered by the new medium. From 1910 to 1920 the NAD produced a variety of films in ASL. In these early films the ear-to-chin form comprised the great majority of examples of DEAF used by deaf signers (Van Manen 1997).

Our choice of a model of rule ordering was also motivated by a desire to understand whether the same processes that underlie phonological variation in spoken languages underlie variation in ASL. The relationship between the three variants of DEAF postulated in table 5.5 involved two clearly understood processes, metathesis and deletion. Thus, in the scenario selected here, we assume that the underlying form is +cf (ear-to-chin). Some of these forms surface as +cf, while a certain proportion (69 percent in this study) undergo metathesis. Tokens that have not undergone metathesis are not available for the second stage of the process. Of the forms that have undergone metathesis, some surface as chin-to-ear, while a certain proportion (20 percent in this study) undergo a further process of deletion of the second element and surface as contact-cheek. As it turns out, deletion is far more common in compounds than in other grammatical categories. Fully 45 percent of the tokens of DEAF in compounds are contact-cheek, compared to 13 percent of nouns, 9 percent of nonpredicate adjectives, and only 6 percent of predicate adjectives. That is, we find deletion where we would most expect to find it in any language, whether spoken or signed.

A further motivation for our choice of a rule-ordering system involving a sequence of variable metathesis followed by variable deletion is based on an analysis of the structure of ASL compounds in which DEAF is the first element, as occurs with CULTURE, RESIDENTIAL SCHOOL, COMMUNITY, FAMILY, CLUB, MAN, PARENTS, BLIND, PERSON, and PEOPLE, among others. These are essentially compound constructions in which lexicalization has occurred. According to Liddell and Johnson's (1989) account of compound formation in ASL, part of that lexicalization may include retaining the initial contacting hold in the first sign of the compound while deleting the other segments that make up the sign. The contact-cheek variant of DEAF, then, is most likely the result of structural reduction occurring in the compounding process.

Finally we offer an additional observation to support the view that the deletion process of which contact-cheek is the result occurs only after metathesis of the hold segments of DEAF. If contact-cheek is the result of reduction as assumed in our model, it would have to be the reduction of the chin-to-ear variant. Were it the reduction of the ear-to-chin form, we would expect it to be produced near the ear (i.e., to retain the first contact hold). However, it is not. In compounds involving DEAF in which the first sign has been reduced, that sign is always produced near the corner of the mouth.

The DEAF Variable: Summary

Perhaps the most surprising result of our analyses of DEAF, as in our analyses of 1 handshape signs, is the very strong influence of grammatical factors on patterns of variation. As we have seen, when we perform VARBRUL analysis on all the tokens, with –cf defined as including both chin-to-ear and contact-cheek forms, the grammatical category and speech genre are the only significant linguistic constraints. The locations of the preceding and following signs have no significant effect. Liddell and Johnson's (1989) suggestion that the ear-to-chin form "typically" follows signs produced in higher facial areas, while the chin-to-ear form is "immediately preceded by a sign in the lower facial regions" finds no empirical support in this study. Moreover, the grammatical category and speech genre remain the only significant linguistic constraints in the analysis even if we accept a restricted definition of the deaf variable and exclude contact-cheek tokens.[3]

Why should the location of the preceding and following signs have failed to affect signers' choice between +cf and –cf forms of DEAF? One possibility is that the grammatical constraints are a synchronic reflex of a change in progress that originates in compounds and then spreads to nouns and adjectives and finally to predicates. A change from ear-to-chin to chin-to-ear, beginning with compounds, a grammatical class that is most subject to change, is arguably a shift in the direction of greater ease of production. Such a change would conform to Kroch's (1978) model of change from below, which, at least in the case of consonants, tends to greater ease of articulation. This explanation is supported by the fact that there exist a number of ASL signs that move from chin to ear in their citation form. Only two of these, however, clearly allow metathesis. They are HEAD and MOTHER⌒FATHER ('parents')[4] Metathesis is not allowed by

3. If our account of the derivation of the contact-cheek variant of DEAF (metathesis followed by deletion) is correct, exclusion of contact-cheek tokens is not justified. We do so here only for the purpose of comparing the results of empirical study with Liddell and Johnson's (1989) claim. When the contact-cheek variant is excluded, the results for the grammatical category factor group are as follows: noun, .521; adjective, .554; predicate adjective, .404; and compound, .492. Discourse genre and age by region are also significant. The change in the value for compounds, from .660 with contact-cheek tokens included to .492 with contact-cheek tokens excluded, is not surprising since contact-cheek is the most common variant of DEAF in compounds. When contact cheek tokens are removed from the analysis, the proportion of +cf to –cf forms for compounds is very close to the proportion for nouns and adjectives.

4. There is some question about whether HOME permits metathesis. Liddell and Johnson (1989) claim that it does, whereas there is disagreement among Deaf informants as to whether it does or not.

other common signs with a phonological structure like DEAF, consisting of a hold, a movement, and a hold (e.g., INDIAN, HOME, YESTERDAY). The fact that metathesis is not allowed by most signs whose citation form is chin-to-ear, that is, signs that move up, while it is allowed by DEAF, where the citation form moves down, suggests that chin to ear movement is the less marked sequence. DEAF, then, may be undergoing a change from a more marked to a less marked form that is characterized by greater ease of production.

In summary, variation in the form of DEAF, like variation in 1 hand-shape signs, is systematic and subject to both linguistic and social constraints. In general, the linguistic processes are similar to processes that are frequently observed in studies of spoken language—metathesis and deletion. With respect to social constraints, although the factor groups that constrain variation—age and geographical region—are certainly familiar to us from studies of spoken language variation, we suggest that their patterning reflects the specific educational experiences and history of Deaf communities in the United States. We return to this suggestion in chapter 6. We turn now to our third phonological variable, the location of a class of signs exemplified by the verb KNOW.

THE LOCATION VARIABLE

The variable we have termed the *location variable* encompasses a set of signs that share a common feature.[5] These signs, of which KNOW is a typically cited example, share features of location and placement of the hand; they are produced at the forehead or temple. In addition to KNOW, signs in this class include verbs of thinking and perception (e.g., BELIEVE, DECIDE, FORGET, REMEMBER, SUPPOSE, SUSPECT, SEE, THINK) as well as a variety of

5. Because variation in location may well be a characteristic of many classes of signs and because the location at which a sign is produced is part of its phonetic description, *location variable* is a somewhat awkward name. However, alternative terms such as "the class of signs represented by the verb KNOW" or "signs normally produced at the forehead or temple but variably produced lower on the face or neck" involve elaborate circumlocutions. We have not entirely avoided such circumlocutions where they were required for clarity. However, in other instances we have settled on the term *location variable* for the sake of brevity.

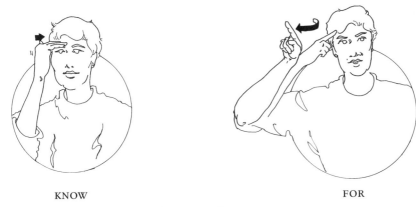

KNOW   FOR

FIGURE 5.3. *Citation forms of* KNOW *and* FOR

adjectives (e.g., DIZZY, FEDERAL, REASONABLE), nouns (e.g., DEER, FATHER, HORSE, PARENTS), prepositions (e.g., FOR), and interrogatives (e.g., WHY). Figure 5.3 is an illustration of KNOW and FOR in their citation forms.

It is well recognized by ASL signers and linguists that signs such as KNOW can "move down" (Frishberg 1975). Variants of these signs are produced at locations that are lower than the forehead or temple. Liddell and Johnson state:

> [M]any signs which are produced with contact at the SFH [side of forehead] location in formal signing may be produced in casual sign-ing at the CK [cheek] location. Similarly, signs produced at the CK lo-cation (including those moved from the SFH location) may be pro-duced at the JW [jaw] location. These same signs also appear at times without contact in the area immediately in front of the iNK [ipsilat-eral neck] location. (1989, 253)

Figure 5.4 shows KNOW and FOR as they are sometimes produced, just above or just below the jaw.

Like DEAF, KNOW has a segmental structure of the form movement-hold (MH). With the location variation that we see in signs such as KNOW, the segmental tier does not change in any way. Rather, the partic-ular features specifying the sign's location vary. Note that what differs between figures 5.3 and 5.4 are the features specifying the target location of the sign and the placement of the fingers relative to that location. This is the kind of variation that we examine here.

The question for us to consider, then, is just what causes signs pro-duced as high as the signer's temple to be produced lower on the head or

KNOW   FOR

FIGURE 5.4. *Noncitation forms of* KNOW *and* FOR

face? Liddell and Johnson state that "the phonological processes that originally must have moved them are still active in contemporary ASL. The rules which account for [these signs] appear to be variably selected by casual signing, and, like vowel reduction rules in spoken languages, have the effect of neutralizing contrasts of location" (1989, 253). Thus, their discussion of this variability suggests that surrounding phonetic material related to location helps to determine where these signs are produced in a given utterance. This suggests a purely phonological process of assimilation, where a sign produced lower than the head or face either immediately prior to or following would make KNOW look more like figure 5.4. Similarly, if the sign in question is preceded or followed by a segment whose location is on the head, the target sign may be more likely to be produced at its specified location. We use multivariate analysis to test the hypothesis that the downward movement of these signs is constrained primarily by the locations of the preceding and following segments.

Sampling and Coding for the Location Variable

Approximately 15 tokens of the variable were sampled from each signer, resulting in a total of 2,862 tokens. Tokens were coded to test the possible effects of a broad range of social and linguistic factors. Social factors were coded for the same categories as for the 1 handshape and DEAF variables.

As with the 1 handshape variable, we coded for features of the preceding and following segments as well as for grammatical function and discourse genre. In coding, we hypothesized that the location of the target sign would be influenced by the location of the preceding or following segment. We also hypothesized that variability in the target sign would be influenced by whether the preceding or following segment contacted the body or face. In order to test both hypotheses and to avoid the problem of having the same factor, pause, appear in more than one factor group, we created separate factor groups for whether the target variable was preceded or followed by a sign or a pause. Pauses in the preceding and following location and contact factor groups were then coded as not applicable, while signs were coded according to their location and contact with the body or the base hand.

We also coded for whether the signers' elbows or forearm were resting on a chair or table while the signers were producing the target sign. This phenomenon is known as "impeded signing." It is somewhat comparable to a hearing person's speaking with food in the mouth. The difference is that impeded signing, which does not carry social stigma, is more common. We predicted that a signer's resting the elbows on a table would result in the sign being produced lower than the temple. However, although results from the initial analysis bore out our prediction, the 268 tokens of impeded signing (less than 10 percent of the total) were eliminated from the final analysis reported here because such signing shows the influence of a constraint that is subject to neither linguistic nor social analysis. The linguistic factors that were coded are as follows:

1. Grammatical function of location sign
   noun (e.g., BOY, FATHER)
   adjective (e.g., BLACK, DIZZY, REASONABLE)
   verb (e.g., KNOW, UNDERSTAND)
   preposition, interrogative (grammatical function words) (e.g.,
   FOR, WHY)
2. Preceding sign
   sign
   pause: no preceding segment; target is first sign
3. Location of preceding segment
   at level of signer's head
   at level of signer's body (neck or below)
   not applicable; target is preceded by a pause

4. Contact of preceding segment with the body
   contact with the head or face
   no contact with the head or face
   contact with the body (i.e., lower than the chin)
   no contact with the body (i.e., lower than the chin)
   at level of signer's body (neck or below) *and* the dominant hand
   contacts the base hand (2-hand contact)
   not applicable, target is preceded by a pause
5. Following sign
   sign
   pause: no preceding segment; target is first sign
6. Location of following segment
   [same codes as for location of the preceding segment, applied to
   the segment following the target sign.]
7. Contact of following segment with the body
   [same codes as for contact of the preceding segment, applied to
   the segment following the target sign.]
8. Genre of text in which location sign occurs: conversation, narrative

Results for Location

Multivariate analysis of 2,594 tokens (the total remaining after examples of impeded signing were excluded) shows that the variation in location of the class of signs represented by KNOW, like variation in the other phonological variables we have considered, is systematic and constrained by multiple internal and external factors. Again, as with the other variables, the noncitation variants of these signs are more common than the citation forms, although the difference is not as great as in the cases of 1 handshape signs or DEAF. Noncitation variants account for 53 percent of the tokens, and citation forms 47 percent. Moreover, younger signers use more noncitation variants than older signers. The following discussion sets out our findings of significant contributions of both internal and external factor groups.

THE LOCATION VARIABLE: LINGUISTIC
FACTORS

In the results reported here, we assumed that the underlying form was the citation form for each sign. As noted, this is the form of the sign that appears in sign language dictionaries and is taught in sign language classes. Among linguistic factors, grammatical function, preceding location, and following contact proved significant at the .05 level. Table 5.6 shows the VARBRUL weights for the significant linguistic factor groups, with –cf as the application value. The table also includes the input probability, a measure of whether a rule is likely to apply (regardless of the presence or absence of any factor in the environment) and the overall totals.

Grammatical category.

As with the choice between citation and noncitation forms of the 1 handshape variable and DEAF, the grammatical category to which a sign belonged proved to be the first-order linguistic constraint, as indicated by the results of a step-up, step-down analysis and the spread in factor values. Within this group, prepositions and other grammatical function words are most likely to be produced at a location lower than the temple ($p = .581$). Nouns and verbs, which comprise the great majority of tokens, form the nearly neutral reference point ($p = .486$), whereas adjectives favor the citation form ($p = .316$). The result for adjectives, however, should be treated with caution. The data contained only 57 adjective tokens. We have no tokens of this category from approximately 75 percent of the signers in the study.

Phonological factors.

With respect to the phonological factors considered, contact and location behaved somewhat differently from what we expected. We coded for location and contact of preceding and following segments because we

TABLE 5.6. *VARBRUL Analysis of the Location Variable: Linguistic Factor Groups (Application Value: –cf)*

Factor Group	Factor	Weight	%	n
Grammatical	Preposition, interrogative	.581	59	485
function	Noun, verb	.486	52	2052
	Adjective	.316	35	57
Preceding	Body	.514	53	1648
location	Head	.463	48	614
Following contact	No contact	.525	55	1323
	Contact	.466	48	991
Input (p_o)	Total	.518	53	2594

Note: χ^2/cell = 1.1702; all factor groups significant at $p < .05$. Results for preceding location and following contact do not include pauses, which were tested in separate factor groups that proved not to be significant.

hypothesized that, as in spoken language variation, something in the immediately preceding and following phonological environments would play a role in the variation. The results show that among the phonological factors, only the location of the preceding sign and contact of the following sign with the body, head, or base hand proved to have statistically significant effects. The other four factor groups, whether the preceding segment was a part of a sign or a pause, whether the following segment was part of a sign or a pause, whether the preceding segment contacted the body or the head, and the location of the following sign, all failed to reach significance and are not discussed further.

The results for the location of the preceding sign suggest that assimilation may be at work. If the preceding segment is produced on the head, the target sign is less likely to be produced in its noncitation location ($p = .463$). Preceding signs produced at the level of the body, which constitute 73 percent of the tokens, represent the neutral reference point ($p = .514$).

As we have noted, the feature [+/− contact] also influences the location where these signs are produced. A [+contact] following segment disfavors –cf ($p = .466$). As with location, the influence is in the direction of the citation form, whereas the factor we expected would account for the signs being produced lower (i.e., –contact) only slightly favors –cf ($p = .525$).

THE LOCATION VARIABLE: SOCIAL FACTORS

Among the social factors, gender, region, age, language background, and ethnicity by social class were found to significantly affect the location of the signs included in this analysis. The values for the factors in these groups are given in table 5.7. As in the table showing the effects of the internal factors, the input probability and the overall totals are included.

The values for the social factors indicate that older signers disfavor –cf ($p = .416$), signers in the 26-to-54 age group are choosing the –cf variant at an intermediate rate ($p = .517$), and younger signers favor the –cf ($p = .602$). Turning to region, signers in the relatively rural sites of Washington and Virginia, all of whom were Caucasian, disfavor –cf ($p = .461$ and .334, respectively). In contrast, the signers in the five other areas favor –cf ($p = .529$). Signers from deaf families who acquired ASL naturally at an early age disfavor the noncitation variant ($p = .444$). Signers from hearing families, many of whom did not acquire ASL until they at-

TABLE 5.7. *VARBRUL Analysis of the Location Variable: Social Factor Groups (Application Value: –cf)*

Factor Group	Factor	Weight	%	n
Age	15–25	.602	61	554
	26–54	.517	54	1133
	55+	.416	46	907
Gender	Male	.544	56	1376
	Female	.451	49	1218
Region	Calif., La., Md.,			
	Kans./Mo.	.529	54	2055
	Wash.	.461	56	259
	Va.	.334	40	280
Language	Hearing parents	.519	53	1940
background	Deaf parents	.444	52	654
Ethnicity, Class	C, MC and WC	.555	56	1882
	AA, MC	.445	55	257
	AA, WC	.314	40	455
Input	Total	.518	53	2594

Note: χ^2/cell = 1.1702; all factor groups significant at $p < .05$. No African Americans participated in Virginia and Washington. African American middle-class signers include persons ages 15–54.

tended residential schools, represent the majority of tokens and the neutral reference point ($p = .519$). Turning to gender, female signers tend to be conservative and disfavor –cf ($p = .451$). Male signers, in contrast, slightly favor –cf ($p = .544$).

Thus far, the results for the social factors have proven to be fairly straightforward, at least statistically. To complete the analysis, however, it was necessary to account for the differential effect of class on African American and Caucasian signers. An early run showed that social class had a significant effect, with middle-class signers slightly favoring and working-class signers slightly disfavoring the noncitation variant. Separate runs by ethnic group, however, indicated that social class was significant only for African Americans. It had no significant effect on the location of signs produced by Caucasian signers. We therefore created a new factor group, ethnicity by social class, consisting of three factors: Caucasian middle- and working-class, African American middle-class, and African American working-class. The results of the analysis that included the combined factor group show that Caucasian signers favor –cf ($p =$

.555), middle-class African Americans disfavor –cf ($p = .445$) and work-ing-class African Americans strongly disfavor the –cf variant ($p = .314$).

In summary, older signers, African Americans, rural signers, native signers, and females all disfavor the noncitation variants of the signs in this study exemplified by KNOW. Second, some of the patterns parallel so-ciolinguistic variation in spoken languages. For example, older speakers and women are often more linguistically conservative than younger speakers and men of the same social class (cf. Eckert 1989; Labov 1990; Trudgill 1974; Wolfram 1969). Some of the patterns, however, seem to be unique to the Deaf community. For example, it is known that African American signers often use the older forms of signs (Aramburo 1989; Woodward 1976). Their preference for citation forms is therefore not surprising. In addition, the preference of native signers for citation forms may be explained by a sense of protectiveness or loyalty toward ASL that leads them to produce what they perceive to be the "proper" or "not lazy" forms of these signs, even in conversation with perceived peers. Note, however, that only in the analysis of the location of signs exempli-fied by KNOW and for the open hand variant of 1 handshape signs was the difference between native and non-native ASL signers significant. That factor did not reach significance either for the 1 handshape or the DEAF variable.

The Location Variable: A Change in Progress?

The results presented here show that variation in location in ASL is sys-tematic and constrained by multiple linguistic and social factors. However, a further question remains to be addressed. Is the systematic variation re-vealed by the multivariate analysis stable, or does it represent a change in progress? The results are generally compatible with the view that variation in location signs represents a change in progress. In this section we focus on evidence from the distribution of citation and noncitation forms by age, grammatical function, social class, and ethnicity. We also consider the application of the apparent time construct to the study of sign languages.

LOCATION: AGE AND GRAMMATICAL
FUNCTION
As noted in the results section, the ordering of constraints within the grammatical function factor group is prepositions and interrogatives > nouns and verbs > adjectives. That is, grammatical function signs such

as prepositions and interrogatives are more likely to be produced in a location lower than the forehead or temple, while content signs are more likely to be produced in citation form. When the data are broken down by age and grammatical function, we find that not only are grammatical function signs more likely than content signs to be produced in an area lower than the citation form, but also that, where we have large numbers of tokens, the numbers of lowered forms within each of the broad grammatical categories increase as the age of the signers decreases. Adjectives represent an exception; however, this category represents only 2 percent of the tokens in the analysis. Table 5.8 shows the percentages and numbers of noncitation forms by age group and grammatical function. Figure 5.5 represents the same information graphically.

The distribution of citation and noncitation variants by age and grammatical function shown in table 5.8 and figure 5.5 indicates that prepositions and interrogatives signs are the most favorable environment for –cf, whereas content signs are somewhat less favorable.

A full account of the mechanism of change is beyond the scope of this book. However, it is not surprising to find that innovations such as the lowering of this class of signs are more common in grammatical function

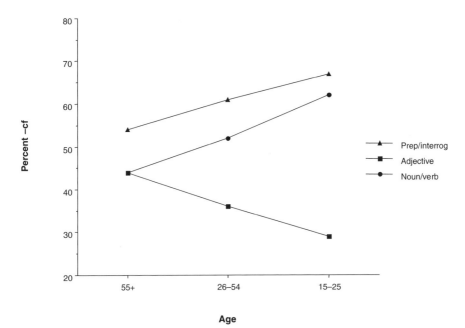

FIGURE 5.5. *The location variable: Age by grammatical function*

TABLE 5.8. *Location: Age by Grammatical Function, Percentage of Noncitation Forms*

Grammatical function	15–25 %	15–25 n	26–54 %	26–54 n	55+ %	55+ n	Total %	Total n
Noun, verb	62	439	52	904	44	709	52	2,052
Adjective	29	28	36	11	44	18	35	57
Preposition, interrogative	67	87	61	218	54	180	59	485
Total	61	554	54	1,133	46	907	53	2,594

signs such as prepositions and interrogatives than in content signs. In many spoken languages, grammatical function words are more subject to processes of phonological reduction and assimilation than are content words.[6]

AGE, SOCIAL CLASS, AND ETHNICITY

Further evidence for the lowering of the class of signs represented by KNOW as a change in progress comes from the distribution of tokens by age, social class, and ethnicity. Among Caucasian middle- and working-class signers and among African American working-class signers, younger people use more noncitation variants, signers aged 26 to 54 show an intermediate value, and signers 55 and older use the fewest noncitation variants. Percentages and numbers of noncitation variants of location signs by age, social class, and ethnicity are shown in table 5.9.

These results conform to the classic pattern of language change: the younger the signer (or speaker), the greater the use of the innovative form. The data from middle-class African Americans, however, fail to conform to the general pattern. Middle-class African Americans aged 26

---

6. In spoken languages, prepositions are often unstressed and hence subject to phonological reduction. It is possible that a similar process is at work here and that the effect of grammatical function may be a reflex of an underlying phonological process. However, stress in ASL is not as clearly understood as it is in spoken languages and therefore presents many difficulties in coding. Moreover, our intention in this study was to test the claim that the location of the preceding and following segments fully accounted for the lowering of the class of signs represented by KNOW.

TABLE 5.9. *Location: Age by Ethnicity and Social Class, Percentage of Noncitation Forms*

	15–25		26–54		55+		Total	
Ethnicity, Class	%	n	%	n	%	n	%	n
C, MC	66	182	60	394	46	292	57	868
C, WC	68	185	53	356	51	473	55	1014
AA, MC	42	64	59	193	—	0	55	257
AA, WC	54	123	38	190	30	142	40	455
Total	61	554	54	1,133	46	907	53	2594

to 54 use innovative variants at approximately the same rate as Caucasian middle-class signers of similar age. Younger middle-class African Americans exhibit a lower percentage of innovative variants than either the 26-to-54-year-old middle-class African Americans or than the other three groups of similar age.

A number of factors might account for these apparently anomalous results. As table 5.9 shows, the number of tokens available from young middle-class African Americans is considerably smaller than from any other group. Indeed, our data contain only about half as many tokens from young middle-class African Americans as from their working-class counterparts. The anomalous results thus may be partially attributable to the low token count. The social situation of young middle-class African Americans may also account for the high incidence of citation forms in the data. We noted in chapter 2 that the effects of the Observer's Paradox (Labov 1972a) are intensified in studies of sociolinguistic variation of sign languages. Speakers who participate in studies of variation in spoken languages can remain relatively secure in their anonymity because such studies have usually relied upon audiotape rather than videotape. Moreover, spoken-language communities are typically much larger than sign language communities. Preserving anonymity is much more difficult in sociolinguistic studies of sign languages. We suggest that the younger middle-class African American signers in this study may have felt the effects of the Observer's Paradox particularly acutely. These signers, as young African American Deaf people, belong to multiple groups that are stigmatized by the dominant society. However, as evidenced by their middle-class status, they are also upwardly mobile. Given the multiple identities and aspirations they represent, as well as the generally conservative nature of African American ASL (Aramburo 1989), it is at least possible that the young middle-class African Americans whose data are included here felt considerable pressure to produce a more standard form of ASL.

When broken down by age and grammatical category on one hand and age, social class, and ethnicity on the other, the distribution of the data suggests that the lowering of the class of signs represented by KNOW may represent a change in progress. This suggestion rests on the assumption that the apparent time construct applies to change in sign as well as to spoken languages. The idea that synchronic variation by age groups reflects diachronic change has proven extremely productive both in early dialectology and in modern sociolinguistics ever since Hermann (1929) confirmed many of the phonological changes predicted by Gauchat (1905) in his study of the Swiss village of Charmey at the end of the nineteenth century. The apparent time construct was also used by Labov in his early work in New York City (1966). More recently, Bailey et al. (1991) provided clear evidence of the utility of the apparent time construct by comparing two random telephone samples of Texas English with data collected 15 years earlier for the *Linguistic Atlas of the Gulf States* (Pederson et al. 1981, 1986). Bailey et al. note that we cannot say with certainty that apparent time differences "universally reflect language change in progress for all kinds of linguistic features" (1991, 263). Nevertheless, the apparent time construct has been used most successfully to understand phonological change in spoken languages, and we suggest that the construct may apply to phonological change in sign languages as well.

SUMMARY: LOCATION

To summarize, the results of the analysis presented here suggest that location is a classic sociolinguistic variable constrained by linguistic, social, and geographical factors. The linguistic constraints we have identified (e.g., the grammatical category to which a sign belongs, features of the surrounding phonological environment) are characteristic of both spoken and signed languages, although the particular form they take, such as the location at which the sign is produced or contact with the body, are of course particular to sign languages. Many of the social constraints we have identified (gender, ethnicity, class, age, and region) also

influence variation in spoken languages. However, as with the two variables previously considered, the particular manifestations of many of
these constraints (e.g., the relatively conservative nature of African
American ASL) are best explained by reference to Deaf history and to the
social structure of the Deaf community. Finally, we have suggested that
the distribution of tokens by age, grammatical function, social class, and
ethnicity provides evidence of a change in progress.

PHONOLOGICAL VARIATION IN ASL: CONCLUSION

Analysis of nearly 10,000 tokens produced by more than 200 signers
and distributed among three variables indicates that phonological variation in ASL, like variation in spoken languages, is systematic. This is not
to say that we can predict whether a signer will produce one or another
variant in any particular instance. We can say, however, that in certain
linguistic environments, signers who belong to particular groups and
who live in a specific region will be more likely to choose one variant
over another. That is, given a sufficient number of tokens in a particular
environment, we can predict in a probabilistic sense the patterns of variation that are likely to be exhibited by signers representing different social categories and geographic regions. In addition, although our data
show social and regional differences, as well as differences in the effects
of linguistic factors, a number of major—and sometimes unexpected—
similarities were found that extend across the three phonological variables. Chief among these are the effect of the grammatical category to
which a sign belongs and regional groupings, especially the close connection between Virginia and Washington. In the following chapter, we explore patterns that extend across more than one phonological variable,
with emphasis on the effect of the grammatical category and the social
and regional patterning of the variants.

Chapter 6

Grammatical and Social Conditioning

of Phonological Variation

In chapters 4 and 5 we looked at the patterns of variation exhibited by three phonological variables: 1 handshape signs, DEAF, and the location of signs represented by KNOW. We saw that all three can be considered classic sociolinguistic variables, in that the variation that they exhibit correlates with both linguistic and social factors. That all three variables exhibit significant correlations with both linguistic and social factors is not at all surprising. As we have seen, these kinds of correlations have been described extensively for variables in spoken languages, and we are not at all surprised to find them in sign languages as well. What is striking and unexpected, however, is the consistent and strong role of grammatical factors in accounting for the behavior of all three phonological variables. Also of interest is the role of social and historical factors unique to the American Deaf community across all three variables. In chapters 4 and 5 we examined each of the three phonological variables separately; in this chapter we consider them together, first in terms of grammatical conditioning of the variables and second in terms of the sociohistorical context in which they occur.

GRAMMATICAL CONDITIONING OF PHONOLOGICAL VARIATION

Sociolinguistic research on spoken languages has shown that linguistic variables may be systematically conditioned by factors operating at different levels of the linguistic system. For example, as we saw in chapter 1, numerous studies have shown that -t,d deletion in English is systematically conditioned by the preceding and following phonological environments, stress, and the grammatical category of the word containing the cluster (e.g., Baugh 1983; Guy 1980; Wolfram 1969). Other sociolinguistic variables, such as verbal -*s* in English, are also constrained by both phonological and grammatical factors (Godfrey and Tagliamonte 1999; Poplack and Tagliamonte 1989), as is final -*s* aspiration and deletion in Puerto Rican Spanish (Poplack 1979).

Although the fact that many sociolinguistic variables are constrained by factors operating at different linguistic levels may be a commonplace for students of spoken languages, phonological variation in ASL and other sign languages has heretofore been accounted for by positing phonological constraints alone, particularly the features of the preceding and/or following segments, without reference to structures other than the sequence of phonological segments. The program of research on ASL until very recently has been to demonstrate that ASL, and by analogy other sign languages, are true languages. This work has proceeded by demonstrating that the structure of ASL parallels that of spoken languages and that its phonology and syntax are subject to the same kinds of processes that operate in spoken languages. In the process, this work has not considered the possibility that factors at different linguistic levels may constrain phonological variation. For example, as we saw in chapters 4 and 5, Liddell and Johnson (1989) explain variation in all three of the variables examined here—1 handshape, DEAF, location signs—exclusively by reference to features of the preceding and/or following segments.

The results of our analysis do not support Liddell and Johnson's claims. Recall that the core of our analysis of each variable involved identifying the linguistic factors that govern the observed variation. Following the model provided by studies of spoken language variation and heeding earlier claims about variation in sign languages, we hypothesized that features of the immediately preceding and following phonological environment would play key roles. For example, we assumed that the location of preceding and following signs would be important for understanding the variation in DEAF and in the location of signs such as KNOW; we assumed that the handshape of the preceding and following signs would play a role in the variation of 1 handshape signs. We therefore included factor groups consisting of the features of the preceding and following segments. However, Lucas's earlier analysis of DEAF (1995), albeit with a small number of tokens, had alerted us to the possible role played by grammatical function in explaining the variation. That analysis, based on 486 tokens, found the syntactic category of DEAF to be the only significant linguistic factor, with adjectives favoring noncitation forms, predicate adjectives slightly disfavoring them, and nouns strongly disfavoring them. In the 1995 pilot study, the locations of the preceding and following segments were found to be not significant. Based on the results of Lucas (1995), in this study we included a factor group for the relevant grammatical categories of each variable along with the phonological and social factor groups.[1] For DEAF, the grammatical categories included predicate adjective, noun, adjective, and adjective in a compound. For the location variable, they included prepositions and interrogatives, nouns, verbs, and adjectives, and for 1 handshape signs, they included pronouns and lexical signs, the latter divided into nouns, adjectives, verbs, adverbs, and grammatical function words. Table 6.1 summarizes the ranking of the factors for all three variables and shows that grammatical function is the most powerful factor for all three variables. This is a very surprising finding with substantial implications. We first discuss its importance in terms of each variable and then offer a more global explanation that unifies all three variables.

The results for variation in 1 handshape signs show grammatical function to be the first-order linguistic constraint on two of the three main variants, +cf and open hand, and a significant constraint on the third, L handshape. The 1 handshape findings suggest that conditioning at the level of discourse structure and information packaging may be more important for phonological variation in sign languages than previously thought. That is, there appears to be an inverse relationship between the distance of a form from the signing subject and the extent to which a handshape may diverge from the citation form. We can view the three variants shown here as points on a continuum of distance from the citation form: the citation form itself, a form in which only the thumb is extended, and a class of forms in which other fingers are also selected and extended. This continuum corresponds inversely to a continuum of grammatical distance from the signing subject in the discourse setting: That is, the most salient referent in the discourse, the signer, is more likely to be referred to with a pronoun whose form may vary maximally from the citation form. The addressee, also salient in the discourse set-

1. Even though the features of the preceding and following environment proved not to be significant in Lucas's pilot study, we included them in this study because we suspected that some features would prove significant, given the much larger number of tokens we were working with. As the results in chapters 4 and 5 show, this turned out to be the case.

TABLE 6.1. *Linguistic Constraints on Phonological Variation: Summary*

Variable	Analysis	Constraint Ranking
1 handshape	+cf vs. –cf	Grammatical function > features of preceding and following handshapes (assimilation)
	L handshape vs. all others	Features of preceding and following handshapes (assimilation) > grammatical function
	Open hand vs. all others	Grammatical function > features of preceding and following handshapes (assimilation)
DEAF	+cf vs. –cf	Grammatical function > discourse genre. Location of preceding and following segments not significant
	Chin-to-ear vs. contact-cheek	Grammatical function > location of following segment (assimilation)
Location	+cf vs. –cf	Grammatical function > contact with body of following sign > location of preceding sign

ting, is more likely to be referred to with a pronominal form that diverges from the citation form only in features of the thumb. Third-person referents, those not present in the setting, are the most likely among the pronouns to be the citation forms. In ASL pronouns, the indexical category is carried by the tips of the fingers, regardless of the handshape used. In nonindexical lexical signs, however, the whole handshape carries part of the semantic load. The handshape in this class is the most likely to be the citation form. Lexical signs may be produced as the L handshape variant, in which the thumb is also extended, but they are less likely to take a handshape that is farther away from the citation form than are pronouns, as this could convey a different meaning or no meaning at all.

Turning to DEAF, we suggested in the previous chapter that the role of grammatical constraints in the choice between a citation and noncitation form may represent a synchronic reflex of a change in progress in which compounds are the most favorable environment for innovative forms, followed by nouns and adjectives and finally predicates. We also see both the chin-to-ear and contact-cheek forms occurring with predicates, nouns, and adjectives. As demonstrated by the results of the VARBRUL analysis, then, when the citation (ear-to-chin) and noncitation forms (chin-to-ear and contact-cheek) of DEAF are compared, grammatical category accounts for the variation.

These findings do not mean that phonological factors never play a role.[2] As we saw in chapter 5, when we compare the noncitation forms to each other, grammatical function is still the most important factor, but the location of the following sign also plays a role, and we have evidence of assimilation: Following locations higher or lower than the usual location for the contact-cheek form slightly favor this form, whereas a following location at the contact-cheek location (as in YESTERDAY or GIRL) and a following pause both disfavor the contact-cheek form and favor the chin-to-ear form.

In the case of the lowering of signs such as KNOW, as with DEAF, grammatical function is again the most important factor. Specifically, prepositions and interrogatives are most likely to be produced at a location lower than the temple. Nouns and verbs represent the neutral reference point. Adjectives favor citation form. And as we explained in chapter 5, the phonological factors of the location of the preceding sign and body contact in a following sign proved to be significant. So, the features of the preceding and following signs do play a role in location variation, but their role is not as strong as the one played by grammatical category.

2. If indeed variation in ASL is similar to variation in spoken languages, as yet unexplored phonological factors may play a role in the patterning of grammatical constraints that we see with DEAF and other phonological variables. The case of -t,d deletion in English offers an example of how phonological factors may influence grammatical factors. Guy (1991a) proposed an exponential model of constraints to explain the relationships observed in the grammatical category factor group, which related the retention of past tense, semiweak, and monomorphemic clusters in the ratio of $x: x^2: x^3$. He explained this ratio as a consequence of the multilevel architecture of lexical phonology (Kiparsky 1985), whereby the three main grammatical categories are subject to one, two, or three passes of a deletion rule. That is, the grammatical categories differ from one another with respect to -t,d deletion as a consequence of the number of times they are operated on by a phonological process. In examining phonological variation in ASL, we do not rule out the possibility that some of our results for the influence of the grammatical category may eventually be explained by phonological processes operating at similarly abstract levels. Rather, our intention is to show that features of the preceding and following segments are not the main constraints on the variables we have examined here.

The analyses summarized here highlight several points. First, we cannot assume that only features of the preceding and/or following signs constrain phonological variation in sign languages. Indeed, the results of the multivariate analyses presented here show that is not the case. Second, just as in the study of variation in spoken languages, studies of variation in sign languages must be based on large amounts of data collected from representative samples of the language community. In her discussion of the basic principles of discourse analysis, Schiffrin states as the first principle that "Analysis of discourse is empirical. Data come from a speech community: data are about people using language, not linguists thinking about how people use language" (1994, 416). And thus it is also with the study of variation. With all three phonological variables, we have clearly seen that although it might seem reasonably correct to assume that most important factors governing variation in 1 handshape signs, the location of signs such as KNOW, and in DEAF have to do with features of the preceding and following segments, this assumption is not always reliable. When examined in light of the actual language produced by real people, the claims and assumptions about all three variables could not be supported. We find this to be the case with syntactic and lexical variation as well, described in chapters 7 and 8 respectively. Third, the consistent pattern observed across all three phonological variables examined here may help us sort out the types of constraints that may be unique to signed languages (e.g., indexicality) and those that are common to all languages, whether spoken or signed.

This pattern is further supported by the results of Hoopes's (1998) study of pinky extension and Mulrooney's (2001) work on variation in fingerspelling. Hoopes looked at signs such as THINK, WONDER, and TOLERATE, all signed in citation form with the pinky closed but variably produced with the pinky extended. Again we might suspect pinky extension to be governed by the handshape of the preceding or following sign, but this turned out to not be the case. Rather, pinky extension tended to occur with lexemes used repeatedly within a discourse topic, before pauses, and with lexemes lengthened to almost twice their usual duration. These findings suggest that pinky extension is itself a prosodic feature of ASL that adds emphatic stress or focus to the sign with which it cooccurs. It is quite analogous to stress in spoken language as indicated by a stronger signal as a result of greater articulatory effort. Thus, in Hoopes's study we do see the possible influence of a phonological factor, stress, as well as a discourse factor, repetition.

The phonological factor, however, is unrelated to the features of the preceding or following signs.[3]

Mulrooney (2001) investigated variation in fingerspelling, with the goal of determining what governs the production of noncitation forms of the individual signs that make up a fingerspelled word. Again one might expect the immediate phonological environment to play some role, specifically the handshape of the immediately preceding or immediately following sign. However, neither the immediately preceding handshape nor the following handshape turned out to have a significant effect. The immediately preceding and following locations had modest roles, but once again, the strongest role was played by the function of the fingerspelled word in which the target form occurred, with proper nouns favoring citation forms, common nouns being neutral, and verbs favoring noncitation forms.

We have strong evidence, then, that grammatical constraints play a more important role than the features of the preceding and following signs in constraining phonological variation in ASL. The challenge is to understand why this is so. The first answer is simply that, as in spoken languages, phonological variation in ASL is not constrained only by phonological factors, at least if phonological factors are restricted to the features of the preceding and following signs. The focus heretofore may have been on features of the preceding and following signs, but large data-based quantitative studies such as ours clearly show that grammatical factors must also be considered. A second answer leads inevitably to thinking about fundamental differences between spoken languages and sign languages. That sign languages are real languages, viable linguistic systems independent from the spoken languages with which they may coexist, has been amply demonstrated and is not the point here. However, having established that sign languages are languages, research on all aspects of sign language structure has begun to reveal some very fundamental and most likely modality-related differences between spoken languages and sign languages. Of most relevance to the present study are the

---

3. It is possible that stress may also be implicated in the predicate adjective effect for DEAF. That is, predicate adjectives may favor +cf because they are frequently stressed. However, we are not in a position to evaluate this possibility at this time because, although we coded the data for a large number of factors, we did not code for stress.

fundamental differences in how morphology functions and how these differences manifest themselves in variation. In many of the spoken languages in which phonological variation has been extensively explored, morphology is a "boundary phenomenon." That is, meaningful segments (bound morphemes) are added to the beginning or to the end of other units in the language in the form of plural markers, person and tense markers, derivational affixes, and so forth. These units are essentially added to an existing phonological environment. It stands to reason that when variation occurs, a good place to look for the cause of this variation is the immediate environment to which the units have been added (i.e., the preceding or following segments). And in fact, many studies of spoken language variation have demonstrated the key role of the immediate phonological environment in governing variation.

However, morphology in sign languages is by and large not a boundary phenomenon, at least not to as great an extent. There exist very few affixes. Morphological distinctions are accomplished by altering one or more features in the articulatory bundle that makes up a hold or a movement segment or by altering the movement path of the sign. That is, segments are not usually added to other segments to provide information about person or aspect. Rather, the location feature of a segment (e.g., near the signer or away from the signer) indicates person, and movement between locations indicates subject and object of the verb in question; similarly, a particular movement path indicates continuative aspect or inceptive aspect. As Emmorey states with specific regard to aspect marking in ASL,

> In many spoken languages, morphologically complex words are formed by adding prefixes or suffixes to a word stem. In ASL and other signed languages, complex forms are most often created by nesting a sign stem within dynamic movement contours and planes in space. . . . ASL has many verbal inflections that convey temporal information about the action denoted by the verb, for example, whether the action was habitual, iterative, continual. Generally, these distinctions are marked by different movement patterns overlaid onto a sign stem. This type of morphological encoding contrasts with the primarily linear affixation found in spoken languages. For spoken languages, simultaneous affixation processes such as templatic morphology (e.g., in Semitic languages), infixation, or reduplication are relatively rare. Signed languages, by contrast, prefer nonconcatenative processes such

as reduplication; and prefixation and suffixation are rare. Sign languages' preference for simultaneously producing affixes and stems may have its origins in the visual-manual modality.

For example, the articulators for speech (the tongue, lips, jaw) can move quite rapidly, producing easily perceived distinctions on the order of every 50–200 milliseconds. In contrast, the major articulators for sign (the hands) move relatively slowly such that the duration of an isolated sign is about 1,000 milliseconds; the duration of an average spoken word is more like 500 milliseconds. If language processing in real time has equal timing constraints for spoken and signed languages, then there is strong pressure for signed languages to express more distinctions simultaneously. The articulatory pressures seem to work in concert with the differing capacities of the visual and auditory systems for expressing simultaneous versus sequential information. That is, the visual system is well suited for simultaneously perceiving a large amount of information, whereas the auditory system seems particularly adept at perceiving fast temporal distinctions. Thus both sign and speech have exploited the advantages of their respective modalities. (1999, 173)

Based on the results of our analyses, it would seem that these fundamental differences manifest themselves in the variable components of the language. That is, the immediate phonological environment turns out to not have the major role in governing the variation of phonological variables, in part because the variables themselves are not of an affixational nature. The grammatical category to which the variable in question belongs consistently is the first-order linguistic constraint.

This is a significant finding: As the modality differences between spoken and signed languages manifest themselves in the basic phonological, morphological, and syntactic components of the language, so do they seem to manifest themselves in the variation found in the language. As phonological and morphological processes go, so apparently goes variation.

Now, the question arises as to the parallels between spoken languages such as Chinese that, like ASL, do not use affixes to any great extent. The gist of the question is whether the variation in these spoken languages resembles variation in ASL, specifically the prominent role of grammatical factors in governing the variation. As of this writing, the question is difficult to answer. Although numerous studies of Chinese dialects exist, relatively few studies of Chinese varieties employ variationist methods. Moreover, a number of the studies that do exist have been concerned with testing Wang's (1969) model of lexical diffusion (e.g., Bauer 1982 on variation in Cantonese). Others, such as Barale's (1982) dissertation on the loss of final nasals in Beijing Mandarin, which used variable rule methodology, have not included grammatical function or category as factor groups. One study, however, Bourgerie's (1990) dissertation on sociolinguistic variation in Hong Kong Cantonese, does consider the effect of grammatical class on phonological variation.

Bourgerie (1990) examined three sociolinguistic variables: initial *n-/l-*, initial *ng-/ø-*, and initial *k-/h-* in third-person pronouns. Although his main focus was on the social dimensions of variation, he found that two of the three phonological variables were constrained by grammatical class. For the *ng-/ ø -* variable, adverbs and nonstative verbs were significantly more likely to be realized by the innovative initial, while stative verbs were much less likely to be realized in the innovative form. Grammatical class was also significant for the *n-/l-* variable. More than 80 percent of the tokens of verbs and adverbs were realized with the [l-] initial, compared to only 40 percent of demonstratives and particles (Bourgerie 1990, 137–38).

Bourgerie's results for grammatical class suggest that differences in modality alone may not account fully for the difference in the strength of grammatical constraints on phonological variation in spoken and sign languages. However, in the absence of substantial studies of sociolinguistic variation in Chinese varieties and other languages that have no or only minimal inflectional morphology, we cannot rule out modality differences as a contributing factor to the patterns reported in the previous chapters. At this point, the role of grammatical factors in conditioning phonological variation in ASL seems to be best described as a *matter of degree:* There clearly are grammatical constraints on spoken language phonological variation, and features of preceding and following signs clearly influence variation in sign languages. What we are suggesting, based on the results of our analyses, is that the difference in modality may make for a difference in the relative importance of the constraints. In the phonological variation observed thus far in sign languages, grammatical constraints are consistently more important than phonological ones. Ironically, it may be the visual nature of sign languages that reinforces the impressions and hypotheses that phonological variation in sign languages is governed by constraints having to do with the features of the preceding and/or following segments. That is, we can actually *see* the lower and higher locations that precede and follow signs such as DEAF and KNOW; we can *see* the handshapes that precede and follow 1 handshape signs. Being able to see the phonological environment surrounding the variation easily leads to hypotheses about this environment accounting fully for the variation. But these hypotheses are simply not supported by our data.

THE SOCIOHISTORICAL CONTEXT OF PHONOLOGICAL VARIATION

We also saw in chapters 4 and 5 that all three phonological variables are conditioned by social factors. As we had hoped to demonstrate at the outset of this project, as in spoken languages, there exists sociolinguistic variation in ASL. For 1 handshape signs, in four of the seven sites, signers are more likely to use the citation form than either of the two main noncitation forms analyzed. Three other sites, Maryland, Virginia, and Washington, exhibit the same pattern: Signers disfavor the citation form and favor the noncitation forms in these three sites. Table 6.2 summarizes the results for the social factors for all three analyses of 1 handshape signs, as well as for the other two variables.

For DEAF, we see a complex interaction between age and region. When comparing the citation form to the two noncitation forms, in six of the seven sites—all except Kansas/Missouri—VARBRUL results show that the signers in the 26-to-54 age group either favor the ear-to-chin citation form or, in the case of Virginia, are neutral (Virginia signers in this group are much more likely to choose the citation form than younger or older signers).[4] In Massachusetts these middle-aged signers are joined by the older and younger signers, and in Maryland they are joined by the younger signers. When comparing the two noncitation forms, we see that older and middle-aged signers in Massachusetts, Louisiana, and California favor the contact-cheek form, whereas the younger signers in these sites disfavor this form. In fact, there were no instances of contact-cheek produced by the younger signers in Louisiana. The younger signers in Kansas/Missouri favor the contact-

Note: In table 6.2, –cf is the application value. Hence, VARBRUL weights, or factor values, between 0 and .5 indicate that signers in that group disfavor –cf and favor +cf.

Table 6.2. Social Constraints on Phonological Variation: Summary

Variable	Analysis	Constraint Ranking
1 handshape	+cf vs. –cf	region > age > social class
	L handshape vs. all others	region > age > language background
	open hand vs. all others	region > age
DEAF	+cf vs. –cf	region by age
	Chin-to-ear vs. contact-cheek	region by age
Location	+cf vs. –cf	region > social class by ethnicity > age > language background > gender

cheek form, as they do in Washington, where they are joined by the older signers. And the older signers in Maryland and Virginia disfavor the contact-cheek form, whereas the middle age and younger signers favor it. A summary of how the age groups pattern for DEAF in different regions is seen in table 6.3.

There are two points of interest here. One is the "old and young vs. mid"-pattern that we see with the citation vs. noncitation forms. We see that in four of the seven sites, the middle age signers are less likely to choose a noncitation form than the older and younger signers in these sites. And in six of the seven sites, the older signers favor the noncitation forms. These results correlate with the history of deaf education in the United States and specifically with the recognition and use of ASL in residential schools. For example, many of these older signers attended residential schools at a time when ASL was actively suppressed and

TABLE 6.3. Age Group Patterning for DEAF

	+cf vs. –cf	Chin-to-ear vs. contact-cheek
Old vs. mid and young	Md.	Md., Va.
Old and mid vs. young	none	Mass., La., Kans./Mo., Calif.
Old and young vs. mid	Va., La., Calif., Wash.	Wash.
All favor +cf	Mass.	n/a
All favor –cf	Kans./Mo.	n/a

forbidden. Although they were certainly fluent users of the language, there was very little metalinguistic awareness or prescriptivism accompanying that use. Indeed, many of the older signers could not provide a name for their language—they did not provide the lexicalized finger-spelling #ASL—as the two younger groups could. Rather, many of the older signers still referred to their fluent language production simply as SIGN. By contrast, the 26-to-54-year-old signers in the sample were in school at the time when ASL was beginning to be recognized and valued as a language separate from English. ASL was still not accepted in classrooms, but there was a rapidly growing awareness in the Deaf community of the need for recognition. The first dictionary of ASL was published in the mid-1960s (Stokoe, Casterline, and Croneberg 1965). In the late 1960s and early 1970s, formal instruction in sign language began, along with the preparation of teaching materials. This new awareness of the status of ASL may help explain the preference among the 26-to-54-year-old signers in the majority of sites for the citation form of DEAF. The prescriptivism seen here in the use of citation forms may be regarded as a tool in maintaining the hard-won recognition of ASL. Finally, the youngest signers in the sample all attended school at a time when, for the most part, the status of ASL was no longer in question. The change in the status of ASL may explain the more frequent use of noncitation forms by younger signers. The status of the language is not threatened by the use of noncitation forms.

The second point of interest is the similar behavior of the Virginia and Washington signers in light of the direct historical connection (outlined in chapter 3) between the American School for the Deaf, the Virginia School for the Deaf and Blind in Staunton, and the Washington State School for the Deaf in Vancouver. Recall that the Virginia school opened in 1839 and the first superintendent was Joseph Tyler, who had been an instructor at the American School for 7 years. The Washington school opened in 1886, and the first principal, W. D. McFarland, was assisted by George Layton, a graduate of the Virginia school. A similarity in signing styles in Virginia and Washington might not be surprising, especially since this same pattern reveals itself in the location variable to which we now turn.

As we explained in chapter 5, the analysis of the location of the class of signs represented by KNOW found region, gender, age, language background, and ethnicity by class to be significant. The gender and age patterns are similar to those found in spoken languages, in which it is frequently found that women and older speakers prefer standard forms, whereas men and younger speakers tend to choose nonstandard forms. In the case of the location variable, women and older signers prefer the citation forms at the forehead level, whereas men and younger signers tend to produce the signs at a lower level. Specifically in terms of age, we suggest that we are seeing change in progress, with the increasing preference for noncitation forms from older to younger signers. This is not to say, of course, that the citation forms will ever be completely replaced by the noncitation ones. The citation forms are the ones that appear in dictionaries, are taught in sign language classes, and are probably most likely to be produced in formal situations such as lectures.

As we saw in chapter 5, the African American signers disfavored the noncitation variant, and this may be indicative of a tendency noted by other researchers (e.g., Aramburo 1989) for African American signers to favor the older forms of signs. We also see that signers from ASL backgrounds (i.e., native signers) prefer the citation variant. The language background factor is not one usually found in studies of spoken language variation, at least not in same way in which it is found in studies of deaf communities in which language background directly reflects the nature of language acquisition. Fewer than 10 percent of ASL users are born to deaf parents and into ASL-using families. The majority of ASL users are born to hearing parents who may or may not sign, and if they do use some form of manual communication, it may not be ASL but rather a manual code for English that may be produced simultaneously with spoken English. These ASL users have traditionally learned ASL in residential school settings from peers who are native signers, but the advent of mainstreaming since the mid-1970s has endangered this means of transmission (Ramsey 1997). Increasingly, however, and as we witnessed in five of our seven sites, ASL is used as the medium of instruction and allowed both in the classroom and for interpersonal communication. Nevertheless, the native signer/non-native signer distinction is still a real one in the Deaf community, and we felt that it needed to be represented among the social factors. This evidently was a good choice at least in the case of the location signs, as we see the distinct difference between natives and non-natives described earlier. The preference of the native signers for the citation variant may reflect a sense of loyalty or protectiveness toward ASL, which leads them to produce what they perceive to be the "proper" or "not lazy" forms of these signs.

As for region and the location variable, we see that signers in five of the seven sites very much favor the noncitation variant. And, as with DEAF, Washington and Virginia exhibit the same pattern, this time with signers in both sites disfavoring the noncitation variant. And again we suggest that this may reflect the direct historical link between these two sites.

To summarize, the results for the social factors show considerable variability in ASL as we move from one region to another. In fact, in all of the analyses, region, sometimes in conjunction with age, proved to be the strongest nonlinguistic factor. Perceptions that signing differs from one region of the country to another, then, have an empirical basis. Despite the regional differences, however, all variants are found in all of the regions we studied. Unlike the case of English phonological variables such as intrusive /r/ that are found only in some regions of the United States, none of the variants examined here is exclusive to a single region or group of regions. Rather, the ASL phonological variables we have reported on more closely resemble -t,d deletion or alveolarization of /ŋ/, which are found to a greater or lesser extent in virtually all English dialects. The patterning of regional groups, though, is surprising, particularly the Virginia-Washington connection. The similarities between these two areas, located 3,000 miles apart, provide evidence of the powerful role of the state schools for Deaf people in the transmission of ASL.

As stated in chapter 1, a major goal of the project was to determine whether the external social constraints on variation such as those defined and described in spoken languages also operate in sign languages. And we have seen that many of the same factors that have been shown to constrain phonological variation in spoken languages, namely social class, ethnicity, and gender, do indeed significantly affect one or more phonological variables in ASL. However, in ASL the effect of these factors seems to be considerably less than it is with many spoken language variables. At this point we can only point to possible explanations. One is methodological in nature and has to do with data-collection procedures. In the case of the limited role that ethnicity played in explaining the variation in this study, it may be that the effect of the interview situation was to preclude the production by the participants of what is commonly identified as "Black ASL." As mentioned before, there is a widespread perception that such a variety exists, a variety distinguished from "white ASL" not only by lexical differences (which we did see) but also by differences in phonological and syntactic structure. It may be that the African American participants in our study did not produce this variety as a result of the Observer's Paradox; it may be that the variation does not manifest itself in the target variables that we chose. At any rate, this is clearly a case where more research is necessary, research that starts with data collected in a way that takes better account of the Observer's Paradox—data collected, for example, exclusively by African American Deaf researchers with no hearing or Caucasian researchers near the collection site. Another possible explanation might be that the factors of deafness and minority language status within the context of a strong majority language and culture simply override or level the effects of gender and social class differences and to a lesser extent (given a segregated educational system) ethnic ones. The shift that Padden (1998, 94) describes from "essentially a one-class community" to one with a growing professional class will no doubt eventually be reflected in linguistic variation.[5] Finally, the most powerful social factors in the study—region and age—cannot be understood in isolation but within the context of the history of the transmission of ASL and deaf education.

5. Indeed, in examining the location variation in a subset of the project participants ($n = 135$, signers in the four sites with both African American and Caucasian signers), Rose (2000) does find social class to be significant.

Chapter 7

Syntactic Variation: Null Pronoun

Variation in ASL Narratives

We now turn our attention to one kind of syntactic variation, variable subject pronoun presence, or null subject variation, in plain verbs. ASL verbs are usually considered to fall into three main categories: plain verbs, pointing or indicating verbs, and spatial-locative (or classifier) predicates. In the latter two categories, characteristics of the verb forms provide additional real-world information. The most important characteristics of classifier predicates are a handshape that represents some aspect of the size and shape of an entity and a movement that either adds to the size and shape information provided by the handshape or indicates the movement path of the entity in three-dimensional space. Classifier predicates make extensive use of the signing space in meaningful ways by mapping real-world space onto the signing space, such that a right-to-left movement in the signing space, for example, would be used to describe a right-to-left movement of the referent in the real world.

Indicating verbs can provide information about their subject and/or object referent via changes in form. These changes typically involve the location and palm-orientation features of a sign. In example 1, to produce GIVE, a signer's hand would move from an area of space associated with the subject referent (A), to an area associated with the object referent (B). If B were the giver and A the recipient, that act of giving could be represented by example 2.

1. $_A$GIVE$_B$ BOOK.
2. $_B$GIVE$_A$ BOOK.

In an actual conversation, the identity of person A and person B and their associations with particular areas of the signing space would have been previously established in the discourse and would be known by both the signer and the addressee. These associations, along with the directional movement of the verb, provide the addressee with the necessary information to determine the subject's and object's respective referents. Similarly, in the verb FLATTER, the palm orientation indicates the subject and the object: in first person-FLATTER-third person, the orientation of the signer's palm is away from the body, whereas in third person-FLATTER-first person, the orientation of the palm is toward the signer's body. With these verbs, the presence of an overt subject or object pronoun may be considered as providing redundant information. These verbs are sometimes produced with separate signs for subject and object. It appears that this happens for purposes of emphasis or disambiguation and therefore is a function of discourse. Woodward (1973a) explored variation in these indicating verbs (see chapter 1), but we are not discussing variation in this class here.

ASL also has a class of so-called plain verbs (Padden 1988) such as THINK, KNOW, and FEEL, which do not incorporate indications of subject and object into their structure. Although these verbs necessarily move through space, their use of space is articulatory. Plain verbs would theoretically have to cooccur with separate signs for subject and object. However, it has been observed that these plain verbs do not always cooccur with separate signs for subject and object. Rather, subject presence is variable. Our goal in this chapter is to understand why this might be. Although subjects can be full noun phrases, our focus is on subject pronouns. For example, we examine sentences such as PRO.1 THINK ('I think'), which also occurs as (PRO.1) THINK with no overt pronoun sign. This examination of variation between overt and null pronominal subjects is based on a set of naturally occurring narratives extracted from the videotaped corpus used for the analysis of phonological variation.

PREVIOUS RESEARCH ON NULL PRONOUNS

Null pronouns have received considerable attention from linguists working in a number of different frameworks and focusing on a variety of areas of linguistics, including formal syntax, first- and second-language acquisition, and variationist sociolinguistics. Here we selectively review recent work in ASL and in sociolinguistic variation. Although much of the work on spoken language null pronouns undertaken within various formal approaches is not without interest, it is not directly relevant to our concern here. Such work deals with questions such as the properties of languages that permit null subjects and those that do not, including the clustering of other features of the grammar (e.g., subject-verb inversion) with the presence or absence of null subjects rather than with the distribution of null pronouns across linguistic and social factors within a particular language, which is the concern of our study (see e.g., Huang 1984; Hyams 1986; Jaeggli and Safir 1989; White 1989).

NULL SUBJECTS IN ASL

Null subjects have been investigated in ASL, although not from a variationist perspective. The main studies are by Lillo-Martin (1986, 1991), Bahan (1996), and Neidle and associates (Neidle et al. 2000). Lillo-Martin noted that in ASL, null subjects occur with both agreeing, or indicating, and plain verbs. She argued that ASL null subjects are licensed in two different ways. With agreeing verbs, null subjects are licensed by Agreement, as is the case with Spanish and Italian. With plain verbs, null subjects are licensed by Topic, as in Chinese.

Lillo-Martin's explanation has been challenged by Bahan and Neidle et al., who argue that, even with plain verbs, agreement is marked by an optional nonmanual "role prominence marker," defined as "a slight shift in the signer's head and/or torso that attributes role prominence to the referent at the target location" (Aarons et al. 1994, 16). This line of thinking was further developed by Bahan, who concluded that "strong evidence in favor of analyzing head tilt as a nonmanual expression of syntactic subject agreement features comes from the finding that null subjects are licensed by head tilt in the same way that they may be licensed by overt agreement morphology" (1996, 154). Although an examination of a subset of the narratives considered in this study did not find evidence of nonmanual agreement markers (Wulf et al. 1999), the existence or nonexistence of such nonmanual markers is not directly related to the study of null pronoun variation except insofar as they might be hypothesized to correlate positively with null rather than overt pronouns. Because we were unable to code consistently for nonmanual agreement markers in our data, we have not considered them here.

Variationist Studies

Null pronoun variation has long been a central topic in quantitative sociolinguistics, particularly in Portuguese and Spanish. Research has been conducted on Brazilian Portuguese speech and writing (e.g., Naro 1981; Paredes Silva 1993) and on many Spanish dialects, including those of Argentina (Barrenechea and Alonso 1977), Chile (Cifuentes 1980–1981), Puerto Rico (Cameron 1992, 1993, 1996; Hochberg 1986a, 1986b; Morales 1986; Poplack 1980), Spain (Cameron 1992, 1993; Enríquez 1984; Ranson 1991), and Venezuela (Bentivoglio 1987). Research has also included Spanish spoken in Mexican-origin communities in the United States (e.g., Bayley and Pease-Alvarez 1996, 1997; Silva-Corvalán 1982, 1994). To date, however, the patterning of null and overt pronouns in ASL has not been examined from a variationist perspective. In this overview of variationist studies of null pronouns, therefore, we are limited to studies of spoken languages.

Research has been motivated by two main considerations. First, the preponderance of the evidence indicates that null pronoun variation is a classic sociolinguistic variable that is subject to a range of both linguistic and social constraints. Second, null pronoun variation offers a convenient locus to test whether language variation is governed by functional constraints or whether other processes are involved. In Andalucian and popular Caribbean Spanish and in popular Brazilian Portuguese, the distinction between second- and third-person singular is variably neutralized by /s/-deletion, so that Spanish *hablas* (2 sg. present), for example, may be realized as *habla/Ø/*(= 3 sg. present). As it turns out, Spanish and Portuguese dialects that exhibit variable /s/-deletion also exhibit higher overall rates of overt pronoun use than those dialects in which /s/-deletion does not occur (Hochberg 1986a, 1986b; Poplack 1980). This finding has been taken as evidence in support of Kiparsky's hypothesis that "there is a tendency for semantically relevant information to be retained in surface structure" (1982b, 87). To the extent that null pronouns are common with ASL plain verbs, which carry no information about person or number, studies of null pronoun variation in ASL should be able to shed some light on this issue.

The results of a considerable body of research on null pronoun variation in spoken languages are not consistent with a functionalist explanation. Enríquez (1984), for example, in a study of Madrid Spanish, found that morphologically ambiguous verb forms such as the first- and third-person singular imperfect (e.g., *hablaba* ['I, he/she/you (formal) spoke']) were no more likely to have overt pronominal subjects than verb forms that preserve person and number distinctions (e.g., *hablo*, *habla* ['I speak,' 'he/she/you (formal) speak(s)']). Ranson (1991) provided further evidence against a functional explanation of null pronoun variation. In a study of the /s/-deleting Andalucian dialect of Puente Genil, she found that ambiguous verb forms exhibited an effect opposite to what the functional hypothesis predicts. Speakers in her study used more overt pronouns with unambiguous than with ambiguous verbs. Ranson explained this result by showing that, in the vast majority of cases, the subjects of ambiguous verbs could be adduced from the context (1991, 149).

The most extensive examination of the functional compensation hypothesis is by Cameron (1996), who compared null pronoun variation in Puerto Rican and Madrid Spanish. Cameron investigated the difference in rates of pronominal expression of second-person singular *tú* ('you'), where the distinction between second- and third-person singular is neutralized in the /s/-deleting dialect of San Juan but not in the /s/-conserving dialect of Madrid. He showed that the source of the difference in the rate of second-person singular pronominal expression was the way the two dialects treat specific and nonspecific *tú*. Speakers in San Juan and Madrid Spanish exhibit the same pattern with respect to formal ambiguity of person marking on finite verbs. However, San Juan speakers "have re-analyzed the quantitative nature of [–spec] *tú* by analogy to [–spec] *uno* or [–spec] *usted*" (Cameron 1996, 102). This reanalysis, rather than functional compensation, explains the higher incidence of pronominal expression of second-person singular *tú* in San Juan.

Recent studies have not supported a functional explanation for the patterning of null pronoun variation at the clause or sentence level. However, research on both Spanish and Portuguese has shown that the ease with which a pronominal subject may be inferred from the discourse is an important constraint on pronoun absence. Cameron (1992), for example, in addition to showing that null pronoun variation in Puerto Rican and peninsular Spanish is constrained by whether the variable is coreferential with the subject of the immediately preceding tensed verb, demonstrated that pronoun presence or absence is also constrained by what he referred to as "reference chains." Thus, when the target variable was coreferential with the subjects of the two preceding tensed verbs, only 28 percent of pronominal subjects were realized overtly. However, when neither subject of the preceding two tensed verbs was coreferential with the target variable, and the two preceding subjects also differed from one another, 62 percent of pronominal subjects were realized overtly (Cameron 1992, 182).

An alternative model was proposed by Paredes Silva (1993) in a study of written Brazilian Portuguese. Rather than examining coreference as a binomial factor group, Paredes Silva considered the more subtle effects of changes in narrative continuity as expressed by changes in tense or aspect even when there is no change in subject. The model accounts for different types of switch reference, ranging from a switch in which the subject was last mentioned in some other syntactic function to a disrupted connection or a change in topic, regardless of whether the same subject is maintained (Paredes Silva 1993, 43–44). Results of VARBRUL analysis demonstrated the efficacy of the model, which was later adapted by Bayley and Pease-Alvarez (1997) in a study of Mexican immigrant and Chicano children's oral and written narratives.

To summarize, recent sociolinguistic research on null pronoun variation does not support the functional compensation hypothesis, at least not in its strong form. Second, research has established constraints that extend across a number of varieties of Spanish and Portuguese. When a subject differs from the subject of the immediately preceding verb, it is more likely to be expressed overtly. We turn now to the examination of null pronoun variation in the visual-gestural modality, specifically in ASL.

THE DATA

The original goal in this analysis was to sample the entire videotaped corpus of 207 signers and to extract 15 examples per signer of pronoun presence and absence. However, this task rapidly became cumbersome, mainly because it was very difficult to identify sentence boundaries in casual conversation. Although the transcription of multiparty casual conversations in any language presents a challenge, ASL, as well as other sign languages, presents an additional challenge. There is no written form of ASL, so we cannot fall back on the conventions for the construction of sentences, for example, that the use of orthographic systems may provide. When several signers are involved in a conversation with rapid turn taking and much overlap, it becomes even more complicated. When one signer was producing a narrative, we were much better able to reliably identify and agree on sentence and clause boundaries. For this reason we focus on individuals' narratives that occurred spontaneously during the course of the group conversations. Narratives provided relatively well-bounded speech events and reduced the relative frequency of turn taking, shared negotiation of reference, and topic changes. Our study, then, is limited to one type of discourse. Although we have no reason not to believe that the constraints we have identified do not also affect null pronouns in other types of discourse, including multiparty casual conversations, a full account of null pronoun variation in ASL awaits further research.

The revised goal in this study was to identify a narrative of 30 seconds or more to represent each possible combination of region and age group, as these two social constraints had proved significant in the analyses of ASL phonological variation. With seven regions and three age groups, this would have yielded a total of 21 narratives. However, one group from Maryland and one group from Virginia did not produce appropriate narratives, so a total of 19 narratives was used. Given the number of qualifying narratives in the data, it was not possible to produce a perfectly even distribution by gender and ethnicity, but these were balanced to the degree possible. The shortest narrative was 39 seconds and the longest, 170 seconds. Each was spontaneously produced during the course of the free conversation; none of the narratives was specifically elicited. Table 7.1 shows the social and de-mographic characteristics of the narrators whose stories are analyzed here.

TABLE 7.1. *Sociodemographic Characteristics of ASL Narrators and Narrative Topics*

Signer	Region	Age	Gender	Social Class	Ethnicity	Topic
1	Mass.	15+	F	MC	C	Flu
2	Mass.	25+	M	WC	AA	Reunion
3	Mass.	55+	F	WC	C	Cards
4	Md.	25+	M	WC	C	Hitchhiker
5	Md.	55+	M	WC	C	New car
6	Va.	55+	M	WC	C	Tobacco story
7	Va.	55+	F	MC	C	Break-in
8	La.	15+	M	WC	AA	Foot race
9	La.	26+	F	WC	C	Casino
10	La.	55+	F	WC	AA	Getting sick
11	Kans.	15+	F	MC	C	Escaped lizard
12	Kans.	26+	M	MC	C	Moment of silence
13	Kans.	55+	M	WC	AA	Encounter
14	Calif.	15+	F	MC	C	Busted
15	Calif.	26+	F	WC	AA	Interview
16	Calif.	55+	F	WC	AA	House burning
17	Wash.	15+	M	WC	C	Canadian traffic
18	Wash.	26+	M	MC	C	At college
19	Wash.	55+	M	WC	C	Run over

Each story was glossed in its entirety. Narratives included both brief and extensive accounts of personal experience as well as reactions to current events. The following example, told by a male resident of Kansas, illustrates the briefer narratives:

AWFUL! PRO.1 THINK-OF-SOMETHING. POSS.1 CLASS index-location. PRO.1 TEACH INTERPRET PRACTICE PROGRAM index-location. HAVE TWO STUDENT FROM O-K-A C-I-T-Y index-location. THAT EXACTLY ONE WEEK (false start)—BOMB ONE WEEK LATER (headnod). ANNOUNCE HAVE TIME NINE-OCLOCK index-location SILENCE FOR ONE MINUTE. FINE. DURING POSS.1 CLASS TIME EIGHT T-(O) TEN. FINE. RESPECT PRO.1 (false start) (rs: PRO.3). PRO.3 WANT HONOR. FINE. WELL GET-UP (cl: people standing in a semicircle). BE-QUIET. STAND. BE-QUIET. (pause) (gesture) #THEN FEW MINUTE PRO.1 OPEN-EYES. THINK ENOUGH TIME. FINISH PRO.1 (cl: eyes look up). (rs: be startled). HOLD-IT. SILLY! STUDENT CRY+++. LOOK-AT. WOW TOUCH-HEART (rs: index-location). FIND POSS.3 SEVERAL FRIENDS DIE index-location SAME AS. S-O PRO.3 KNOW SOME PEOPLE index-location. WOW LOOK-AT WONDER TOUCH-HEART WOW.

'How awful! That makes me think of something that happened in the class I teach over in the interpreter training program. There are two students in it from Oklahoma City. This was exactly one week— this was one week after the bombing. It was announced that there would be a moment of silence at nine o'clock. No problem. It would be during my class that runs from eight to ten o'clock. It's important to have a time to pay respect, and that's what the students wanted to do. So we all got up. We were completely silent. We just stood there and kept quiet. After a few minutes, I opened my eyes because I thought enough time had gone by. When I looked up, I was really surprised to see one of the students really crying. Wow—that sure got to me. It turned out she'd had friends who died there. So she actually knew people involved. Wow—I couldn't imagine how she felt. Seeing that was really moving.'[1]

---

1. The glossing style used in this and the other narratives was intended to aid coders to focus on pronouns and is not strict with respect to notational conventions. A number of features are not indicated (e.g., representation of classifiers). The translation is intended to provide readers without ASL with a sense of the types of narratives coded.

All +animate subjects associated with plain predicates were identified, and each token was coded according to a number of factors. Because this is the first variationist examination of null pronouns in ASL, we coded broadly. Given the modality differences, we considered it possible that constraints might differ from those that apply to spoken languages. On the other hand, because both modalities produce natural human languages, we also recognized that ASL might follow patterns observed in the study of spoken pro-drop languages. The linguistic factors we coded for include coreference with the subject of the preceding clause, person, number, constructed action/dialogue, and English influence. The social factors we coded for are gender and age.

Coreference

As noted in the review of previous research, coreference with the subject of the preceding tensed verb has often been shown to be a robust constraint on subject pronoun behavior in spoken languages. In order to test the influence of this factor on a language in the visual-gestural modality, we coded tokens for switch or coreference with the subject of the preceding verb. That is, is the referent of the subject of a given clause or verb in a narrative the same as the referent of the subject in the clause or verb immediately preceding (as in example 3), or is it different (as in example 4)? Our hypothesis is that subject pronouns are more likely to appear when there is a switch in reference to clarify who the subject of the verb is; a switch reference environment without a subject pronoun might easily result in ambiguity:

3. (Ø) STAND. (Ø) BE-QUIET.
    '(We) just stood there. (We) were completely silent.'
4. STUDENT CRY+++. (Ø) LOOK-AT.
    'A student was really crying. (I) looked at her and reacted.'

Person and Number

Coding for person and number was straightforward. Because there were very few tokens of second- and third-person plural ($n = 4$ and $n = 14$, respectively), these factors were combined. Additionally, six tokens could not be coded for number because the referent was unresolvably ambiguous. These tokens were excluded from the person/number analysis.

The five factors in this group were first-person singular, second-person singular, third-person singular, first-person plural, and second-person/third-person plural.

Sentence Type

Each token was coded by the type of sentence in which it occurred: declarative, yes-no question, *wh*-question, conditional, and so forth. Because only an extremely small number of sentences were not basic declaratives, this factor group was not used in the final analysis.

Constructed Dialogue and Constructed Action

Tannen (1986) suggests the term *constructed dialogue* for a speaker's act of directly reporting what others have said. Winston (1992) observes that ASL has both constructed dialogue and constructed action, as signers frequently perform acts of demonstrating what others have done (see also Metzger 1995). Constructed action/dialogue is a discourse strategy in which reference, as well as the meaning of the utterance, depends largely on context. A signer takes on the role of some referent, which frequently also involves adopting certain behaviors, features of appearance, and other characteristics of that referent. We hypothesized that comprehension of the discourse would be facilitated by the established context and less dependent on frequent articulation of pronominal subjects. It is then reasonable to expect a lower rate of subject pronouns in utterances that include constructed action and dialogue.

English Influence

The coexistence of ASL and English in the Deaf communities of the United States means that most Deaf people are bilingual to a greater or lesser extent and creates a wealth of language contact phenomena, including some unique to contact between languages in different modalities (Lucas and Valli 1992).[2] Many ASL signers, therefore, use structures

2. This is not to say, of course, that most Deaf people are fluent in spoken English. However, because ASL does not have a commonly agreed upon written form, Deaf children are normally expected to acquire written English as part of their schooling.

or expressions that result from the intimate contact of ASL with spoken and written English. For example, the lexicon of ASL contains several signs that have developed over time from the repeated fingerspelling of the associated English words. These signs are now lexicalized and have undergone additional phonological changes that differentiate them from letter-by-letter fingerspelling of the English word. Beyond the natural outcomes of language contact, which are generally accepted and usually go unnoticed, some signers may also exhibit unexpected or unusual English-influenced structures that may be judged as ungrammatical and unacceptable by native ASL users. We hypothesized that use of these types of structures may have a relationship to subject pronoun presence or absence. Because English is not a pro-drop language, whereas ASL is, a signer might be more likely to use a subject pronoun while "under the influence of English," so to speak.

Utterances 5 and 6 are examples from the data that exhibit obvious English influence:

5. BUT THRILL (claps hands) L- HAPPY LIZARD I-S #BACK HOME.
   'But (he) was thrilled! (claps hands) The liz- (he's) happy the lizard is back home.'
6. ANYWAY PRO.1pl GET HOME.
   'So anyway, we got home.'

In example 5, the English present singular copula is present through fingerspelling. The copula, however, is not part of ASL grammar, so I-S is an example of English influence. Without the presence of the fingerspelled English copula, the utterance would be judged as ASL. In example 6, the influence of English is identifiable in the use of GET. In ASL, GET is not used with locatives to construct the meaning of "arrive," as it is in English. The acceptable ASL alternative was provided by the same signer just shortly afterward, when she performed a repair by replacing GET with ARRIVE.

Other features of English influence observed in the data include silent mouthing of an equivalent English word instead of producing the expected manual sign, nonlexicalized initialization of signs (replacing the handshape of a sign with a different handshape representing the first letter of a semantically similar English word), and the use of word-by-word transliterations of English colloquialisms and idioms. In no case was an utterance coded as having English influence based on the presence or absence of a subject pronoun.

Gender and Age

Tokens were coded as being produced by a male or female signer aged 15–25, 26–54, or 55 and older. As we saw in chapter 2, the choice of these age groups for the project as a whole was motivated by the history of language in education policies in U.S. Deaf schools in the past century. As we have seen, these policies affected the choice of language for classroom instruction and the relative status of ASL and English. English was—and to a certain extent still is—perceived in the Deaf community to have a higher status than ASL and to be an indicator of both intelligence and education. These attitudes might very well have an impact on the occurrence of subject pronouns. That is, the influence of the structure of English might lead a signer to produce a subject pronoun with a plain verb, when, absent such influence, the pronoun might not be produced.

RESULTS

As with the phonological variables, the variable subject data were analyzed with Rand and Sankoff's (1990) Macintosh version of VARBRUL. Overall, even with plain verbs, signers omitted manual pronouns more often than they supplied them. In our corpus, only 35 percent of pronominal subjects are marked with manual signs. The results of the multivariate analysis show that the presence of a subject pronoun with plain verbs is conditioned by multiple constraints. Statistically significant factor groups are English influence, person/number, coreference, constructed action/dialogue, age, and gender. That is, all of the groups except for sentence type proved to have a significant effect on signers' choice between null and overt pronouns. Table 7.2 shows the VARBRUL weights and percentages of overt pronoun use for all significant factor groups, with pronoun presence as the application value. Factors groups are displayed in the order in which they were selected in the step-up step-down analysis. Because this is the first examination of this phenomenon in ASL, we cannot be sure whether pronoun presence or pronoun absence represents the marked variant. We chose pronoun presence as marked, and therefore the application value, for two reasons: to enable more straightforward comparisons with the results of studies of other languages and to emphasize the fact that even though we chose to use only plain verbs, overall results show less than 40 percent occurrence of subject pronouns.

TABLE 7.2. *Null Pronoun Variation: VARBRUL Results (Application Value: +Overt Pronoun)*

Factor Group	Factor	VARBRUL Weight	%	n
English influence	Yes	.763	63	52
	No	.459	31	377
Person/number	1 sg.	.610	41	261
	2/3 pl.	.471	39	18
	2 sg.	.456	38	34
	3 sg.	.282	21	95
	1 pl.	.210	13	15
Coreference with subject of preceding clause	Switch reference	.631	46	169
	Same reference	.414	28	260
Age	55+	.602	42	136
	15–54	.452	32	293
Gender	F	.585	41	218
	M	.413	29	211
Constructed action	None	.571	40	224
	Action	.422	29	205
Total	Input	.325	35	429

Note: χ2/cell = 0.9857; all factor groups significant at *p*<.05.

English Influence

English influence proved to be the strongest constraint on variation, although this finding must be tempered by the fact that the distribution of tokens is highly unbalanced. However, it is worth noting that while only 52 tokens were +English, these tokens were contributed collectively by more than half of the signers. As predicted, an environment characterized by other types of obvious influence from English favored pronoun presence (*p* =.763) while the absence of English influence disfavored pronoun use (*p* = .459).

Coreference

Coreference with the subject of the preceding verb constrained pronoun subject variation as predicted. Pronominal subjects were more likely to be produced in switch-reference environments than in environments in which the target variable was coreferential with the subject of the preceding verb. Only 28 percent ($p = .414$) of subjects that were coreferential with the subject of the preceding verb were expressed by overt pronouns. In contrast, 46 percent ($p = .631$) of subjects that involved a switch in reference showed pronoun presence.

Person and Number

As in studies of other languages, first-person singular pronominal subjects were most likely to be present ($p = .610$) (cf. Bayley and Pease-Alvarez 1997; Cameron 1992). Third-person singular pronouns were much less likely to be realized overtly ($p = .282$). The order of the remaining factors was 2 pl./3 pl. ($p = .471$) > 2 sg. ($p = .456$) > 1 pl. ($p = .210$). The numbers of tokens in the second-person/third-person plural and the first-person plural groups ($n = 18$ and 15, respectively) each represent less than 5 percent of the data and are likely too small to provide a reliable quantitative analysis. One contributing cause to the greater likelihood of overt pronoun use for first-person singular concerns the fact that the signers (and speakers) have only a binomial choice between an overt pronoun and null. Other than in special discourse contexts, signers and speakers are not likely to refer to themselves by name (i.e., a full NP). With third-person pronouns, the choice is trinomial: overt pronoun, null pronoun, or full NP. Thus, whenever the context requires an expressed subject, signers and speakers have essentially no choice but to use a pronoun to refer to themselves. However, in ordinary discourse, users of pro-drop languages may choose between a pronoun and a full NP to refer to a third person.

Constructed Action

Constructed action/dialogue environments also had a significant effect on subject pronoun variation. These environments disfavored the presence of subject pronouns ($p = .422$), whereas their absence favored pronoun presence ($p = .571$). Initially, three separate factors had been established for this group: constructed action, constructed dialogue, and absence of either. However, analysis of the resulting VARBRUL weightings showed no significant difference between the results for action and for dialogue, and because constructed dialogue is a special instance of constructed action, these two factors were combined into a single factor.

Gender

The results for gender can be analyzed from multiple perspectives. Women favored subject pronoun presence ($p = .585$), whereas men disfavored it ($p = .413$). It may be that women produce more pronouns than men because overt pronouns represent a prestige variant. As mentioned earlier, ASL has made great strides in the last 35 years in gaining recognition as a natural human language. Nevertheless, English, which is not a pro-drop language, enjoys a certain prestige in the Deaf community, in recognition of the fact that access to power and resources is still very restricted for people who do not have a working command of English.

Another possible explanation for the gender results would recognize how women in the United States are socialized from the earliest years and how they come to perform on scales measuring features of conversational interaction such as feedback and clarity (Tannen 1986). It may be that these women are working harder in specific ways to ensure their message gets across clearly, padding their message with a larger amount of redundant information in an attempt to minimize possible ambiguity or confusion.

Age

The results for the younger and middle age groups were not significantly different. Together, they disfavored pronoun presence ($p = .452$) whereas the older group favored it ($p = .602$). Although social constraints such as gender, age, and ethnicity might be common to all studies of sociolinguistic variation, many of these need to be articulated more fully when they are put into research practice in a particular community such as the American Deaf community. As we have seen in the results for the phonological variables, even seemingly simple notions such as age cannot be borrowed whole from studies of variation in spoken language communities. Constraints such as "age" have labels with a common application but can have a different meaning considering the history of Deaf communities in this country.

As we explained in chapter 3, age as a sociolinguistic variable may have effects on linguistic variation in sign languages that are different from those in spoken languages because of the differences in language policies in Deaf schools in the last century. Thus, while observed differences in the signing of older and younger people may exhibit the same pattern as age group differences or language change over time (such as occurs in all languages), these differences may also be the result of changes in educational policies such as the shift from oralism to Total Communication or from Total Communication to a bilingual-bicultural approach (Padden 1998). These language policies affected not only what language was used in the classroom but also teacher hiring (i.e., Deaf signers of ASL or hearing teachers who knew no ASL) and the practices of adult language models. These language policies would have affected deaf children's access to appropriate language models, and this access may have varied across time to such an extent as to affect the kind of variation we see in ASL today. Participants who were 25 or younger at the time of data collection began school at a time when a shift toward greater use of ASL in the classroom was occurring, whereas most signers in the middle and older age groups attended residential schools at a time when policies promoting either oral communication only or English-based invented sign systems prevailed—a possible explanation for the pattern we see here.

DISCUSSION AND CONCLUSIONS

In the most general sense, the results for null pronoun variation parallel the results for the phonological variables analyzed in previous chapters. That is, the results for linguistic factors are very similar to the results of studies of variation in spoken languages, while the results for the social factors, particularly for age, are best explained by reference to the social historical circumstances of Deaf communities in the United States. Thus, as in Portuguese and Spanish, a switch in reference favors an overt pronominal subject, even though in the ASL narratives considered here the majority of subjects of plain verbs that involve a switch in reference are realized as null. In addition, as in studies of spoken languages, in the ASL narratives examined here, first-person singular pronouns are most likely to be overt, and plural subjects in general are more likely to be null than are singular subjects.

Turning to the influence of English, the effects of language contact have been a central concern in several studies of Mexican-American Spanish (e.g., Silva-Corvalán 1994; Bayley and Pease-Alvarez 1996, 1997). These studies tested the hypothesis that the influence of English would manifest itself in a higher incidence of overt pronouns, the option that is congruent with English, in the Spanish of speakers who were in the process of shifting to English. The results of three separate studies failed to confirm the hypothesis. Silva-Corvalán found that English-dominant bilinguals in Los Angeles do not express a higher overall percentage of subjects overtly, although they do not always adhere to the same constraints on subject absence as Spanish-dominant speakers (1994, 162). Bayley and Pease-Alvarez (1996), in a study of the Spanish of Mexican immigrant and Chicano children representing four different immigrant groups, found no significant difference in the rate of pronominal expression across immigrant generations. In a later study of oral and written narratives by Mexican immigrant and Chicano children in northern California, Bayley and Pease-Alvarez (1997) reported that English-dominant children were less likely to use overt pronouns than were children born in Mexico. That is, the results were the opposite of what an interference hypothesis would predict.

The ASL results for the influence of English thus represent a departure from the results of studies of contact between spoken languages. However, it should be noted that this study operationalized the influence of English in a manner different from that of the studies of U.S. Spanish varieties. Here, we considered whether the influence of English was obvious in the immediate environment of the target variable in the form of English word order, fingerspelling, and so forth. The studies of U.S. Spanish we have been considering, in contrast, operationalized English influence in a much more global manner by dividing speakers according to immigrant generations or depth of ties to the United States. The results of this study, then, suggest that one way in which the possible effects of contact between null subject and non-null subject languages might be investigated in more detail is by examining possible correlations between rate of overt pronoun use and contact phenomena such as lexical borrowings, calques, and changes in word order in the immediate linguistic environment.

As to the question of functional compensation that has motivated much of the research on null pronoun variation in spoken languages, our results suggest that the need to preserve a surface morphological distinction has relatively little explanatory power. ASL plain verbs carry no indication of person; however, we still see clear differences in the likelihood of subject pronoun absence by person and number. Although we have not explored the question in depth here, the results for person and number in this study suggest that factors other than the need to preserve a surface distinction are better able to explain null pronoun variation.[3]

As we have suggested, the results for gender are subject to varying interpretations. The fact that women tend to use more overt pronouns than men may be attributed higher status accorded to English and the general tendency of women to prefer prestige forms. On the other hand, it might also be attributed to the greater attentiveness to clarity on the part of the women in this study. However, we do not wish to overinterpret the results from a small-scale study. Whereas the results for the phonological variables are based on data from a reasonable representation of the Deaf community across the United States, the results discussed in this chapter are based on only 19 signers, selected because they happened to produce narratives that were appropriate for analysis. A full analysis of the correlations between social factors and the extent of null pronoun usage awaits larger studies based on more representative samples of the Deaf community.

To summarize, the results of this study suggest that null pronoun variation in ASL is systematic and subject to many of the same constraints observed in spoken languages. More detailed examination of the effects of the various constraints, however, is dependent on the examination of many more tokens than we have analyzed here.

3. Spoken languages (such as Chinese) that allow null subjects but do not mark person or number on the verb would of course provide a better comparison than Spanish or Portuguese for null pronoun variation in ASL. However, to our knowledge, there are no variationist studies of null pronoun variation in Chinese or similar languages.

Chapter 8

Lexical Variation

As we explained in chapter 2, the last part of each data collection session
consisted in showing the participants a set of 34 stimuli—mostly pictures
but fingerspelling in some cases—to elicit their responses. The selection of
the 34 stimuli was motivated by earlier work on lexical variation in ASL,
work that we described in chapter 1. We were interested in reexamining
specific claims made about the correlation of lexical variation with social
factors such as region, ethnicity, and age and claims pertaining to the
course of language change. Most of the early work on lexical variation in
ASL was done during the mid-1970s, and we were interested in seeing how
the results of our analysis compared to the results of those studies. It is important to note that these early studies are actually studies of phonological
variation, as they almost invariably focus on variation in some parameter
of signs, such as handshape (pinky extension, thumb extension), location
(on the face, on the hands), or handedness (two-handed or one-handed).

For example, in comparing signs that can be produced on the face or
on the hands, Woodward, Erting, and Oliver (1976) claimed that New
Orleans signers and Caucasian signers produced more signs on the face
than did signers from Atlanta and African American signers; they make
no specific claims about language change. Woodward and DeSantis, in
their 1977 study of two-handed signs that can be signed one-handed,
claim that Southerners, older signers, and African American signers produce more two-handed signs than do non-Southerners, younger signers,
and Caucasian signers. They describe the variation between two-handed
and one-handed signs as "one on-going change" (1977b, 329) seen in
both ASL and French Sign Language. One of the stated goals of this
study was "to specify how the change is in the process of occurring"
(329) and to demonstrate that the rate of change depends on specific social factors such as age and ethnicity. Frishberg (1975) also examined
variation in location and in handedness. More recently, Liddell and
Johnson observed that "Assimilation of the hand configuration of the
weak hand to that of the strong hand in two-handed signs is quite common" and that other examples of assimilation include "two-handed

signs becoming one-handed as a result of assimilation to a one-handed sign in the same string" (1989, 252). Shroyer and Shroyer (1984) also present a broad nontechnical picture of lexical variation in ASL. For example, although many of the variants that they present are actually related phonological variants of the same basic sign, they present them as separate variants.

In this chapter, then, we examine the results of our analysis of the 34 signs, and we focus on three specific questions:

1. What is the relative proportion of lexical variation to phonological variation within lexical items? That is, is a given concept represented by a number of lexical items that are unrelated to each other phonologically, or is a given concept represented by one or two lexical items, each of which shows several phonological variants?

2. Is there any semantic or functional pattern in the variation? That is, do signs for food and animals show more variation than others? Do nouns show more variation than verbs, adjectives, or adverbs?

3. In terms of phonological variation, do we have any evidence of the language change in progress suggested by the earlier studies (e.g., signs produced at the head being produced on the hands, two-handed signs becoming one-handed, assimilation, and so forth)? And what about lexical innovation, as in AFRICA and JAPAN—how widespread is the use of the recently introduced signs for these two concepts? In the case of JAPAN, the traditional ASL sign is a J handshape, twisting at the corner of the eye; both one-handed and two-handed versions occur. In Japanese Sign Language (JSL), JAPAN is a two-handed sign in which the thumb and the index fingers trace the islands of Japan. This sign has been borrowed into ASL. In traditional ASL, AFRICA is an A handshape that circles the face and sometimes ends on the nose. Some signers feel that this sign is racist, with its focus on physical characteristics, and some signers prefer the newer sign that traces the outline of the continent. This is not a sign that originated in Africa; rather it seems that it was proposed by one person in the course of a formal lecture. Recent anecdotal evidence suggests that both African and African American signers are expressing a preference for the A handshape version that

simply circles the face and are *rejecting* the "new" sign in part because it closely resembles the sign for a part of the female anatomy (Anthony Aramburo, personal communication).

SEPARATE LEXICAL VARIANTS OR PHONOLOGICAL VARIATION?

The first issue is whether a given concept is represented by a number of lexical items that are unrelated to each other phonologically or whether it is represented by one or two lexical items, each of which has several phonological variants. We can illustrate this with two signs, PIZZA and BANANA.

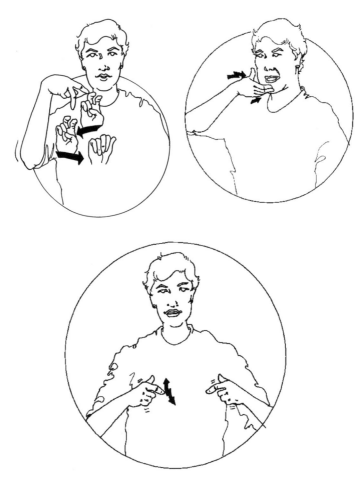

FIGURE 8.1. *Lexical variants of* PIZZA

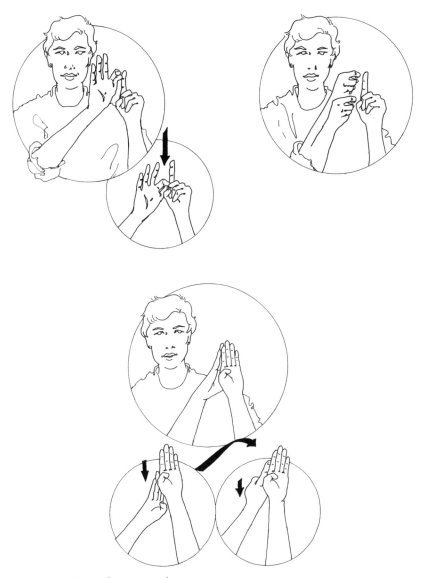

FIGURE 8.2. *Lexical variants of* BANANA

Pizza is commonly represented fingerspelling, sometimes with every letter of the English word represented—#PIZZA—and sometimes with the i deleted—#PZZA—or simply as #ZZA, with the two z's being simultaneously produced with a bent V handshape. However, there exist several other signs for PIZZA that have no relation to fingerspelling whatsoever— a bent B handshape, palm up, fingertips pointing toward the mouth, a two-handed sign with bent L handshapes representing the round shape of a pizza, and so forth. These are clearly separate lexical variants, unrelated phonologically to each other or to fingerspelling.

BANANA also has a number of separate, phonologically unrelated variants, but at first glance, separating out what is truly a separate variant from what is a phonological variant of another variant is not always completely straightforward. For example, one variant consists of the nondominant hand in a 1 handshape (extended index, all other fingers and thumb closed). The dominant hand moves down from the tip of the nondominant index to its base as if removing the peel of the banana. The handshape of the dominant hand can be an F, an A, an X, a 1, a G, or a V. This is one variant with five "subvariants," distinct from another variant in which the nondominant hand is a flat O or a B handshape and the dominant hand is a flat O or a 5, again moving down or sweeping around the nondominant hand. This categorization of variants and subvariants seems much preferable to the alternative, which would be to say that BANANA has eight separate and unrelated variants, especially when it is clear that the subvariants share many phonological features and usually differ in only one feature, usually the handshape.

The responses to the 34 stimuli, then, were categorized as follows: variants that were clearly unrelated phonologically to other variants were counted as separate lexical items; variants such as the ones described for BANANA (and, for that matter, for variations in the fingerspelling of *pizza*) were grouped together as subvariants of one variant (See Appendix B for a full description of all variants). Table 8.1 shows the total number of variants and subvariants for each stimulus.

The separate lexical variants are numbered consecutively, and the number of subvariants associated with each separate variant appears in parentheses next to the variant. Thus, AFRICA has five distinct variants, and Variant 2 has four subvariants; DOG has three distinct variants, and Variant 1 has four subvariants, and so forth. The separate lexical variants were assigned their number in order of their mention on the data tapes, so that Variant 1 was the first one mentioned on the first tape reviewed, Variant 2 the second, and so forth. On some tapes, Variants 1 and 2 were not mentioned at all, and only higher-numbered variants occurred, for example. When we compared the numbered variants across all seven sites in the study, we found that for 27 of the 34 signs, some form of Variant 1 was shared by all sites. That is, 79 percent of the signs

TABLE 8.1. *Variants and Subvariants for Each Stimulus*

Sign	Overall Number of Lexical Variants and Their Phonological Variants												
AFRICA	1	2(4)	3	4	5								
ARREST	1(2)	2	3	4	5	6	7	8	9	10	11		
BANANA	1(4)	2(3)	3(2)	4(3)	5								
CAKE	1(9)	2	3	4									
CANDY	1(2)	2(2)	3(2)	4(4)	5	6							
CEREAL	1(4)	2(2)	3	4	5	6	7	8	9	10	11		
CHEAT	1(4)	2	3(4)	4	5	6	7	8	9	10	11		
CHERRIES	1(4)	2(3)	3(4)	4(2)	5								
CHICKEN	1(4)	2	3	4	5								
COMPUTER	1(4)	2(3)	3(4)	4	5								
DEER	1(4)	2	3(2)	4									
DELICIOUS	1(4)	2	3(3)	4									
DOG	1(4)	2	3										
EARLY	1(3)	2	3	4	5	6	7	8	9	10	11	12	13
FAINT	1(4)	2(6)	3(4)	4	5	6	7	8	9	10	11		
FEAR	1(5)	2(4)	3										
GLOVES	1(5)	2											
JAPAN	1(2)	2(3)											
MICROWAVE	1(8)	2	3	4	5	6							
MITTENS	1(4)	2(4)	3	4(2)	5								
PANTS, men	1(4)	2	3	4									
PANTS, women	1(3)	2(2)	3	4									
PERFUME	1(2)	2(4)	3(3)	4	5	6							
PIZZA	1(4)	2(3)	3(4)	4(3)	5								
RABBIT	1(4)	2	3										
RELAY	1(4)	2(7)	3	4	5	6							
RUN	1(4)	2	3	4									
SANDWICH	1(4)	2	3	4(4)	5								
SNOW	1(4)												
SOON	1(3)	2	3	4(4)	5	6	7	8(2)	9				
SQUIRREL	1(5)	2	3(2)	4(4)									
THIEF			3	4	5								
STEAL	1	2											
TOMATO	1(2)	2	3	4	5								
Phonological variation:	31	14	11	8									
	34	34	34	34									
	91%	41%	32%	23.5%	[For variants 5–13, only one sign (SOON) has phonological variation in one variant]								

Note: Numbers in parentheses indicate subvariants.

had a shared variant across all sites for Variant 1. This number includes cases in which both Variant 2 and Variant 3 might also be shared across all groups. When considered without Variants 2 and 3, Variant 1 was shared for 20 out of 34 signs (58.8 percent), and Variant 2 or 3 (independent of Variant 1) was shared for 3 signs (8 percent). There were no shared variants at all for CEREAL.

We also see from table 8.1 that Variants 1, 2, and 3 have the highest number of subvariants: Variant 1 usually has the highest number for each sign, with subvariants found in 31 of the 34 signs, or 91 percent. Variant 2 has subvariants in 14 signs (41 percent), Variant 3 in 11 (32 percent), and Variant 4 in 8 (23.5 percent). For Variants 5–13, only one sign, SOON, has two subvariants in one variant. This seems to indicate that the lexical items most frequently used and most widely distributed also have the highest number of phonological variants, and this is true even with the lexical items such as EARLY that have the highest number of distinct lexical variants. So even though EARLY has 13 distinct variants, only Variant 1, the most widely used, has subvariants. There would seem to be a link, then, between frequency of use, distribution, and phonological variation.

As concerns the second question, table 8.2 shows the functional breakdown of the signs.

We see from this that the signs having the highest overall number of distinct variants are EARLY (13), ARREST (11), FAINT (11), CEREAL (11), CHEAT (10), and SOON (9). Nouns average four distinct variants each, verbs 8.7, and adverbs 11. (There was only one adjective stimulus, DELICIOUS, not enough to classify.) Both the verb and adverb distinct variant averages are markedly higher than the noun average, and were the verbs and adverbs to be combined, the average of distinct variants would be 9.5. Because adverbs such as EARLY can function as predicates in ASL (e.g., BOY EARLY, 'The boy is early'), combining the verbs and the adverbs is not unreasonable. It would seem, then, that lexical items that function as predicates have the highest number of distinct variants. This is a somewhat surprising finding because we expected nouns to show the most variation. (The noun with the highest number of distinct variants is CEREAL.)

The explanation of these findings may have to do in part with the grammatical function of the verbs and adverbs; it may also have to do with their morphological structure. Many of the variants for ARREST, FAINT, and RUN, for example, are examples of classifier predicates, that

TABLE 8.2. *Functional Breakdown of Stimuli*

Nouns	# of Variants	Verbs	# of Variants
AFRICA	5	ARREST	11
BANANA	5	CHEAT	10
CAKE	4	FAINT	11
CANDY	6	RUN	3
CEREAL	11	Average:	8.7
CHERRIES	5		
CHICKEN	5		
COMPUTER	5	Adverbs	
DEER	5	EARLY	13
DOG	4	SOON	9
FEAR	3	Average:	11
GLOVES	2		
JAPAN	2		
MICROWAVE	6		
MITTENS	5		
PANTS, m & w	4	Adjectives	
PERFUME	6	DELICIOUS	4
PIZZA	5		
RABBIT	3		
RELAY	6		
SANDWICH	5		
SNOW	1		
SQUIRREL	4		
THIEF	3		
TOMATO	5		
Average:	4.4		

is, predicates that consist of a movement and a handshape that together represent various aspects of the size, shape, and movement of an entity in three-dimensional space. Many of the nouns in our data clearly have their origins in classifiers, with the possible exception of CANDY, DOG, FEAR, and RELAY. However, although they have classifier origins, they are also completely lexicalized at this point. They refer to a specific entity now and no longer to the activity that led to their lexicalization. For example, a common sign for CEREAL looks like a classifier predicate that could be glossed BRING-FOOD-TO-MOUTH-WITH-SPOON; signs for GLOVES look like predicates that could be glossed as PULL-ON-GLOVES. However, these signs do not refer to the actions of bringing food to the mouth or pulling on gloves; they refer to the *nouns* associated with these actions.

So although the classifier origins of these nouns are plain to see, these signs are not "active" classifiers; they are lexicalized.[1] In contrast, although each community we interviewed provided a sign for ARREST (i.e., attesting to the fact that there is an established lexical item for this concept in each community), ARREST is an action verb, not a noun, and its status as a verb may make its classifier features not only visible but available to signers for immediate productive use and hence for variation. ARREST revealed 11 distinct variants, including alternately grasping the wrists, putting on handcuffs, grasping the nondominant index finger, and so forth. In short, the verbs in the sample do not seem to be as far along in the process of lexicalization precisely because they represent actions and not things and hence may be more prone to variation.

Finally, as we see in table 8.3, signs for food average 5.7 distinct variants and signs for animals average 4, so variation with food and animal signs does not seem to be exceptionally high. As we saw earlier, the highest number of distinct variants is seen with verbs and adverbs.

Before addressing the third question, we provide a brief summary of lexical variation in the data as it relates to each one of the six social factors—region, age, ethnicity, gender, social class, and language background. A brief account is given of the overall findings for each factor.

TABLE 8.3. *Semantic Breakdown of Stimuli: Food and Animals*

Food	# of Variants	Animals	# of Variants
BANANA	5	CHICKEN	5
CAKE	4	DEER	5
CANDY	6	DOG	3
CEREAL	11	RABBIT	3
CHICKEN	5	SQUIRREL	4
PIZZA	5		
SANDWICH	5	Average:	4
TOMATO	5		
Average:	5.7		

1. These may be related to the large attested class of noun-verb pairs in ASL (Supalla and Newport 1978) in which the members of each pair share handshape, location, and orientation and differ only in their movement specification. Examples of these pairs include FLY-AIRPLANE and SIT-CHAIR.

As we mentioned earlier, for 27 of the 34 signs, Variant 1 was shared across all seven sites. This brings to mind the observations by Croneberg (1965) and Padden and Humphries (1988) about the close social ties and the sharing of ASL among American Deaf people. These observations seem to be clearly born out in our lexical data: Despite some forms unique to each site, there are also lexical forms shared across the seven sites. And an understanding of why this might be so comes directly from the history of the deaf community and of deaf education, as outlined in chapter 3 (see figure 3.1). Residential schools in our seven sites were very commonly founded either by graduates of ASD or by graduates of other schools themselves educated by ASD graduates or instructors. What figure 3.1 in chapter 3 shows is the steady progression of ASL users from Hartford, Connecticut, all the way to Washington. Based on this picture, it is not at all surprising that signers in our seven sites share lexical variants. Upon hearing about our findings, Robert C. Johnson, editor in the Graduate School and Research Department at Gallaudet University, remarked that "It really is an *American* sign language" (personal communication, April 2000), and this would seem to be the case. And of course, the facts about language use in residential schools are supplemented by the powerful role played by sports, civic, and religious organizations in the deaf community, organizations that have had, since their inception, the effect of bringing into contact signers from all over the country.

Some forms unique to each site were produced, and two sites emerged as having high numbers of unique forms: Boston with eleven and Kansas/Missouri with eight. This result for Boston is not at all surprising in light of the patterns of phonological variation that we saw in Massachusetts. Boston signers seem to be generally conservative in their usage and to diverge from the rest of the country. The fairly high number of unique forms in Kansas is somewhat more puzzling.

Age

Although there were 10 signs shared by at least two of the three age groups, there were also some variants unique to each age group. Older signers produced unique forms for PERFUME, SNOW, and SOON; the middle-aged signers fingerspelled #BANANA and #GLOVES and had unique forms for DELICIOUS, MICROWAVE, and RELAY, the telephone service provided for communication between hearing and Deaf people; the younger signers had unique signs for DOG and PIZZA. It is interesting that the middle-aged signers have unique forms for MICROWAVE and RELAY, as signs for these concepts were introduced in their generation. This may be because the coining of signs for a new concept may lead to the coexistence of several variants before a community settles on one or two variants.

Ethnicity

For 28 of the 34 signs, the African American signers in the sample use signs that the Caucasian signers do not. The only 6 signs for which the African American signers do not have their own unique variants are CAKE, MICROWAVE, JAPAN, SANDWICH, THIEF, and STEAL. Furthermore, whereas the Caucasian signers have fingerspelled variants of ARREST, BANANA, FEAR, and GLOVES, the African American signers do not. And whereas the African American signers fingerspell DEER and RABBIT, the Caucasian signers do not. Most striking, however, is the large number of signs used only by African Americans. Woodward and Erting (1975) hypothesized that African American signers tend to use older forms of signs. It is not clear whether the unique forms that we see in our data are in fact older forms of signs (and we will see later on that this hypothesis does not exactly pan out), but it is clear that although African American and Caucasian signers share a lexicon to some extent, not all areas of the lexicon overlap.

Gender

Men and women also have nonoverlapping parts of their respective lexicons. For only 8 of the 34 signs do men and women not have unique variants, and these 8 signs include the fairly recent additions COMPUTER, JAPAN, and MICROWAVE. Interestingly, for 2 signs for which we expected to find differences between men and women, namely MEN'S PANTS and WOMEN'S PANTS (where we expected to find differences akin to 'pants' versus 'slacks'), we found no difference at all. Most signers agreed that the same sign—two-handed B handshapes, palms facing and alternatingly descending each thigh—was used for both concepts. This finding coincides exactly with Mansfield (1993), who found that in addition to using this sign, both male and female informants fingerspelled #PANTS.

Social Class

For 25 of the 34 signs, differences were seen between the middle-class signers and the working-class signers. With the exception of JAPAN, all of the fairly new signs (MICROWAVE, COMPUTER, AFRICA, RELAY, and PIZZA) have forms unique to each social group, even though the two groups also share forms for these same concepts. The middle-class signers also tend to fingerspell more than the working-class signers.

Language Background

The crucial distinction here is between signers who were raised in ASL-using families as opposed to signers who are fluent users but who learned to sign at an early age in a residential school setting, and the difference between these two groups in our data is striking. For only 4 of the 34 signs, we see no difference between the two groups for CAKE, GLOVES, JAPAN, and SQUIRREL. For 23 of the signs, the non-ASL-family signers have variants that the ASL-family signers do not display; for 9 of the signs, the ASL-family signers use variants that the non-ASL-family signers do not. This difference may mirror the same differences that we saw in the results for the location variable, with the ASL-family signers tending to be more conservative in their lexical choices and the non-ASL-family signers having perhaps been exposed also to a wider range of variants both at home with hearing parents who are non-native signers and in a variety of educational programs, a range not tempered by the steady influence of an ASL-using family (Supalla 1986; Claire Ramsey, personal communication 2000).

LANGUAGE CHANGE IN PROGRESS?

We turn finally to the third question asked at the beginning of this chapter, namely, do we have any evidence from our analysis of language change in progress? To explore this question, we focused on 6 of the 34 signs. We selected DEER, RABBIT, SNOW, and TOMATO because claims have been made in earlier work as to how phonological variation in these signs represented change in progress; we focused on AFRICA and JAPAN because these are examples of lexical innovation. For the latter two signs, the focus is on the difference between older forms such as an A handshape circling the face for AFRICA and a J produced at the side of the eye for JAPAN, and the outlining of the continent for AFRICA and the outlining of the Japanese islands (a sign borrowed from Japanese Sign Language).

The overall picture for the DEER, RABBIT, SNOW, and TOMATO is one of variation but not necessarily of completed language change. Overall, signers in all seven sites and in all three age groups use both the older and newer versions of these signs. So, signers in all regions and all age groups produce both two-handed and one-handed DEER, RABBIT at the head and on the hands, SNOW as a compound (WHITE‿SNOW and without WHITE, TOMATO with an O base hand (unassimilated to the 1 handshape of the dominant hand) or with a 1 handshape (assimilated). If the change were complete, we would not expect the younger signers to produce two-handed DEER, RABBIT on the head, WHITE‿SNOW, or unassimilated TOMATO. However, we see these forms in all three age groups. And the overall picture for AFRICA and JAPAN is that all regions and most age groups produce both older forms and the newly introduced forms of these signs. In the case of AFRICA and JAPAN, it would seem that the introduction of new forms has been successful and that lexical innovation is complete.

TABLE 8.4. RABBIT: *High Form (Forehead)*

Site	55+		26–54		15–25	
	AA	C	AA	C	AA	C
Calif.	+	+	+	+	+	+
Kans./Mo.	+	+	+	+	+	+
La.	−	−	+	+	+	+
Md.	na	−	na	−	na	−
Mass.	+	+	+	+	+	+
Va.	na	+	na	−	na	+
Wash.	na	+	na	+	na	−

Note: + indicates use of the variant by at least one signer; − indicates no use by signers in this group; Tables 8.4–8.9 reflect only the variants named, not other variants of these six signs.

TABLE 8.5. DEER: *2-Handed*

Site	55+		26–54		15–25	
	AA	C	AA	C	AA	C
Calif.	+	+	+	+	+	+
Kans./Mo.	+	+	+	+	+	+
La.	+	+	+	+	+	+
Md.	na	+	na	+	na	+
Mass.	+	+	+	+	+	+
Va.	na	+	na	+	na	+
Wash.	na	+	na	+	na	+

We emphasize that this is the *overall* picture because there are some details within the big picture that make it very interesting. These are summarized in tables 8.4–8.9.

For example, the older signers in Boston prefer the head form of RAB-BIT, whereas this form is not produced in any age group in Maryland, by young signers in Washington, by older signers in New Orleans, and by middle-aged signers in Virginia. In Kansas and Washington, only middle-class signers produce the head form. Older Boston signers and middle-aged and younger Maryland signers do not produce the compound form of SNOW, whereas younger and older signers in Kansas, middle-aged signers in Virginia, and middle-aged and older signers in Washington produce only the compound form. African American signers in Kansas/Missouri also produce only the compound form, as do ASL-family signers from Kansas/Missouri and Virginia. And whereas middle-class signers in Boston and Maryland do not use the compound form, middle-class

TABLE 8.6. *TOMATO: Unassimilated (Nondominant Is Flat O or S)*

| | 55+ | | 26–54 | | 15–25 | |
Site	AA	C	AA	C	AA	C
Calif.	+	+	+	–	+	+
Kans./Mo.	+	+	+	+	+	+
La.	+	+	+	+	+	+
Md.	na	–	na	–	na	+
Mass.	+	+	+	+	+	+
Va.	na	+	na	+	na	+
Wash.	na	+	na	+	na	+

TABLE 8.7. *SNOW: compound,* WHITE‒FALL

| | 55+ | | 26–54 | | 15–25 | |
Site	AA	C	AA	C	AA	C
Calif.	+	+	+	+	+	+
Kans./Mo.	+	+	+	+	+	+
La.	+	+	+	+	+	+
Md.	na	+	na	–	na	–
Mass.	–	–	+	+	+	+
Va.	na	+	na	+	na	+
Wash.	na	+	na	+	na	+

TABLE 8.8. *AFRICA: Outline Continent, New Form*

Site	55+ AA	C	26–54 AA	C	15–25 AA	C
Calif.	+	+	+	+	+	+
Kans./Mo.	–	–	+	+	+	+
La.	–	–	+	+	+	+
Md.	na	+	na	+	na	+
Mass.	+	+	+	+	+	+
Va.	na	+	na	+	na	+
Wash.	na	+	na	+	na	+

TABLE 8.9. *JAPAN: Trace Islands, New Form*

Site	55+ AA	C	26–54 AA	C	15–25 AA	C
Calif.	+	+	+	+	+	+
Kans. Mo.	–	–	+	+	+	+
La.	+	+	+	+	+	+
Md.	na	+	na	+	na	+
Mass.	+	+	+	+	+	+
Va.	na	–	na	+	na	+
Wash.	na	+	na	+	na	+

signers in Kansas use only the compound form. Middle-aged California signers and middle-aged Maryland signers use only the assimilated form of TOMATO, whereas older Kansas and younger Virginia signers use only the nonassimilated form. ASL-family signers from Boston and Maryland use only the assimilated form, whereas ASL-family signers from Kansas and Virginia use only the nonassimilated form. Older signers in Kansas do not use the new form for AFRICA, whereas younger signers in California, Virginia, and Maryland do not use any of the older forms at all. Older signers in Kansas and Virginia do not use the new sign for JAPAN, whereas younger signers in Virginia and Maryland do not use the old sign. In Kansas, only non-ASL-family signers used the new sign, whereas non-ASL-family signers in Virginia used only the old sign. Older African American signers did not produce the new sign, nor did older ASL-family signers in general.

This more detailed picture, then, shows that there is definitely change in progress and that in some cases, as with RABBIT in Maryland, the change is probably close to being complete. But in many cases and in light of the claims about language change in progress made in the 1970s, the change would seem to be still very much in progress. And in the case of DEER, which is produced in all regions and in all age groups either two-handed or one-handed, it is not clear that any change is really taking place.

Finally, with regard to AFRICA and JAPAN, even though some groups do not use the new forms, we need to point out the difference between these two signs and the other four. It is clear that AFRICA and JAPAN represent instances of fairly rapid lexical innovation, cases in which new forms were introduced to respond to specific societal or political pressures. JAPAN was borrowed at the same time that a number of other country signs were borrowed, no doubt as a direct result of the increased contact between American deaf people and deaf people from communities all over the world. A common reason cited for the borrowing is to show respect for other cultures and to not impose the ASL sign on the Deaf citizens of other nations who have signs in their own sign languages for their respective countries. And this in turn is no doubt a reflection of the anger that American Deaf people have felt, justifiably, at having their own language tampered with by educators and educational administrators. AFRICA is believed to have been introduced as a direct response to ASL signs for AFRICA that focus on the nose and are widely perceived to be racist. However, as noted earlier, current attitudes seem to indicate a rejection of this innovation despite widespread knowledge and use of it by our informants. The course of this rejection bears watching.

The life of AFRICA and JAPAN is quite different from that of the other four signs, DEER, RABBIT, SNOW, and TOMATO. In the latter, instead of rapid lexical innovation, we see the usual and natural unfolding of phonological processes, of phonological variation followed by change, very similar to what we see in spoken languages.

Chapter 9

Sociolinguistic Variation in

American Sign Language

We now return to the two basic research questions that structured the original proposal written to the National Science Foundation in 1993, questions that guided the progress of the project and that open this volume: (1) Can the internal constraints on variation such as those defined and described in spoken languages be identified and described for variation in ASL? and (2) Can the external social constraints on variation such as those defined and described in spoken languages be identified and described in ASL?

The first answer to both questions is simply "yes." Our analysis reveals internal constraints on sign variation that are the same as those found in spoken language variation: phonological and grammatical factors occurring in the immediate linguistic environment of a target variable that play a role in the behavior of that variable. Our analysis also reveals the role of external constraints in variation, factors such as region, age, ethnicity, and gender. We also find that similar kinds of units are variable in sign languages and spoken languages (i.e., parts of segments vary, segments may be added, deleted, or rearranged, and word-sized units participate in lexical and syntactic variation). And we find the same kinds of processes at work—assimilation, metathesis, neutralization, and so forth. So we found what we had expected, based on what we knew.

However, we also encountered some unexpected findings. In the first place, we had not anticipated the strong role of grammatical function in phonological variation. As we explain in chapter 6, this would seem to be a direct reflection of modality differences between sign languages and spoken languages. Fundamental differences in basic structure seem to be manifested in variation. Second, although the social factors that play a role in sign language variation are the same ones that we find in spoken language variation, the two that consistently play the strongest role—

region and age—must necessarily be considered and understood within the specific context of the Deaf community and deaf education. Both the history of the relationship between the Hartford school and the residential schools in the seven project sites and the history of language policy in deaf education have direct bearing on the regional and age variation that we have described. Furthermore, we have had to consider the nature of families into which deaf children are born as a factor in variation because we observed differences between signers born into ASL-using families and those born into hearing, nonsigning families.

So we found many things that we expected and some that we did not. This brings us to the issue with which we close this volume, that is, the importance of this kind of research both in general and for Deaf communities in particular.

In discussing what guided them in the preparation of the *DASL* as early as 1957, Stokoe et al. cited the thinking of George Trager and Henry Lee Smith: "They insisted that language could not be studied by itself, in isolation, but must be looked at in direct connection to the people who used it, the things they used it to talk about, and the view of the world that using it imposed on them" (1965, 333). This perspective clearly prompted Stokoe and his associates to include Croneberg's appendices in the *DASL,* appendices that showed "how language and culture as well as deafness formed a special community" (1965, 334). The importance of studying variation is three-fold. First, the recognition that ASL exhibits variation like other systems that we recognize as languages reinforces the status of ASL as a real language. As a corollary, because variation is often the precursor to change (Milroy 1992), the study of variation in ASL, as in other languages, leads us to an understanding of how the language changes.

Second, the study of variation reinforces the position that rather than being just a curiosity or an anomaly, variation is an integral part of the structure of a language. That is, if we are to truly understand the nature of a language, we must account for variation. In this regard Weinreich et al. (1968), in their work on the role of variation in language change, introduced the idea of "orderly heterogeneity" as the most useful metaphor for understanding the nature of language:

[I]f a language has to be structured in order to function efficiently, how do people continue to talk while the language changes, that is, while it passes through periods of lessened systematicity?

Alternatively, if overriding pressures do force a language to change, and communication is less efficient in the interim . . . why have such inefficiencies not been observed in practice?

This, it seems to us, is the fundamental question with which a theory of language change must cope. The solution, we will argue, lies in the direction of breaking down the identification of strucuredness and homogeneity. The key to a rational conception of language change — indeed, of language itself — is the possibility of describing orderly differentiation in a language serving a community. We will argue that nativelike command of heterogeneous structures is not a matter of multidialectalism or "mere" performance, but is part of unilingual linguistic competence. One of the corollaries of our approach is that in a language serving a complex (i.e., real) community, it is the *absence* of structured heterogeneity that would be dysfunctional. (99–100)

And, indeed, as we have demonstrated in this volume, the way that heterogeneity is ordered has to do to some extent with whether the language in question is an aural-oral one or a visual-gestural one. That is, the nature of the orderly heterogeneity has to do in part with modality.

Third, the study of sign language structure and variation has had a direct impact on the lives of Deaf people in terms of educational and employment opportunities. Indeed, it seems fair to say that this impact has been very tangible. Research on sign language structure and variation has led to the recognition of sign languages as real languages and has had the effect of legitimizing them. This legitimization has allowed at least for the discussion of what the medium of instruction should be in deaf education and to, as Johnson, Liddell, and Erting said in 1989, the unlocking of the curriculum at least for some deaf students. That is, it has made the content of the curriculum accessible to a limited number of Deaf students via ASL. It has led to the improvement of services for Deaf people such as interpreting and has opened up new career paths for Deaf people as teachers both of Deaf children and adolescents and as teachers of sign language. The research on sign language structure and variation that Bill Stokoe initiated has ultimately contributed to the continuing empowerment of Deaf people all over the world.

APPENDIX A

Transcription Conventions

Notation	Explanation
SMALL CAPS	English gloss of signs
F-I-N-G-E-R-S-P-E-L-L-I-N-G	A fingerspelled word
#ASL	A lexicalized, fingerspelled sign
HYPHENATED-WORDS	A single sign represented by multiple English glosses
COMPOUND⌒WORDS	Compounds
+	Reduplication of a sign
PRO.1	PRO = pronoun, 1 = 1st person, 2 = 2nd person, 3 = 3rd person
POSS.1	Possessive pronoun (and person)
CL:	Classifier predicate
Bob-ASK-TO-Mary	Indicating verbs that include the subject-object referents
₁FOLLOW₂	Actions of or directions relative to the signer
<u>gaze left LOOK-AT-THEM</u>	Nonmanual features of a signed expression

Sign Variants

Sign: AFRICA

Variants:

1. "New sign": outline continent
2. A handshape or 8 handshape, circle face, may end on nose
3. A handshape, thumb brush forehead like BLACK
4. F handshape, ring in nose
5. A-F-R-I-C-A

Sign: ARREST

Variants:

1. Wrists cross back to back as 5 handshape closes to S handshape or dominant palm to back of nondominant, or dominant 5 handshape closes to S handshape on wrist of nondominant B handshape
2. B handshape palm down on relaxed B handshape, maybe alternating dominance
3. Bent V (thumb extended or not), two-handed forward movement
4. Two-handed or one-handed open 5 handshape move forward, close to S
5. Open 8 CL: PUT-ON-HANDCUFFS
6. Like JAIL, two 5 handshapes, back of dominant on palm of nondominant, palms in, or two-handed open 5 handshape, hands move forward, fingers interlock
7. #ARREST
8. Like SUE, two-handed B handshape, dominant in nondominant palm, perpendicular
9. C or bent V dominant grasps 1 nondominant or closes on side of it
10. Two-handed 1234 extended, rounded, hands move together, dominant close over nondominant
11. Two-handed A handshape palms up, ulnar contact

Sign: BANANA

Variants:

1. Index nondominant, dominant handshape (may be F, A, X, 1, G, V, flat O, B) "remove peel"
2. Nondominant flat O or B, dominant flat O or 5, pull off end of nondominant, repeat; or 5, sweep around nondominant
3. Two-handed G handshape, move apart in neutral space, or two-handed H handshape, extend thumb, tips touch, move up and down
4. (Related to 1) nondominant is whole forearm, S or 5 or B, dominant is flat O or B or H
5. #BANANA

Sign: CAKE

Variants:

1. Some variant of nondominant B handshape, palm up and dominant C, E or bent 5, palm down
2. #CAKE
3. Like PIE

Sign: CANDY

Variants:

1. 12 fingers on chin, oscillate
2. Some variation of twisting at cheek, dominant is index or X
3. Baby O, twist at side of mouth or circle on cheek
4. 1 or L or H brush cheek
5. Like SWEET
6. Radial side of index finger slides across lips, repeat

Sign: CEREAL

Variants:

1. Some variant of nondominant palm up, dominant is C or B or H or U or A or X, palm up, sweep nondominant
2. 1 handshape on chin or cheek
3. Nondominant 1, dominant index brush nondominant

4. Nondominant 1 or X, dominant X brush nondominant
5. C handshape, palm to face, thumb contact cheek, repeat
6. Dominant F or 1 handshape from mouth to nondominant index or just tap index
7. Full forearm, S handshape, base hold dominant elbow, shake back x 2
8. Shake C (CL: POUR-CEREAL-FROM-BOX)
9. #CEREAL
10. Like CONFUSE, near ear
11. Two-handed C handshape palms facing, repeat tap tips

Sign: CHEAT

Variants:

1. Some variant of dominant interlocking with nondominant
2. Index and/or pinky down nondominant forearm
3. Some variant of PUNISH or STEAL
4. Like COST
5. C-H-E-A-T
6. Same as DIRTY
7. V on chin, palm out, repeat movement
8. Two-handed 1 handshape dominant rub top of nondominant, repeat, pinky extended
9. Bent L oscillates at temple ('infidelity')
10. Nondominant palm down B handshape, dominant B palm down, brushes tips of nondominant

Sign: CHERRIES

Variants:

1. Some variant of E or O twist on index or pinky of nondominant
2. Some variant of 12 fingers or C on cheek
3. Some variant of F on mouth, sometimes with RED
4. Fingerspell C-H-E-R-R-Y or C-H-E-R-R-I-E-S
5. V handshape in hook around ear, reduplicate

Sign: CHICKEN

Variants:

1. Some variant of index and thumb at mouth
2. For live chicken, X handshape at nose, palm out, fingertip down to palm
3. Like TURKEY, G or R from chin or cheek to chest
4. Two-handed G handshape at waist palm in index oscillate
5. Bent 3 handshape palm out, thumb on chin, oscillate or bounce (like ROOSTER)

Sign: COMPUTER

Variants:

1. Some variant of C moving on arm
2. Some variant of open 8 or C palm out circling
3. Some variant of C on forehead
4. Like typing
5. C across face, like SEARCH (can be two-handed)

Sign: DEER

Variants:

1. Some variant of open 5 handshape on temple, two-handed or one-handed
2. #DEER
3. Bent 3, two-handed, on temple, may move lower
4. ILY handshape on forehead, one-handed

Sign: DELICIOUS

Variants:

1. Some variation of 8 handshape snapping
2. Lexical sign? B handshape rubs stomach
3. Some variation of open 8 on mouth, palm in
4. One-handed index and pinky extended, palm down, index brush chin then hand move away from face

Sign: DOG

Variants:

1. Some combination of slap thigh and snap finger
2. #DG or D-O-G
3. P shaking

Sign: EARLY

Variants:

1. Some variant of open 8 on back of nondominant fist or open 5
2. #EARLY
3. L handshape (two-handed) thumb on chest, palm neutral, hand move out from chest
4. Modified form of morning, S opens to 5, palm in
5. Two-handed B handshape, horizontal, palm in, dominant hand comes up to back of nondominant, like NEAR
6. Dominant V handshape, palm against elbow of nondominant
7. Open 8, palm in, move down cheek
8. 3 handshape on forehead, like ROOSTER
9. Like GET-UP
10. Like OPEN-CHAMPAGNE
11. Like WHAT'S-UP
12. 3 handshape on cheek, palm in, move forward
13. 2 handshape S crossed in neutral space (like STATISTICS), both open to 5

Sign: FAINT

Variants:

1. Some variant of FALL or THINK-FALL or THINK-DROP
2. Some variant of bent 5 or index on forehead, close to A or S or open to 5
3. Some fingerspelled variant: #FAINT, #PO, BLACK O-U-T, K at forehead then O in neutral space
4. SHOCK or THINK-SHOCK
5. HEART-DEFLATE
6. F handshape move side to side, move down from neck to stomach

Sign: FEAR

Variants:

1. Some variant of 5 handshape or S/A open to 5, palm in
2. Some variant of palms move down, in or out
3. #FEAR

Sign: GLOVES

Variants:

1. Some variant of pulling on gloves
2. G-L-O-V-E-S, full fingerspelling

Sign: JAPAN

Variants:

1. Some variant of "new" sign, "trace islands"
2. Old sign, J handshape or 1 handshape at corner of eye

Sign: MICROWAVE

Variants:

1. Some variant of S opening to V or U or W
2. Fingerspelling
3. Outline machine, two-handed M handshape or W handshape
4. Some variant of W (one-handed or two-handed) move toward or away
5. COOK + CL: SQUARE BOX, CL: OPEN-DOOR; CL: SQUARE + OVEN
6. Two-handed 8 handshape move in semicircle, palms facing, then flick fingers at each other

Sign: MITTENS

Variants:

1. Some variant of dominant tracing outline of nondominant
2. Same as GLOVE, dominant sweeps over back of nondominant
3. Dominant C handshape cup nondominant B handshape, pull mitten on

4. Like GLOVE, dominant A or 5 close to A on back of nondominant B or open 5
5. #MITTENS

Sign: PANTS, men's

Variants:

1. Some variant of 5 or B, flat O, J (JEANS), P brush up on thigh
2. 4 or B handshape, two-handed, parallel tips move down each leg
3. S or A handshape, pull up pants
4. Fingerspell J-E-A-N-S, #BJ, #PANTS

Sign: PANTS, women's

Variants:

1. Some variant of open 5 handshape, B handshape, J, P, flat O, brush up thigh
2. 4 handshape or 5 handshape, two-handed, parallel down each leg
3. S handshape, pull up pants
4. Fingerspell #JEANS, #BLUEJEANS, #SLACKS, #PANTS

Sign: PERFUME

Variants:

1. Some variant of spraying, 1 handshape to X, L handshape
2. Open 8 or P touches both sides of neck or upper chest
3. Various handshapes oscillate on neck or torso
4. Flat B or 5 at base of neck
5. One-handed, index finger contact below earlobe, twisting
6. Dominant index touch nose, pinky extended, then dominant X touch nondominant palm and rotate

Sign: PIZZA

Variants:

1. Some fingerspelled variant: #PZZA, #PIZZA, #ZZA, P-I-Z-Z-A
2. Some variant of fingertips at chin, B handshape, palm up
3. Some variant of B or P dominant slicing palm

4. PIZZA L-classifier, 2 hands in neutral space
5. CL, PUT-PIZZA-IN-OVEN

Sign: RABBIT

Variants:

1. Low or high form of 12 fingers wiggle, palm in or out
2. #RABBIT
3. Bent V on forehead, palm out, fingers oscillate

Sign: RELAY

Variants:

1. Some variation of R-E-L-A-Y
2. Some variant with R handshapes, crossing and oscillating
3. Dominant flat O across nondominant 3
4. Two-handed 5 handshapes, palms facing, fingers aligned, fingers curl to 1234 hooked, contact opposite hand then release
5. Like TRANSLATE
6. Open 8, NETWORK

Sign: RUNNER/RUN

Variants:

1. Some variant of index hooks dominant thumb, index oscillates
2. Body CL, run in place
3. Like run a company, B handshapes
4. Like COMPETE (effect of stimulus picture?)

Sign: SANDWICH

Variants:

1. Some variant of two-handed B handshape, at or near mouth, either both palms down or palms facing
2. Like HAMBURGER
3. Instrumental CL, HOLD-SANDWICH-AT-MOUTH
4. Some variant of two-handed B handshape, all palms up, interlocking in some way
5. Like SCHOOL, dominant may start at mouth then move down

Sign: SNOW

Variants:

1. Some variant of WHITE⁀SNOW, with or without WHITE
2. Fingerspell snow then 5 handshape wiggle down

Sign: SOON

Variants:

1. Some variant of F on chin or lips
2. Some variant of fingerspelling, #SN, #SOON
3. Two-handed H handshapes, palms facing, repeat movement
4. Some variant of '12' on cheek
5. WILL
6. Same as FAST
7. LATER
8. A open like FEW on chin or A on cheek open to L
9. 8 handshape oscillates on chin

Sign: SQUIRREL

Variants:

1. Some variant of two-handed bent V, tap
2. Fingerspell #SQUIRREL
3. Some variant of O handshape
4. Some variant of F, X, V or 3 on cheek

Sign: THIEF/STEAL

Variants:

STEAL

1. V → bent V, at elbow
2. Some variant of 5 or B or V cross and close

THIEF

3. STEAL⁀AGENT
4. Some variant of L or R away from body
5. Some variant of outlining mustache

Sign: TOMATO

Variants:

1. Some variant of RED⌢SLICE
2. Two-handed 5 handshape, dominant from ulnar to radial on back of base hand, fingers wiggle
3. #TOMATO
4. CL: BALL, OR RED-CL: BALL
5. T hand on cheek, twist

REFERENCES

A Brief Summary of the Activities at the Louisiana State School for Deaf Negroes. 1952. Archival clipping.

Aarons, D., B. Bahan, J. Kegl, and C. Neidle.1994. Subjects and agreement in American Sign Language. In *Perspectives on sign language structure: Papers from the Fifth International Symposium on Sign Language Research,* ed. I. Ahlgren, B. Bergman, and M. Brennan, 13–28. vol. 1. Durham: International Sign Language Association.

Aramburo, A. 1989. Sociolinguistic aspects of the Black Deaf community. In *The sociolinguistics of the Deaf community,* ed. C. Lucas, 103–19. San Diego: Academic Press.

Asante, M. K. 1990. African elements in African American English. In *Africanism in American culture,* ed. J. Holloway, 19–23. Bloomington: Indiana University Press.

ASD [Connecticut Asylum for the Education and Instruction of Deaf and Dumb Persons]. 1817. First report of the directors of the Connecticut Asylum for the Education and Instruction of Deaf and Dumb Persons.

———. 1818. Second report of the directors of the Connecticut Asylum for the Education and Instruction of Deaf and Dumb Persons.

——— [Asylum for the Education and Instruction of the Deaf and Dumb]. 1819. Third report of the directors of the Asylum, at Hartford, Conn., for the Education and Instruction of the Deaf and Dumb.

———. 1820. Fourth report of the directors of the Asylum, at Hartford, Conn., for the Education and Instruction of the Deaf and Dumb.

———. 1827. Eleventh report of the directors of the Asylum, at Hartford, Conn., for the Education and Instruction of the Deaf and Dumb.

———. 1830. Fourteenth report of the directors of the Asylum, at Hartford, Conn., for the Education and Instruction of the Deaf and Dumb.

———. 1844. Twenty-eighth report of the directors of the Asylum, at Hartford, Conn., for the Education and Instruction of the Deaf and Dumb.

———. 1845. Twenty-ninth report of the directors of the Asylum, at Hartford, Conn., for the Education and Instruction of the Deaf and Dumb.

———. 1857. Forty-first report of the directors of the Asylum at Hartford, Conn., for the Education and Instruction of the Deaf and Dumb.

Bahan, B. 1996. Non-manual realization of agreement in American Sign Language. Ph.D. diss., Boston University.

Bailey, G., T. Wikle, J. Tillery, and L. Sand. 1991. The apparent time construct. *Language Variation and Change* 3:241–64.

Baker, C., and D. Cokely, 1980. *American Sign Language: A teacher's resource text on grammar and culture.* Silver Spring, Md.: T. J. Publishers.

Barale, C. 1982. A quantitative analysis of the loss of final consonants in Beijing Mandarin. Ph.D. diss., University of Pennsylvania.

Barrenechea, A. M., and A. Alonso. 1977. Los pronombres personales sujetos en el español hablado en Buenos Aires. In *Estudios sobre el español hablado en los principales ciudades de America,* ed. J. Lope Blanch, 333–49. México City: Universidad Nacionál Autónoma de México.

Bass, R. 1949. *History of the education of the Deaf in Virginia, 1839–1948.* Staunton: Virginia School for the Deaf and the Blind.

Battison, R. 1978. *Lexical borrowing in American Sign Language.* Silver Spring, Md.: Linstok Press.

Battison, R. M., H. Markowicz, and J. C. Woodward. 1975. A good rule of thumb: Variable phonology in American Sign Language. In *Analyzing variation in language,* ed. R. W. Fasold and R. Shuy, 291–302. Washington, D.C.: Georgetown University Press.

Bauer, R. 1982. Cantonese sociolinguistic patterns. Ph.D. diss., University of California, Berkeley.

Baugh, J. 1983. *Black street speech: Its history, structure, and survival.* Austin: University of Texas Press.

Bayley, R. 1991. Variation theory and second language learning: Linguistic and social constraints on interlanguage tense marking. Ph.D. diss., Stanford University.

———. 1994. Consonant cluster reduction in Tejano English. *Language Variation and Change* 6: 303–26.

———. 1997. VARBRUL analysis of linguistic variation. Workshop presented at the American Dialect Society Meeting, Chicago, January 2.

Bayley, R., C. Lucas, and M. Rose. 2000. Variation in American Sign Language: The case of DEAF. *Journal of Sociolinguistics* 4(1):81–107.

Bayley, R., and L. Pease-Alvarez. 1996. Null and expressed subject pronoun variation in Mexican-descent children's Spanish. In *Sociolinguistic variation: Data, theory, and analysis,* ed. J. Arnold, R. Blake, B. Davidson, S. Schwenter, and J. Solomon, 85–99. Stanford: Center for the Study of Language and Information.

———. 1997. Null pronoun variation in Mexican-descent children's narrative discourse. *Language Variation and Change* 9:349–71.

Baynton, D. C. 1996. *Forbidden signs: American culture and the campaign against sign language.* Chicago: University of Chicago Press.

Beebe, L. M., and H. Giles. 1984. Speech-accommodation theories: A discussion in terms of second-language acquisition. *International Journal of the Sociology of Language* 46:5–32.

Bentivoglio, P. 1987. *Los sujetos pronominales de primera persona en el habla de Caracas.* Caracas: Universidad Central de Venezuela, Consejo de Desarrollo Científico y Humanístico.

Biber, D., and E. Finegan, eds. 1993. *Sociolinguistic perspectives on register.* Oxford: Oxford University Press.

Blattberg, S., L. Byers, E. Lockwood, and R. Smith. 1995. Sociolinguistic variation in American Sign Language: Phonological variation by age group in fingerspelling. In *Communication Forum,* ed. L. Byers, J. Chaiken, and M. Mueller, 157–82. Washington, D.C.: Gallaudet University, Department of ASL, Linguistics, and Interpretation.

Bourgerie, D. S. 1990. A quantitative study of sociolinguistic variation in Cantonese. Ph.D. diss., Ohio State University.

Boyes-Braem, P. 1985. Studying sign language dialects. In *SLR '83: Proceedings of the Third International Symposium on Sign Language Research, Rome, June 22–26, 1983,* ed. W. Stokoe and V. Volterra, 247–53. Silver Spring, Md.: Linstok Press.

———. 1994. An overview of current sign language projects in Switzerland. In *The Deaf way: Perspectives from the International Conference on Deaf Culture,* ed. C. Erting, R. Johnson, D. Smith, and B. Snider, 382–87. Washington, D.C.: Gallaudet University Press.

Braddock, G. C. 1975. *Notable Deaf persons.* Washington, D.C.: Gallaudet College Alumni Association.

Brelje, H. W., and V. Tibbs. 1986. *The Washington State School for the Deaf: The first hundred years, 1886–1986.* Vancouver: The School.

Bridges, B. 1993. Gender variation with sex signs. Gallaudet University Department of Linguistics and Interpreting, Washington, D.C. Manuscript.

Bright, W. 1997.Social factors in language change. In *The handbook of sociolinguistics,* ed. F. Coulmas, 81–91. Oxford: Basil Blackwell.

Burnes, C., and C. Ramger. 1960. *History of the California School for the Deaf, 1860–1960.* Berkeley: California School for the Deaf.

Cameron, R. 1992. Pronominal and null subject variation in Spanish: Constraints, dialects, and functional compensation. Ph.D. diss., University of Pennsylvania.

———. 1993. Ambiguous agreement, functional compensation, and nonspecific *tu* in the Spanish of San Juan, Puerto Rico, and Madrid, Spain. *Language Variation and Change* 5:305–34.

———. 1996. A community-based test of a linguistic hypothesis. *Language in Society* 25:61–111.

Campos de Abreu, A. 1994. The deaf social life in Brazil. In *The Deaf way: Perspectives from the International Conference on Deaf Culture,* ed. C. Erting, R. Johnson, D. Smith, and B. Snider, 114–16. Washington, D.C.: Gallaudet University Press.

Cedergren, H. 1973a. The interplay of social and linguistic factors in Panama. Ph.D. diss., Cornell University.

———. 1973b. On the nature of variable constraints. In *New ways of analyzing variation in English,* ed. C. J. Bailey and R.W. Shuy, 13–22. Washington, D.C.: Georgetown University Press.

———. 1987. The spread of language change: Verifying inferences of linguistic diffusion. In *Language spread and language policy: Issues, implications, and case studies,* ed. P. Lowenberg, 45–60. Georgetown University Roundtable on Languages and Linguistics. Washington, D.C.: Georgetown University Press.

Cedergren, H., and D. Sankoff. 1974. Variable rules: Performance as a statistical reflection of competence. *Language* 50:333–55.

Chambers, J. 1995. *Sociolinguistic theory.* Oxford: Basil Blackwell.

Chomsky, N. 1981. *Lectures on government and binding.* Dordrecht: Foris.

Cifuentes, H. 1980–1981. Presencia y ausencia del pronombre personal sujeto en el habla culta de Santiago de Chile. *Homenaje a Ambrosio Rabanales. Boletín de Filología de la Universidad de Chile* 31:743–52.

Clarke School for the Deaf. 2000. Historical information [online]. Northampton, Mass.: Clarke School for the Deaf. Retrieved May 11, 2000, from the World Wide Web: http://www.clarkeschool.org/history.html.

Collins, S., and K. Petronio. 1998. What happens in tactile ASL? In *Pinky extension and eye gaze: Language use in Deaf communities,* ed. C. Lucas, 18–37. Sociolinguistics in Deaf Communities Series, vol. 4. Washington, D.C.: Gallaudet University Press.

Collins-Ahlgren, M. 1991. Variation in New Zealand Sign Language. Paper presented at NWAVE twentieth conference, Georgetown University, Washington, D.C.

Coulter, G. 1990. Emphatic stress in ASL. In *Linguistics,* ed. S. Fischer and P. Siple, 109–25. Theoretical Issues in Sign Language Research, vol. 1. Chicago: University of Chicago Press.

———., ed. 1992. *Current issues in ASL phonology.* Phonetics and Phonology, vol. 3. San Diego: Academic Press.

Croneberg, C. 1965. The linguistic community: Sign Language Dialects. In *A dictionary of American Sign Language,* ed. W. Stokoe, D. Casterline, and C. Croneberg, 297–311. Washington, D.C.: Gallaudet University Press.

CSD [California Institution for the Education of the Deaf and the Blind at Berkeley]. 1862. Third report of the board of directors and officers of the California Institution for the Education of the Deaf and the Blind.

———. 1865. Sixth report of the board of directors and officers of the California Institution for the Education of the Deaf and the Blind.

———. 1875. Eleventh report of the board of directors and officers of the California Institution for the Education of the Deaf and the Blind.

———. 1880–1882. Fifteenth report of the board of directors and officers of the California Institution for the Education of the Deaf and the Blind.

———. 1886–1888. Eighteenth report of the board of directors and officers of the California Institution for the Education of the Deaf and the Blind.

———. 1888–1890. Nineteenth report of the board of directors and officers of the California Institution for the Education of the Deaf and the Blind.

———. 1908–1910. Twenty-ninth report of the board of directors and officers of the California Institution for the Education of the Deaf and the Blind.

——— [California School for the Deaf and the Blind]. 1912–1914. Thirty-first biennial report of the California School for the Deaf and the Blind.

——— [California School for the Deaf]. 1922–1924. Biennial report of the California School for the Deaf.

———. 1934–1936. Seventh biennial report of the California School for the Deaf.

———. 1958–1960. Nineteenth biennial report of the California School for the Deaf.

Davis, J., and S. Supalla. 1995. A sociolinguistic description of sign language use in a Navajo family. In *Sociolinguistics in Deaf communities,* ed. C. Lucas, 77–106. Sociolinguistics in Deaf Communities Series, vol. 1. Washington, D.C.: Gallaudet University Press.

Denton, D. 1976. The philosophy of total communication. Supplement to the *British Deaf News.* Carlisle, Britain: The British Deaf Association.

DeSantis, S. 1977. Elbow to hand shift in French and American Sign Languages. Paper presented at the annual NWAVE conference, Georgetown University, Washington, D.C.

Deuchar, M. 1984. *British Sign Language.* London: Routledge and Kegan Paul.

Dubois, S., and B. Horvath. 1999. When the music changes, you change too: Gender and language change in Cajun English. *Language Variation and Change* 11:287–313.

Eckert, P. 1989. The whole woman: Sex and gender differences in variation. *Language Variation and Change* 1:245–68.

———. 2000. *Linguistic variation as social practice: The linguistic construction of identity in Belten high.* Oxford: Blackwell.

Edwards, W. F. 1986. Vernacular language use and social networking in Eastside Detroit. In *Proceedings of Eastern States Conference on Linguistics (ESCOL),* 117–28. Columbus: Ohio State University Department of Linguistics.

———. 1992. Sociolinguistic behavior in a Detroit inner city black neighborhood. *Language in Society* 12:295–311.

Ely, C. W. 1893. *History of the Maryland School for the Deaf and Dumb.* Frederick City: Maryland School for the Deaf and Dumb.

Emmorey, K. 1999. The Confluence of Space and Language in Signed Languages. *In Language and Space,* ed. P. Bloom and M. A. Peterson, L. Nodel, and M. F. Garrett, 171–209. Cambridge: The MIT Press.

Enriquez, E. V. 1984. *El pronombre personal sujeto en la lengua Espanola hablada en Madrid*. Madrid: Consejo Superior de Investigaciones Científicas, Instituto Miguel de Cervantes.

Fasold, R. 1990. *Sociolinguistics of language*. Oxford: Blackwell.

Fischer, J. 1958. Social influences on the choice of a linguistic variant. *Word* 14:47–56.

Frishberg, N. 1975. Arbitrariness and iconicity: Historical change in American Sign Language. *Language* 51:696–719.

———. 1976. Some aspects of the historical development of signs in American Sign Language. Ph.D. diss., University of California, San Diego.

Galindo, D. L., and M. D. Gonzales, eds. 1999. *Speaking Chicana: Voice, power and identity*. Tucson: University of Arizona Press.

Gannon, J. R. 1981. *Deaf heritage: A narrative history of Deaf America*. Silver Spring, Md.: National Association of the Deaf.

Gauchat, L. 1905. L'unité phonétique dans le patois d'une commune. *Aus Romanischen Sprachen und Literaturen: Festschrift Heinrich Mort*. Halle: Max Miemeyer. 175–232.

Gerner de García, B. 1995. Communication and language use in Spanish-speaking families with deaf children. In *Sociolinguistics in Deaf communities,* ed. C. Lucas, 221–52. Sociolinguistics in Deaf Communities Series, vol.1. Washington, D.C.: Gallaudet University Press.

Godfrey, E., and S. Tagliamonte. 1999. Another piece of the verbal –s story: Evidence from Devon in southwest England. *Language Variation and Change* 11:87–119.

Guggenheim, L. 1993. Ethnic variation in ASL: The signing of African Americans and how it is influenced by conversational topic. In *Communication forum,* ed. E. Winston, 51–76. Washington, D.C.: Gallaudet University Department of Linguistics and Interpreting.

Guy, G. 1980. Variation in the group and in the individual: The case of final stop deletion. In *Locating language in time and space,* ed. W. Labov, 1–36. New York: Academic Press.

———. 1988. Advanced VARBRUL analysis. In *Linguistic contact and change: Proceedings of the Sixteenth Annual Conference on New Ways of Analyzing Variation,* ed. K. Ferrara, R. Brown, K. Walters, and J. Baugh, 124–36. Austin: University of Texas Department of Linguistics.

———. 1990. Explanation in variable phonology: *t/d* deletion. Paper presented at NWAVE nineteenth annual conference, University of Pennsylvania, Philadelphia.

———. 1991a. Explanation in variable phonology: An exponential model of morphological constraints. *Language Variation and Change* 3(1):1–22.

———. 1991b. Contextual conditioning in variable lexical phonology. *Language Variation and Change* 3(2):223–39.

————. 1993. The quantitative analysis of linguistic variation. In *American dialect research,* ed. D. Preston, 223–49. Philadelphia: John Benjamins.

————. 1997. Violable is variable: Optimality theory and linguistic variation. *Language Variation and Change* 9:333–47.

Guy, G. R., and R. Bayley. 1995. On the choice of relative pronouns in English. *American Speech* 70:148–62.

Guy, G. R., and C. Boberg. 1997. Inherent variability and the obligatory contour principle. *Language Variation and Change* 9:149–64.

Haas, C., E. Fleetwood, and M. Earnest. 1995. An analysis of ASL variation within DeafBlind interaction: Question forms, back channeling, and turn-taking. In *Communication Forum,* ed. L. Byers, J. Chaiken, and M. Mueller, 103–40. Washington, D.C.: Gallaudet University Department of ASL, Linguistics, and Interpretation.

Hall, K., and M. Bucholtz, eds. 1995. *Gender articulated: Language and the socially constructed self.* London: Routledge.

Halliday, M.A.K., and R. Hasan. 1976. *Cohesion in English.* London: Longman.

Henry, A.. 1995. *Belfast English and Standard English: Dialect variation and parameter setting.* New York and Oxford: Oxford University Press.

Hermann, M. E. 1929. Lauteränderungen in der Individualsprache einer Mundart. *Nachrichten der Gesellschaften der Wissenschaften zu Göttigen, Philosophisch-historische Klasse* 11:195–214.

Hilles, S. 1986. Interlanguage and the pro-drop parameter. *Second Language Research* 2:3–52.

Hochberg, J. 1986a. Functional compensation for /s/ deletion in Puerto Rican Spanish. *Language* 62(3):609–21.

————. 1986b. /s/ deletion and pronoun usage in Puerto Rican Spanish. In *Diversity and diachrony,* ed. D. Sankoff, 199–210. Amsterdam: John Benjamins.

Hoopes, R. 1998. A preliminary examination of pinky extension: Suggestions regarding its occurrence, constraints, and function. In *Pinky extension and eye gaze: Language use in Deaf Communities,* ed. C. Lucas, 3–17. Sociolinguistics in Deaf Communities Series, vol. 4. Washington, D.C.: Gallaudet University Press.

Hopper, P. J., and E. C. Traugott. 1993. *Grammaticalization.* Cambridge: Cambridge University Press.

Houston, A. 1991. A grammatical continuum for (ING). In *Dialects of English: Studies in grammatical variation,* ed, P. Trudgill and J. Chambers, 241–57. London: Longman.

Huang, J. 1984. On the distribution and reference of empty pronouns. *Linguistic Inquiry* 15:531–74.

————. 1989. Pro-drop in Chinese: A generalized control theory. In *The null subject parameter,* ed. O. Jaeggli and K. J. Safir, 185–244. Dordrecht: Kluwer.

Hyams, N. M. 1986. *Language acquisition and the theory of parameters.* Dordrecht: Reidel.

————. 1989. The null subject parameter in language acquisition. In *The null subject parameter,* ed. O. Jaeggli and K. J. Safir, 215–38. Dordrecht: Kluwer.

Jacobs, L. 1980. *A Deaf adult speaks out.* Washington, D.C.: Gallaudet University Press.

Jaeggli, O. 1982. *Topics in romance syntax.* Dordrecht: Foris.

Jaeggli, O., and K. J. Safir. 1989. The null subject parameter and parametric theory. In *The null subject parameter,* ed. O. Jaeggli and K. J. Safir, 1–44. Dordrecht: Kluwer.

Johnson, E. 1993. The relationship between lexical variation and lexical change. *Language Variation and Change* 5(3):285–303.

Johnson, R., S. Liddell, and C. Erting. 1989. *Unlocking the curriculum: Principles for achieving access in Deaf education.* Gallaudet Research Institute Working Paper 89–3. Washington, D.C.: Gallaudet University.

Keep, J. R. 1857. The mode of learning the sign language. In *Convention of American Instructors of the Deaf, Proceedings,* 133–53.

Kiparsky, P. 1982a. *Explanation in phonology.* Dordrecht: Foris.

————. 1982b. Lexical morphology and phonology. In *Linguistics in the morning calm,* ed. S. Yang, 3–91. Seoul: Hanshin.

————. 1985. Some consequences of lexical phonology. In *Phonology yearbook* 2, ed. C. McEwen and J. Anderson, 85–138. Cambridge: Cambridge University Press.

————. 1994. An optimality-theoretic perspective on variable rules. Paper presented at NWAVE twenty-third annual conference, Stanford University.

Kleinfeld, M., and N. Warner. 1996. Variation in the Deaf community: Gay, lesbian, and bisexual signs. In *Multicultural aspects of sociolinguistics in Deaf communities,* ed. C. Lucas, 3–35. Sociolinguistics in Deaf communities Series, vol. 2. Washington, D.C.: Gallaudet University Press.

Klima, E., and U. Bellugi. 1979. *The signs of language.* Cambridge: Harvard University Press.

Kroch, A. 1978. Toward a theory of social dialect variation. *Language in Society* 7:17–36.

KSD [Kansas Asylum for the Education of the Deaf and Dumb]. 1876. Eleventh annual report of the trustees and principal of the Kansas Asylum for the Education of the Deaf and Dumb.

————. 1886. Fifth biennial report of the Kansas Institution for the Education of the Deaf and Dumb.

————. 1890. Seventh biennial report of the Kansas Institution for the Education of the Deaf and Dumb.

Kyle, J., and B. Woll. 1985. *Sign language: The study of deaf people and their language.* Cambridge: Cambridge University Press.

Labov, W. 1963. The social motivation of a sound change. *Word* 19:273–309.

———. 1966. *The social stratification of English in New York City.* Washington, D.C.: Center for Applied Linguistics.

———. 1969. Contraction, deletion, and inherent variability of the English copula. *Language* 45:715–62.

———. 1972a. *Sociolinguistic patterns.* Philadelphia: University of Pennsylvania Press.

———. 1972b. The transformation of experience in narrative syntax. In *Language in the inner city: Studies in the Black English Vernacular,* 354–97. Philadelphia: University of Pennsylvania Press.

———. 1981. Field methods used by the project on linguistic change and variation. Sociolinguistic Working Paper 81. Austin, Texas: Southwestern Educational Development Laboratory.

———. 1982. Objectivity and commitment in linguistic science: The case of the Black English trial in Ann Arbor. *Language in Society* 11:165–201.

———. 1984. Field methods of the Project on Language Change and Variation. In *Language in use: Readings in sociolinguistics,* ed. J. Baugh and J. Sherzer, 28–53. Englewood Cliffs, N.J.: Prentice-Hall.

———. 1989. The child as linguistic historian. *Language Variation and Change* 1:85–97.

———. 1990. The intersection of sex and social class in the course of linguistic change. *Language Variation and Change* 2:205–54.

———. 1994. *Internal Factors* Vol. 1, *Principles of Linguistic Change,* Language in Society, no. 20. Oxford: Basil Blackwell.

———. 1997. Resyllabification. In *Variation, change and phonological theory,* ed. F. Hinskens, R. van Hout, and W. L. Wetzels, 145–79. Amsterdam: John Benjamins.

Labov, W., P. Cohen, C. Robins, and J. Lewis. 1968. A study of the nonstandard English of Negro and Puerto Rican speakers in New York City. Philadelphia: U.S. Regional Survey.

Lane, H. 1984. *When the mind hears: A history of the Deaf.* London: Penguin.

———. 2000. E-mail to C. Lucas.

Lane, H., R. Hoffmeister, and B. Bahan. 1996. *Journey into the DEAF-WORLD.* San Diego: DawnSignPress.

Lane, H., R. Pillard, M. French. 2000. Origins of the American Deaf-world: Assimilating and differentiating societies and their relation to genetic patterning. *Sign Language Studies* 1(1): 17–44. First published in *The signs of language revisited,* ed. K. Emmorey and H. Lane (Mahwah, N.J.: Erlbaum, 2000), 77–100.

Lavendera, B. 1978. Where does the sociolinguistic variable stop? *Language in Society* 7:171–82.

LeMaster, B. 1990. The maintenance and loss of female and male signs in the Dublin Deaf community. Ph.D. diss., University of California at Los Angeles.

Le Page, R. B. 1997. The evolution of a sociolinguistic theory of language. In *The handbook of sociolinguistics,* ed. F. Coulmas, 15–32. Oxford: Basil Blackwell.

Le Page, R. B., and A. Tabouret-Keller. 1985. *Acts of identity: Creole-based approaches to language and ethnicity.* Cambridge and New York: Cambridge University Press.

Lewis, J. 1996. Parallels in communication styles of hearing and Deaf African Americans. Gallaudet University, Washington, D.C. Manuscript.

Lewis, J., C. Palmer, and L. Williams. 1995. Existence of and attitudes toward black variations of sign language. In *Communication forum,* ed. L. Byers, J. Chaiken, and M. Mueller, 17–48. Washington, D.C.: Gallaudet University Department of ASL, Linguistics, and Interpretation.

Liberman, H. 1966. Early history of the Kansas School for the Deaf, 1861–1873. Master's thesis, George Washington University.

Liceras, J. 1989. On some properties of the "pro-drop" parameter: Looking for missing subjects in non-native Spanish. In *Linguistic perspectives on second language acquisition,* ed. S. M. Gass and J. Schacter, 109–33. Cambridge: Cambridge University Press.

Liddell, S. K. 1980. *American Sign Language syntax.* The Hague: Mouton.

———. 1984. THINK and BELIEVE: Sequentiality in American Sign Language signs. *Language* 60:372–99.

———. 1992. Holds and positions: Comparing two models of segmentation in ASL. In *Current issues in ASL phonology,* ed. G. Coulter, 189–211. Phonetics and Phonology, vol. 3. San Diego: Academic Press.

Liddell, S. K., and R. E. Johnson. 1989. American Sign Language: The phonological base. *Sign Language Studies* 64:195–278.

———. 1995. ASL handshape inventory. Department of ASL, Linguistics, and Interpretation, Gallaudet University, Washington, D.C. Manuscript.

Lillo-Martin, D. 1986. Two kinds of null arguments in American Sign Language. *Natural Language and Linguistic Theory* 4:415–44.

———. 1991. *Universal grammar and American Sign Language.* Dordrecht: Kluwer.

Long, J. Schuyler. 1910. *The sign language: A manual of signs.* Des Moines: Robert Henderson.

LSD [Louisiana Institution for the Education of the Deaf and Dumb]. 1852. First annual report of the administrators and superintendent of the Louisiana Institution for the Education of the Deaf and Dumb.

———. 1853. Second annual report of the administrators and superintendent of the Louisiana Institution for the Education of the Deaf and Dumb.

———. 1860. Eighth annual report of the administrators and superintendent of the Louisiana Institution for the Education of the Deaf and Dumb.

———. 1861. Ninth annual report of the administrators and superintendent of the Louisiana Institution for the Education of the Deaf and Dumb.

———. 1867. Eleventh annual report of the administrators and superintendent of the Louisiana Institution for the Education of the Deaf and Dumb.

———. 1869. Thirteenth annual report of the administrators and superintendent of the Louisiana Institution for the Education of the Deaf and Dumb.

———. 1870. Fourteenth annual report of the administrators and superintendent of the Louisiana Institution for the Education of the Deaf and Dumb.

———. 1872. Sixteenth annual report of the administrators and superintendent of the Louisiana Institution for the Education of the Deaf and Dumb.

———. 1874. Annual report of the trustees and officers of the Louisiana Institution for the Education of the Deaf and Dumb.

———. 1888–1890. Biennial annual report of the trustees and officers of the Louisiana Institution for the Education of the Deaf and Dumb.

———. 1906–1908. Biennial report of the trustees and officers of the Louisiana Institution for the Education of the Deaf and Dumb.

Lucas, C. 1994. The importance of interviewer characteristics in data collection. Paper presented at symposium, Issues in Collecting Visual Data: Links between Signed and Spoken Languages. NWAVE twenty-third annual meeting, Stanford University.

———. 1995. Sociolinguistic variation in ASL: The case of DEAF. In *Sociolinguistics in Deaf communities*, ed. C. Lucas, 3–25. Sociolinguistics in Deaf Communities Series, vol. 1. Washington, D.C.: Gallaudet University Press. Originally published in H. Bos and G. Schermer, eds., *Sign language research 1994: Proceedings of the Fourth European Congress on sign language research*, (Hamburg: Signum, 1995).

Lucas, C., M. Rose, R. Hoopes, S. Collins, A. Wulf, K. Petronio, and R. Bayley. 1998. November. Linguistic variation in sign languages. Workshop conducted at the Sixth International Conference on Theoretical Issues in Sign Language Research, Gallaudet University, Washington, D.C.

Lucas, C., and C. Valli. 1992. *Language contact in the American Deaf community.* San Diego: Academic Press.

Malloy, C., and J. Doner. 1995. Variation in ASL discourse: Gender differences in the use of cohesive devices In *Communication forum*, ed. L. Byers, J. Chaiken, and M. Mueller, 183–205. Washington, D.C.: Gallaudet University Department of ASL, Linguistics, and Interpretation.

Mansfield, D. 1993. Gender differences in ASL: A sociolinguistic study of sign choices by Deaf native signers. In *Communication forum 1993*, ed. E. Winston, 86–98. Washington, D.C.: Gallaudet University Department of Linguistics and Interpreting.

McCarthy, J. 1986. OCP effects: Gemination and antigemination. *Linguistic Inquiry* 17:203–63.

MDSD [Maryland Institution for the Education of the Deaf and Dumb]. 1870. Second annual report of the Maryland Institution for the Education of the Deaf and Dumb.

———. 1871. Third annual report of the Maryland Institution for the Education of the Deaf and Dumb.

———. 1873. Fifth annual report of the Maryland Institution for the Education of the Deaf and Dumb.

———. 1874. Sixth annual report of the Maryland Institution for the Education of the Deaf and Dumb.

——— [Maryland School for the Deaf and Dumb].1883. Third biennial report of the Maryland School for the Deaf and Dumb.

———. 1889. Sixth biennial report of the Maryland School for the Deaf and Dumb.

———. 1897. Tenth biennial report of the president and visitors of the Maryland School for the Deaf and Dumb.

Medina-Rivera, A. 1991. Interaction of (s) and subject expression in the Spanish of Choluteca and El Paraiso, Honduras. Paper presented at NWAVE twentieth annual conference. Georgetown University, Washington, D.C.

Meier, R., and E. Newport. 1985. The acquisition of ASL. In *The cross-linguistic study of language acquisition: The data,* ed. D. Slobin, 881–938. Vol. 1. Hillsdale, N.J.: Erlbaum.

Metzger, M. 1993. Pronoun variation in formal and informal discourse. In *Communication forum 1993,* ed. E. Winston, 132–43. Washington, D.C.: Gallaudet University Department of Linguistics and Interpreting.

———. 1995. Constructed dialogue and constructed action in American Sign Language. In *Sociolinguistics in Deaf communities,* ed. C. Lucas, 255–71. Sociolinguistics in Deaf Communities Series, vol. 1. Washington, D.C.: Gallaudet University Press.

———. 1998. Eye gaze and pronominal reference in American Sign Language. In *Pinky extension and eye gaze: Language use in Deaf communities,* ed. C. Lucas, 170–82. Sociolinguistics in Deaf Communities Series, vol. 4. Washington, D.C.: Gallaudet University Press.

Milroy, J. 1992. *Linguistic variation and change. On the historical sociolinguistics of English.* Oxford: Basil Blackwell.

Milroy, J., and L. Milroy. 1997. Varieties and variation. In *The handbook of sociolinguistics,* ed. F. Coulmas, 47–64. Oxford: Basil Blackwell.

Milroy, L. 1980. *Language and social networks.* Oxford: Basil Blackwell.

———. 1987. *Observing and analyzing natural language.* Oxford: Blackwell.

Morales, A. 1986. La expresión del sujeto pronominal en el Español de Puerto Rico. In *Gramáticas en contacto: Analisis sintacticos sobre el Español de*

Puerto Rico, ed. A. Morales, 89–100. San Juan: Editorial Playor.

MSD [Deaf and Dumb Asylum of the State of Missouri]. 1855. Report of the commissioners of the Deaf and Dumb Asylum, with accompanying reports to the eighteenth general assembly.

———. 1857. Reports of the commissioners and superintendent of the Deaf and Dumb Asylum of the state of Missouri for the years 1855–1856.

——— [Missouri School for the Deaf]. 1864. Fifth biennial report of the Missouri School for the Deaf.

———. 1876. Eleventh biennial report of the Missouri School for the Deaf.

———. 1882 Fourteenth biennial report of the Missouri School for the Deaf.

———. 1888. Seventeenth biennial report of the Missouri School for the Deaf.

———. 1912. Twenty-ninth biennial report of the Missouri School for the Deaf.

Mulrooney, K. 2001. Gender variation in American Sign Language fingerspelling. Paper presented at the American Dialect Society, Washington, D.C., January.

Nagy, N., and W. Reynolds. 1997. Optimality theory and variable word-final deletion in Faetar. *Language Variation and Change* 9:37–56.

Naro, A. J. 1981. Morphological constraints on subject deletion. In *Variation omnibus,* ed. D. Sankoff and H. Cedergren, 351–57. Edmonton, Alberta: Linguistic Research.

Neidle, C., J. Kegl, D. MacLaughlin, B. Bahan, and R. G. Lee. 2000. *The syntax of American Sign Language: Functional categories and hierarchical structure.* Cambridge: MIT Press.

Norušis, M. J. and SPSS Inc, 1996. *SPSS advanced statistics 6.1.* Chicago: SPSS Inc.

Nowell, E. 1989. Conversational features and gender in ASL. In *The sociolinguistics of the Deaf community,* ed. C. Lucas, 273–88. San Diego: Academic Press.

Oviedo, A. 1996. Bilingual Deaf education in Venezuela: Linguistic comments on the current situation. In *Multicultural aspects of sociolinguistics in Deaf communities,* ed. C. Lucas, 61–79. Sociolinguistics in Deaf communities Series, vol. 2. Washington, D.C.: Gallaudet University Press.

Padden, C. 1988. *Interaction of morphology and syntax in American Sign Language.* New York: Garland Publishing.

———. 1998. From the cultural to the bicultural: The modern Deaf community. In *Cultural and language diversity and the Deaf experience,* ed. I. Parasnis, 79–98. Cambridge: Cambridge University Press.

Padden, C., and T. Humphries. 1988. *Deaf in America: Voices from a culture.* Cambridge: Harvard University Press.

Paredes Silva, V. L. 1993. Subject omission and functional compensation: Evidence from written Brazilian Portuguese. *Language Variation and Change* 5:35–50.

Patrick, P. 1992. Linguistic variation in Urban Jamaican Creole: A sociolinguistic study of Kingston, Jamaica. Ph.D. diss., University of Pennsylvania.

Patrick, P., and M. Metzger. 1996. Sociolinguistic factors in sign language research. In *Sociolinguistic variation: Data, theory, and analysis. Selected papers from NWAV 23 at Stanford*, ed. J. Arnold, R. Blake, B. Davidson, S. Schwenter, and J. Solomon, 229–40. Stanford: Center for the Study of Language and Information.

Pederson, L., S. Leas, G. Bailey, and M. Bassett. 1981. *LAGS: The basic materials*. Ann Arbor, Mich.: University Microfilms.

———. 1986. *Handbook*. Vol. 1 of *Linguistic atlas of the Gulf States*. Athens: University of Georgia Press.

Perlmutter, D. 1971. *Deep and surface structure constraints in syntax*. New York: Holt, Rinehart, and Winston.

———. 1992. Sonority and syllable structure in American Sign Language. In *Current issues in ASL phonology*, ed. G. Coulter, 227–61. Phonetics and Phonology, vol. 3. San Diego: Academic Press.

Pintzuk, S. 1988. VARBRUL programs for MS-DOS (computer software). Philadelphia: University of Pennsylvania Department of Linguistics.

Poplack, S. 1979. Function and process in a variable phonology. Ph.D. diss., University of Pennsylvania.

———. 1980. Deletion and disambiguation in Puerto Rican Spanish. *Language* 56:371–85.

Poplack, S., and S. Tagliamonte. 1989. There's no tense like the present: Verbal -*s* inflection in early Black English. *Language Variation and Change* 1:47–84.

Radutzky, E., ed., 1992. *Dizionario bilingue elementare della Lingua Italiana dei Segni*. Rome: Edizioni Kappa.

Ramsey, C. L. 1997. *Deaf children in public schools: Placement, context, and consequences*. Sociolinguistics in Deaf Communities Series, vol. 3. Washington, D.C.: Gallaudet University Press.

———. 2000. On the borders: Families, culture, and schooling for Mexican-heritage deaf children in a transnational region. In *Deaf plus: A multicultural perspective*, ed. K. Christensen, 121–47. San Diego: DawnSignPress.

Rand, D., and D. Sankoff. 1990. GoldVarb: A Variable Rule Application for the Macintosh Version 2.0 (computer program). Centre des recherches mathématiques, Université de Montréal.

Ranson, D. 1991. Person marking in the wake of /s/ deletion in Andalusian Spanish. *Language Variation and Change* 3:133–52.

Rickford, J. R. 1979. Variation in a Creole continuum: Quantitative and implicational approaches. Ph.D. diss., University of Pennsylvania.

———. 1987. *Dimensions of a Creole continuum: History, texts, and linguistic analysis of Guyanese Creole*. Stanford: Stanford University Press.

Romaine, S. 1999. *Communicating gender*. Mahwah, N.J.: Lawrence Erlbaum.

Rose, M. 2000. Gender and phonological variation in ASL: Lowering (and forehead) signs. Stanford University. Manuscript.

Rose, M., C. Lucas, R. Bayley, and A. Wulf. 1999. January. Sociolinguistic variation in American Sign Language: The l handshape variable. Paper presented at the annual meeting of the American Dialect Society, Los Angeles.

Rousseau, P. 1989. A versatile program for the analysis of sociolinguistic data. In *Language change and variation*, ed. R. W. Fasold and D. Schiffrin, 295–409. Amsterdam: John Benjamins.

Rousseau, P., and D. Sankoff. 1978. Advances in variable rule methodology. In *Linguistic variation: Models and methods*, ed. D. Sankoff, 57–69. New York: Academic Press.

Sandler, W. 1992. Linearization of phonological tiers in ASL. In *Current issues in ASL phonology*, ed. G. Coulter, 103–29. Phonetics and phonology, vol. 3. San Diego: Academic Press.

Sankoff, D. 1988. Variable rules. In *Sociolinguistics:An international handbook of the science of language and society*, ed. U. Ammon, N. Dittmar, and K. J. Mattheier, 984–97, vol. 2. Berlin: de Gruyter.

Sankoff, D., and D. Rand. 1990. *Goldvarb, version 2.0 on-line manual*. Montréal: Centre de recherches mathématiques, Université de Montréal.

Sankoff, D., and P. Rousseau. 1989. Statistical evidence for rule-ordering. *Language Variation and Change* 1:1–18.

Sankoff, G., and H. Cedergren. 1972. Sociolinguistic research on French in Montréal. *Language in Society* 1(1):173–74.

Sankoff, D., and W. Labov. 1979. On the uses of variable rules. *Language in Society* 9:189–222.

Schatz, S. 1995. Objectivity and commitment in ASL Research. Paper presented at NWAVE twenty-fourth annual conference, University of Pennsylvania, Philadelphia.

Schein, J. D. 1987. The demography of deafness. In *Understanding Deafness socially*, ed. P. C. Higgins and J. E. Nash, 3–28. Springfield, Ill.: Thomas.

Schein, J. D., and M. T. Delk. 1974. *The Deaf population of the United States*. Silver Spring, Md.: National Association of the Deaf.

Schermer, T. 1985. Analysis of natural discourse of deaf adults in the Netherlands: Observations on Dutch Sign Language. In *SLR '83: Proceedings of the Third International Symposium on Sign Language Research, Rome, June 22–26, 1983*, ed. W. Stokoe and V. Volterra, 281–88. Silver Spring, Md.: Linstok Press.

———. 1990. *In search of a language: Influences from spoken Dutch on Sign Language of the Netherlands*. Delft: Eburon.

Schiffrin, D. 1994. *Approaches to discourse analysis*. Cambridge: Blackwell.

Shapiro, E. 1993. Socioeconomic variation in American Sign Language. In *Communication forum 1993*, ed. E. Winston, 150–75. Washington, D.C.: Gallaudet University Department of Linguistics and Interpreting.

Shroyer, E., and S. Shroyer. 1984. *Signs across America*. Washington, D.C.: Gallaudet University Press.

Shuy, R., W. Wolfram, and W. Riley. 1968. *Field techniques in an urban language study*. Washington, D.C.: Center for Applied Linguistics.

Sicard, R.-A. 1808. *Théorie des signes pour servir d'introduction a l'étude des langues*, vol. 1. Paris: Rorêt et Mongie.

Silva-Corvalán, C. 1982. Subject expression and placement in Mexican-American Spanish. In *Spanish in the United States: Sociolinguistic aspects*, ed. J. Amastae and L. Elias-Olivares, 93–120. New York: Cambridge University Press.

———. 1994. *Language contact and change: Spanish in Los Angeles*. Oxford: Clarendon.

Smith, N. 1989. *The twitter machine*. Oxford: Basil Blackwell.

Stokoe, W. C. 1960. *Sign language structure: An outline of visual communication systems of the American Deaf*. Studies in Linguistics: Occasional Paper 8. Buffalo, N.Y.: University of Buffalo, Linguistics Department.

Stokoe, W. C., D. C. Casterline, and C. G. Croneberg. 1965. *A dictionary of American Sign Language on linguistic principles*. Silver Spring, Md.: Linstok Press.

Supalla, S. 1986. Manually coded English: The modality question in signed language development. Master's thesis, University of Illinois at Champaign-Urbana.

Supalla, T., and E. Newport. 1978. How many seats in a chair? In *Understanding Language through Sign Language Research*, ed. P. Siple, 91—138. New York: Academic Press.

Sutcliffe, R. 1975. A study of language as a determinant of group cohesiveness. Master's thesis, University of Maryland.

Sutton-Spence, R., B. Woll, and L. Allsop. 1990. Variation and recent change in fingerspelling in British Sign Language. *Language Variation and Change* 2:313–30.

Tabouret-Keller, A. 1997. Language and identity. In *The handbook of sociolinguistics*, ed. F. Coulmas, 315–26. London: Blackwell.

Tannen, D. 1986. *That's not what I meant*. New York: Ballantine.

Tarone, E. 1985. Variability in interlanguage use: A study of style-shifting in morphology and syntax. *Language Learning* 35:373–404.

Thibault, P., and M. Daveluy. 1989. Quelques traces du passage du temps dans le parler des Montréalais, 1971–1984. *Language Variation and Change* 1:19–45.

Trudgill, P. 1974. *The social differentiation of English in Norwich*. Cambridge: Cambridge University Press.

Uyechi, L. 1994. The geometry of visual phonology. Ph.D. diss., Stanford University.

Van Cleve, J., and B. Crouch. 1989. *A place of their own. Creating the Deaf community in America.* Washington, D.C.: Gallaudet University Press.

Van Manen, J. W. 1997. DEAF: A journey through the film history of a sign. Gallaudet University, Washington, D.C. Manuscript.

VSDB [Virginia Institution for the Education of the Deaf and Dumb and the Blind]. 1846. Eighth annual report of the Virginia Institution for the Education of the Deaf and Dumb and the Blind.

———. 1852. Fourteenth annual report of the Virginia Institution for the Education of the Deaf and Dumb and the Blind.

———. 1853. Fifteenth annual report of the Virginia Institution for the Education of the Deaf and Dumb and the Blind.

———. 1872. Report of the board of visitors of the Deaf, Dumb, and Blind Institution.

———. 1881. Annual report of the Virginia Institution for the Education of the Deaf and Dumb and the Blind.

———. 1882. Annual report of the Virginia Institution for the Education of the Deaf and Dumb and the Blind.

——— [Virginia School for the Deaf and the Blind]. 1911–1913. Biennial report of the Virginia School for the Deaf and the Blind at Staunton, Va., to the board of visitors.

———. 1952. *The handbook: The Virginia School for the Deaf and the Blind.* Staunton, Va.: Virginia School for the Deaf and Blind.

Wang, W. S.-Y. 1969. Competing changes as a cause of residue. *Language* 45:9–25.

Weinreich, U., W. Labov, and M. Herzog. 1968. Empirical foundations for a theory of language change. In *Directions for historical linguistics,* ed. W. P. Lehmann and Y. Malkiel, 95–189. Austin: University of Texas Press.

White, L. 1985. The "pro-drop" parameter in adult second language acquisition. *Language Learning* 35:47–62.

———. 1989. *Universal grammar and second language acquisition.* Amsterdam: John Benjamins.

Wilbur, R., and B. Schick. 1987. The effects of linguistic stress on sign movement in ASL. *Language and Speech* 20:301–23.

Wilcox, S., and P. Wilcox. 1991. *Learning to see: American Sign Language as a second language.* Englewood Cliffs, N.J.: Prentice Hall.

Winston, E. 1992. Space and involvement in an American Sign language lecture. In *Expanding horizons: Proceedings of the 12TH National Convention of the Registry of Interpreters for the Deaf,* ed. J. Palnt-Moeller, 93–105. Silver Spring, Md.: RID Publications.

Wodak, R., and G. Benke. 1997. Gender as a sociolinguistic variable: New perspectives on variation studies. In *The handbook of sociolinguistics,* ed. F. Coulmas, 127–50. Oxford: Blackwell.

Wolfram, W. 1969. *A sociolinguistic description of Detroit Negro speech.* Washington, D.C.: Center for Applied Linguistics.

———. 1974. *Sociolinguistic aspects of assimilation.* Arlington: Center for Applied Linguistics.

———. 1989. Structural variability in phonological development: Final nasals in Vernacular Black English. In *Language change and variation,* ed. R. Fasold and D. Schiffrin, 301–32. Amsterdam: John Benjamins.

———. 1991a. *Dialects and American English.* Englewood Cliffs, N.J.: Prentice Hall.

———. 1991b. The linguistic variable: Fact and fantasy. *American Speech* 66(1):22–32.

———. 1993. Identifying and interpreting variables. In *American dialect research,* ed. D. Preston, 193–221. Philadelphia: John Benjamins.

———. 1997. Dialect in society. In *The handbook of sociolinguistics,* ed. F. Coulmas, 107–26. Oxford: Basil Blackwell.

Wolfram, W., and D. Christian. 1976. *Appalachian speech.* Washington, D.C.: Center for Applied Linguistics.

Wolfram, W., and N. Schilling-Estes. 1995. Moribund dialects and the endangerment canon: The case of the Ocracoke Brogue. *Language* 71(4):696–721.

Woll, B. 1981. Borrowing and change in BSL. Paper presented at the Linguistics Association of Great Britain Annual Meeting, York.

Woodward, J. C. 1973a. Implicational lects on the Deaf diglossic continuum. Ph.D. diss., Georgetown University.

———. 1973b. Interrule implication in American Sign Language. *Sign Language Studies* 3:47–56.

———. 1973c. Some observations on sociolinguistic variation and American Sign Language. *Kansas Journal of Sociology* 9(2):191–200.

———. 1974. A report on Montana-Washington implicational research. *Sign Language Studies* 4:77–101.

———. 1975. Variation in American Sign Language syntax: Agent-beneficiary directionality. In *Analyzing variation in language,* ed. R. Shuy and R. Fasold, 303–11. Washington, D.C.: Georgetown University Press.

———. 1976. Black southern signing. *Language in Society* 5:211–18.

———. 1979. *Signs of sexual behavior.* Silver Spring, Md.: T. J. Publishers.

———. 1980. *Signs of drug use.* Silver Spring, Md.: T. J. Publishers.

Woodward, J. C., and S. DeSantis. 1977a. Negative incorporation in French and American Sign Languages. *Language in Society* 6(3):379–88.

———. 1977b. Two to one it happens: Dynamic phonology in two sign languages. *Sign Language Studies* 17:329–46.

Woodward, J. C., and C. Erting. 1975. Synchronic variation and historical change in American Sign Language. *Language Sciences* 37: 9–12.

Woodward, J. C., C. Erting, and S. Oliver. 1976. Facing and hand(l)ing variation in American Sign Language. *Sign Language Studies* 10:43–52.

Woodward, J. C., and H. Markowicz. 1975. Some handy new ideas of pidgins and creoles: Pidgin sign languages. Paper presented at the Conference on Pidgin and Creole Languages, Honolulu.

WSD [Washington School for Defective Youth]. 1887–1889. Second biennial report of the trustees of the Washington School for Defective Youth.

———— [Washington School for the Deaf]. 1906–1908. Biennial report of the superintendent.

————. 1910–1912. Biennial report of the superintendent.

Wulf, A. 1998. Gender-related variation in ASL signing space. Guided research paper, Gallaudet University Department of ASL, Linguistics, and Interpretation.

Wulf, A., P. Dudis, R. Bayley, and C. Lucas. 1999. Null subject variation in ASL narratives. Paper presented at the Conference on New Ways of Analyzing Variation 28, Toronto.

Yau, S., and J. He. 1990. How do deaf children get their name signs during their first month in school? In *SLR '87: Papers from the Fourth International Symposium on Sign Language Research, Lappeenranta, Finland, July 15–19, 1987*, ed. W. H. Edmondson and F. Karlsson, 243–54. Hamburg: Signum Press.

Yip, M. 1988. The obligatory contour principle and phonological rules: A loss of identity. *Linguistic Inquiry* 19:65–100.

Young, R., and R. Bayley. 1996. VARBRUL analysis for second language acquisition research. In *Second language acquisition and linguistic variation,* ed. R. Bayley and D. R. Preston, 253–306. Philadelphia: John Benjamins.

Young, R., and B. Yandell. 1999. Top-down versus bottom-up analyses of interlanguage data: A reply to Saito. *Studies in Second Language Acquisition* 21:477–88.

Index

American Sign Language *(continued)*
  pro-drop language, 3, 26, 42, 168
  recognition of as full-fledged
    language, 1, 35, 143, 194
  research on variation in, 7–21. *See
    also* Variation in ASL
  segments that compose, 81–84
  socioeconomic status and variation
    of users, 6
  sociolinguistic variation research,
    5–6, 8–21. *See also* Variation
    in ASL
  speech community of users, 107–10
  structure of, 1, 19–21
Analogy, 27, 28
Animal signs, 184, 187–88, 191
Anonymity of study participants. *See*
    Observer's Paradox
Aramburo, A., 18, 32, 136, 140
ARREST sign, 182–84, 196
Articulation. *See* Oralism
Assimilation, 27, 28, 134, 138, 146,
    176, 192

Back channeling, 18
Bahan, B., 160
Bailey, G., et al., 140
BANANA sign, 178, 180, 197
Barale, C., 151
Battison, R.M., H. Markowicz, and
    J.C. Woodward, 11, 28
Baugh, J., 46–47, 48
Bayley, R., 44, 47, 48, 90
Bayley, R., and L. Pease-Alvarez, 163,
    174
Baynton, D.C., 58
Beebe, L.M., and H. Giles, 40
Bell, Alexander Graham, 61
Beverly School, 61
Biber, D., and E. Finegan, 24
Black signing. *See* African Americans
Blattberg, S., et al., 17
Boundary phenomenon, 29, 149
Bound morphemes, 149
Bourgerie, D.S., 151

Bowles, Theodore C., 76
Braddock, G.C., 64
Braidwood, Thomas, 53
Brelje, H.W., and V. Tibbs, 64
Bridges, B., 15
Brill, Richard G., 60–61
Brown, James S., 57–58, 70

Caldwell, William A., 74
California School for the Deaf,
    Berkeley
  history of, 58–59
  language policies and attitudes at,
    72–75
California School for the Deaf at
    Riverside, 60–61
Cameron, R., 162
Cedergren, H., 4
Chamberlayne, Lewis W., 57
Chinese language, 150–51, 160, 175
Citation form of signs
  age differences among signers using,
    153–54
  content signs, 137–38
  DEAF sign, 115, 116–18, 145–46,
    152–53
  KNOW and like verb signs, 132–33
  1 handshape signs, 16, 91, 144, 152
  pronouns and, 144–45
Clark, Pomeroy B., 59
Clarke School, 58, 61
Class differences in signing, 6, 10, 15,
    156
  DEAF sign, 153, 156
  lexical variation, 187
  location of KNOW and like verb
    signs, 135
  location variable and, 138
  1 handshape variation, 104–5, 111
  study participants to represent,
    36–37
Classifier predicates, 158
Clerc, Laurent, 52, 54, 55, 62
Coalescence, 22, 26
Codeswitching, 19, 40

language policies and attitudes at, 70–72
Louisiana State School for Deaf Negroes, 58
Lucas, C., 16, 17, 21, 28, 29, 46, 114, 115, 117, 143–44
Lucas, C., and C. Valli, 1, 40, 167

Mainstreaming, 35
Malloy, C., and J. Doner, 18
Mansfield, D., 15, 186
Maryland School for the Deaf history of, 59–60
language policies and attitudes at, 77–78
McFarland, W.D., 60, 154
Meier, R., and E. Newport, 1
Metathesis, 22, 112–14, 126–28, 192
Methodology of study, 32–50
    age groups, 35
    contact people, 39
    database creation, 41–43
    data collection, 37, 39–40
    demographics of participants, 37–38
    exclusion of thumb-only variant from study of 1 handshape signs, 90–91
    expectations, 24–31
    factors influencing signer's choice, 46
    goals of study, 6–7, 37
    null pronoun variation, 163–69
    participant selection, 33–38
    recruitment process, 39
    representative communities, 32–33
    transcription conventions, 195
    VARBRUL as analysis tool, 43–49
    videotaping participants, 32, 39–40
Metzger, M., 16, 90, 167
Mexican-American Spanish, 44, 47, 173–74
Mexico, 64
Middle-class signers. See Class differences in signing

Milan Conference, 51, 66, 80
Milligan, L.E., 74
Milroy, J., 3, 4, 14, 39, 193
Milroy, L., 4, 24
Missouri School for the Deaf history of, 57
language policies and attitudes at, 67–70
Modality differences between spoken and sign languages, 149–52
Morphological and syntactic variation
    ASL, 3, 12–13, 26, 27, 28
    boundary phenomenon, 149
    null subject variation in plain verbs, 158–75. See also Null pronoun variation
    spoken language, 2, 22–23, 27, 28
Movement segments in ASL signs, 82
Mulrooney, K., 147, 148

Narratives for study of null pronoun variation, 163–66
National Association of the Deaf (NAD), 9, 125
National Congress of Jewish Deaf (NCJD), 9
National Fraternal Society of the Deaf (NFSD), 9
Native signers, 51
    citation variant use by, 155
    lexical variation, 187, 190
    location of KNOW and like verb signs, 134
    1 handshape variation of signer, 106
    significant factor in variation, 193
Negative incorporation, 13, 20, 26
Neidle, C., et al., 160
Noncitation form of signs
    African American signers' use of, 138, 155
    age differences among signers and, 138
    DEAF sign, 115, 116–18, 152–53
    choice between two forms, 118–22, 145–46

Total Communication, 35, 62
Trager, G., 193
Transcription conventions, 195
Trudgill, P., 4, 36, 106
Turner, Job, 64, 65
Turn-taking strategies, 18
Two-handed signs, 12, 14
    changing into one-handed signs, 26,
        176
Tyler, Joseph D., 57, 64, 65, 154

VARBRUL, 43–49, 85
Variation in ASL
    alternation with fingerspelling, 17
    change in progress and, 136, 138,
        187–91
    compared with spoken languages,
        24–31
    diachronic variation, 13–15
    discourse, 18
    early research on, 8–15
    external constraints. *See* External
        constraints
    factors influencing signer's choice,
        46
    horizontal variation, 9
    internal constraints. *See* Internal
        constraints
    lexical variation. *See* Lexical
        variation
    linguistic. *See* Linguistic
        variation
    morphological and syntactic
        variation, 3, 12–13
    null subject variation, 158–75. *See
        also* Null pronoun variation
    perspectives on structure of sign
        languages, 19–21
    phonological variation. *See*
        Phonological variation in ASL
    recent research on, 15–19
    shared linguistic norm, 106
    social factors. *See* Social factors
    sociolinguistic. *See* Sociolinguistic
        variation

standard sign language,
    determination of, 10
vertical variation, 9
Verbs
    classifier predicates, 158
    directionality and, 20
    indicating verbs, 158–59
    plain verbs. *See* Plain verbs
    reduplication, 13, 20, 26
    types of, 158–59
Vernacular use. *See* Discourse
Vertical variation, 9
Videotaping study participants, 32,
    39–40
Virginia School for the Deaf and Blind
    (VSDB)
    history of, 57, 64
    language policies and attitudes at,
        65–67

Walker, S.T., 76
Wang, W.S.-Y., 151
Washington State School for the Deaf
    history of, 60, 64
    language policies and attitudes at,
        78–79
Watson, Joseph, 53
Weakening, 27, 28
Weinrich, U., W. Labov, and M.
    Herzog, 1, 14, 193
Weld, Lewis, 56
Wilkinson, Warring M., 8, 59, 72–74
Willard, William, 62
Williams, Job, 66
Winston, E., 167
Wolfram, W., 3, 11, 22, 23, 24, 29,
    36, 41, 85
Women vs. men signers. *See* Gender
    differences in signing
Woodward, J.C., 1, 10, 12, 13, 15, 20,
    26, 104, 136, 159
Woodward, J.C., and S. DeSantis,
    12–13, 176
Woodward, J.C., and C. Erting,
    186

Woodward, J.C., C. Erting, and S. Oliver, 12, 176
Working-class signers. *See* Class differences in signing
Wulf, A., et al., 160

Young, R., and R. Bayley, 45, 117
Young, R., and B. Yandell, 50
Younger vs. older signers. *See* Age differences among signers